The "Shabbes Goy"

THE "SHABBES GOY"
A Study in Halakhic Flexibility

Jacob Katz
translated by Yoel Lerner

A MARTHA H. AND JOSEPH L. MENDELSON BOOK

THE JEWISH PUBLICATION SOCIETY

PHILADELPHIA · JERUSALEM   5749/1989

Library of Congress Cataloging in Publication Data

Katz, Jacob, 1904–
  The "Shabbes goy."

  Translation of: Goi shel Shabat.
  Bibliography: p.
  Includes index.
  1. Shabbas goy.   I. Title.
BM523.3.P7K3713   1989   296.1'8   88-13528
Cloth, ISBN 0–8276-0320–7
Paperback, ISBN 0–8276–0413–0

Designed by Adrianne Onderdonk Dudden

The publication of this book was made possible by
a gift from Martha H. and Joseph L. Mendelson
in memory of their parents, Alexander and Celia Holstein
and Abraham and Dora Mendelson.

Contents

Preface

A writer can rarely claim with certainty that his treatment of a subject is the first time that the subject matter has been considered. This, however, is what I experienced with the topic dealt with in this volume. This is so, despite the fact that I had at my disposal no sources that my predecessors or contemporaries lacked. Volumes of halakhah, Jewish law, mostly of the responsa type, which I used are the same texts constantly studied by Torah scholars and rabbis ruling on halakhic questions. Modern scholars, especially historians, study these sources for the purposes of their own types of research and are thus also familiar with them. If my treatment of the selfsame volumes has led to unique results, this is because I made use of both approaches to learning: that of traditional scholarship and that of critical research. In accordance with these two perspectives of analysis, I trust that the book will be regarded as a contribution to both the history of society and the study of halakhah. Although the book itself is essentially historical, scholars may find in it a key to the understanding of some modern problems as well, in that the question of the application of halakhah to changing conditions of life has not ceased to intrigue us. To trace the hesitation that characterizes the adaptation of halakhah regarding the question of the Sabbath Gentile may well afford us a glimpse of the limits of the adaptability of halakhah in other fields as well.

In this study I have made considerable use of the relevant professional libraries—the National and University Library and Yad Maimon, both in Jerusalem, and, while abroad in New York during the winter of 1982/1983, the library of the Jewish Theological Seminary. I was in New York as the guest of Yeshiva University, where I led a seminar on the topic dealt with in this book. Studying the sources with students already familiar with the patterns of halakhic thought often helped me attain a precise clarification of detail. Dr. Avraham Grossman of Jerusalem read the opening chapters of the book, and I am indebted to him for several constructive comments.

Throughout the years I have spent on this subject, I have made inquiry of many specialists—librarians, bibliographers, halakhic experts, and historians. I take this opportunity to thank them all.

Preface to the English Translation

Shabbes goy is an expression likely to conjure up some jocular association in the mind of people whose knowledge of Yiddish or of Jewish religious practice is slight or even nonexistent. Having heard that a book had been published on the subject, many friends and acquaintances expressed their wish to see it translated into English. I warned them that the treatise was not folklore but the tracing of a metamorphosis in religious law, the *halakhah*, reflecting changes in the life of the Jewish community through the ages. It is based on analysis of rather involved source material, the very translation of which would be a formidable task. Still, seeing that the Hebrew version of the book had attracted the attention of reviewers in English periodicals, I overcame my hesitation. I hope that the result presented in this volume will justify the decision.

The rendering into English is the work of Yoel Lerner, Jerusalem; it has been reviewed by Moshe Sherman, New York. Professor Nahum M. Sarna, academic consultant for the Jewish Publication Society, also reviewed the manuscript and contributed substantially to its readability.

J. K.

January 1988, The Hebrew University of Jerusalem

The "Shabbes Goy"

Introduction

The expression "Sabbath Gentile," apparently derived from the Yiddish phrase *shabbes goy,*[1] has in the Hebrew tongue a derogatory connotation implying criticism of the Jewish religious tradition for rendering Jews dependent on the assistance of non-Jews in their religious observance. This criticism results from an aspiration to absolute national independence, an aspiration that has on occasion led to conflicts with traditional patterns of living.[2] Yet during the period that Jewish tradition reigned supreme, this dependence caused no signs of embarrassment whatever. Halakhic sources recommend the use of a Gentile's services with little

1. The expression "Sabbath Gentile" is not found in halakhic sources. Its Yiddish counterpart is common in Yiddish literature, and, according to Professor Dov Sadan, its oral use precedes its written traces.
2. In practice, members of the religious kibbutz movement (Ha-Kibbutz ha-Dati) in the 1930s objected to the use of a Sabbath Gentile in connection with milking cows on the Sabbath, not only for practical reasons—considerations of security involving the introduction of Arabs onto kibbutz property—but also for reasons of principle: because they aspired to live "full, complete" Jewish lives. See Arieh Fishman, "Ha-Kibbutz ha-Dati: A Study of the Mutual Influence of Religion and Ideology in the Context of Modernization" (in Hebrew) (Ph.D. diss. Hebrew University, 1976), 190, 205–207.

hestitation, provided the service is permissible according to the rules of halakhah.[3] Such permission, however, depended upon the fulfillment of numerous conditions. The problem halakhic experts confronted was how to define the boundaries of the permitted and the prohibited and how to ensure that the Jewish public would indeed remain within the realm of the permitted and not stray into that which is forbidden.

Regarding various questions arising in everyday life, there was always a certain tension between basic halakhic teachings and the ability and readiness of the public to adapt its behavior. It seems, however, that in no area was such tension more apparent than in questions of a Gentile doing the work of a Jew on Jewish Sabbaths and festival days. Our research is studded with examples of this phenomenon, a fact that invites thorough consideration, for its historical evaluation is twofold. The problems dealt with by halakhic authorities in this field indicate that Jews were involved in the economic life of their non-Jewish environment, for the use of the Sabbath Gentile is not limited to having a Gentile light the oven of a Jew on a cold winter day and the like. The Sabbath Gentile fulfills an important function resulting from the interdependence of Jew and non-Jew in various economic fields. For example, Gentile servants and laborers work in Jewish households; Jews enter into partnerships with non-Jews in the business world; they rent fields and factories to non-Jews and lease them from non-Jews; they set sail in their ships and journey in caravans led by non-Jews. Even if the Jew himself refrains from doing anything on the Sabbath, he is still liable to benefit from work performed by the Gentile. And so the question arises: Is this benefit permitted or prohibited?

From the types of questions dealt with by halakhic experts in every generation we can gain insight into contemporary sources of Jewish livelihood, which vary from place to place and from one period to another. Jewish involvement in economics was sometimes limited, a fact demonstrated by a small number of questions put to authorities for their consideration. Nevertheless, a large number of questions, especially if original in nature and unprecedented in halakhic tradition, indicates the

3. Traditional halakhic authorities defended the use of a Sabbath Gentile in connection with milking and rejected other permissive rulings whose justification depended on the need for "Jewish labor." See the responsum of Rabbi Abraham Isaac Kook in Yehuda Noah Brawer, *Melekhet Mefarek* (Jerusalem, 1929), 27a–b; the letters of R. Hayyim Ozer Grodzinsky in Shmuel Rothstein, *Ahiezer* (Jaffa and Tel Aviv, 1942), 457–461. For this reference I am indebted to Dr. Menahem Friedman.

expansion of Jewish economic activity. Halakhic literature, in particular volumes of responsa, thus serves as a valuable source of information concerning the economic history of the Jews over the centuries. Historians have indeed made use of this source,[4] though it is doubtful if they have fully exploited it. Our doubt is rooted in the fact that the attention of historians has generally been focused upon questions containing descriptions of events that led to the questions being asked and not upon the halakhic discussions that enabled halakhic authorities to phrase a decision. Nevertheless, it sometimes occurs that the reasoning of the halakhic expert as revealed in his reply uncovers the true nature of the enterprise under consideration, as well as the position it occupied in the life of the Jews. It thus becomes evident that a search for documentation of Jewish economic activity requires a careful perusal not only of the questions posed but also of the answers proffered—even more so when the scholar wishes to learn the halakhic problems involved. Thus, the major interest in the case of the Sabbath Gentile is to be found in its reflection on the history of the halakhah. Tracing the solutions to problems of this kind, whether suggested or actually adopted, may clarify important aspects of the development of halakhah.

Modern halakhic research accepts the premise that whenever the halakhic tradition confronted economic difficulties, such as matters of charging interest on loans, refraining from idolatrous practices, and so forth, decisions were taken under pressure of existing conditions, so that there evolved a kind of generalization whereby it was not the source material "or even Talmudic proofs that was decisive," but rather "existing conditions forced the acceptance (by the scholars) of precise definitions and differentiations" which then formed the basis of their rulings.[5] No other issue presented the aspiration to uphold existing

4. See, e.g., Ben-Zion Dinur, *Toledot Yisrael* (Tel Aviv, 1960–1971), where the chapters dealing with economic conditions always include sources from responsa involving the religious observance of Sabbaths and festivals. See Hayyim Hillel Ben-Sasson, "The Regulations Concerning Sabbath Restrictions in Poland and Their Economic and Social Significance" (in Hebrew), *Zion* 21 (1956): 183–206.
5. So Ephraim E. Urbach, *Baalei ha-Tosafot*, 2d ed. (Jerusalem, 1980), 177; and also 91–92, 351. A similar wording is to be found in Avraham Grossman, *Hakhmei Ashkenaz ha-Rishonim* (Jerusalem, 1981), 126: "This approach of Rabbenu Gershom Meor ha-Golah and the scholars of Ashkenaz who followed his ruling must not be viewed merely as the result of the study of the relevant talmudic item. It stems to a large extent from the historical reality and the aforementioned trends." By "trends" he means the desire to restore apostates to Judaism. Trends of this kind are occasionally a factor in halakhic rulings; the circumstances merely presented the problem.

halakhic tradition with more difficulties than that of employing a Gentile in the service of a Jew. The pressure of contemporary economic conditions can clearly be sensed in each one of the questions and answers concerned with this problem. We have already noted the tension and actual difference between what halakhic authorities considered obligatory under Jewish law and what was prevalent in practice and even approved of retroactively by these authorities. Nevertheless, not every request was approved, and we occasionally encounter scholarly attempts to root out practices already entrenched. We are thus obliged to search out the limits of the influence of contemporary conditions, influence that was certainly finite in its scope. In addition, distinctions are noticeable between one scholar and another, between one period and another, and between one community and another. It is thus justified to inquire if a consistent approach exists in the rulings of various halakhic authorities and in the trends characteristic of entire Jewish communities. These are problems that historians have pondered greatly. A case study in the history of halakhah, such as that presented in this book, may be able to contribute significantly to the solution.

A study of our subject must, it seems, open with a review of the talmudic sources that later served as a basis for the rulings handed down by geonic, medieval, and more recent talmudic authorities. In this field, just as with most other halakhic issues, the talmudic literature is not unambiguous in its rulings. If this were not so, there would have been no room for the doubts and disagreements that plagued post-talmudic generations. Vacillation and change affected the regulations governing this matter in the Mishnaic and talmudic era as well, and while our research does not include these early periods, we are still obliged to describe the developments that occurred at that time as determined by scholars of talmudic halakhah. This is necessary to enable us to obtain a realistic picture of the development of practices affecting future generations and guiding future scholars in their decisions. In attempting to understand the considerations weighed by these scholars, we shall have to ignore our historical findings and hypotheses; we shall view the sources as they viewed them, systematically and dogmatically, rather than historically.

For post-talmudic scholars—the geonim, the earlier and later decisors (Hebrew *poskim*)—the source material contained in talmudic literature dealing with problems of the Sabbath Gentile (as with any other problem) is considered a single, unified corpus. If this corpus is found to be internally inconsistent due to contradictions in details, halakhic authorities resolve the differences by means of certain rules. These rules serve as guidelines that may not be ignored; yet leave the halakhic scholar sufficient room for innovation and original solution. A compromise reached between mutually contradictory sources may have practical significance. It may provide the difference between permission and prohibition. This too applies to the interpretation of individual sources, which may not always be unambiguous: One interpretation may lead to a more lenient ruling and another to a stricter ruling. A halakhic authority may make use of this relative flexibility of halakhic tradition in confronting contemporary problems as well. This fact contributes to the various kinds of halakhic rulings reached in different areas of the Diaspora and to the evolution of the halakhah over a period of time. It is our task here to trace this variation and evolution from the Babylonian geonic period through medieval Jewish life with its Sephardic and Ashkenazic centers until the Jewry of eastern Europe at the turn of the twentieth century.

Polish Jewry is a separate issue in this concern, for the profound Jewish involvement in non-Jewish Polish economy gave rise to unprecedented problems. Moreover, we encounter even deeper involvement at the onset of the modern era, in the eighteenth and nineteenth centuries. We shall trace the attempts of halakhic authorities to wrestle with these new conditions, which gave rise to solutions that would not have occurred to their predecessors.

New permissive rulings, especially regarding the bill of sale, enabled the Jews to participate in modern economic enterprises under the aegis of halakhah—although the modern era is characterized as well by many Jews no longer seeking halakhic permission for their acts. Sabbath observance was no longer characteristic of the entire Jewish community, and there were places, especially in Western countries, where halakhic observance was characteristic of a minority of Jews. Halakhic rulings concerning the Sabbath Gentile pertained henceforth only to those Jews who recognized their authority. This development gave rise to a new consideration for the halakhic authority: Should one rule leniently, lest one deter the questioner from accepting the decision? Or, on the contrary, should one rule strictly and thus try to limit Sabbath desecration? Signs of the attempts to deal with this problem will arise in the final chapters of our discussion.

1

Talmudic Sources

The basis of the problem of the Sabbath Gentile is that only Jews are obliged to observe the Sabbath, non-Jews being exempt from this requirement. On the contrary, the Talmud states (*Sanhedrin* 58b) that "if a Gentile observes the Sabbath, he is liable to the death penalty."[1] This means that a Jew having a Gentile perform creative labor on the Sabbath is not encouraging transgression, whereas a Jew would be liable, were he to have a Gentile rob or eat flesh torn from a living animal, acts included in the seven Noachide prohibitions.[2] Thus it was never dis-

---

1. In the printed texts the wording is "an idolator who observed the Sabbath," but in *Haggadot ha-Talmud* the word used is "non-Jew." Ha-Meiri, ibid., *Sanhedrin* 58b (*Beit ha-Behirah* to *Sanhedrin*, ed. A. Sofer [Frankfurt am Main, 1930], 229), paraphrases the item: "A Noachide whom we see . . . setting aside for himself rest days [like] Sabbath or festivals . . ."

2. The example of a limb taken from a living animal is brought explicitly in *Pesahim* 22b. Another example involving emasculation, according to the opinion that non-Jews were warned of this, may be found in *Bava Metsia* 90b. In this connection *Or Zarua, Bava Metsia* 286 rules that "any precept about which the non-Jew is not warned, a Jew may ask a non-Jew to do, whereas a precept about which the non-Jew is warned, a Jew may not ask a non-Jew to do because we are commanded not to put a stumbling block before the blind."

puted that a Gentile could engage in his own creative labor on the Sabbath, and no demand was made requiring him to observe the Sabbath in his own residence or in the public domain. This was true even when and where Jewish law prevailed.[3] It was not the Gentile involved in his own labor that was viewed as a desecration of the Sabbath but rather the Gentile engaged in creative labor for the benefit of Jews. This prohibition was adopted some time during the early Second Commonwealth, at which time the basic guidelines of Sabbath observance crystallized and thus determined the character of the Sabbath for future generations. To the best of my knowledge, modern research has no adequate answers to the question as to why these specific features evolved. In this particular matter, however, regarding the labors of a Gentile for the needs of a Jew, the explanation seems to be analogous to that of the reaction of recent generations at the relaxation of a prohibition even where formal permission has been obtained. Such relaxation is termed a "desecration of God's Name" or a "source of ridicule."[4] The idea of a Jew observing the Sabbath while a Gentile performs labor for him is viewed as evading the divine precept and holding it up to ridicule. Feelings of this kind were apparently the original source of the prohibition, which, like all other prohibitions that contributed to the formulation of the character of the Sabbath, was felt to derive from the Torah commandment to observe the Sabbath in its entirety.[5] A literary expression of this idea may be found in the homily brought by the Mekhilta to Exodus 12:17: "'No work at all shall be done on them': 'You may not do any, your fellow Jew may not do any, and neither may a Gentile do your labor.'"[6]

3. According to the reading of Nahmanides in the Mekhilta to be considered in n. 6 explicitly: "but the non-Jew does his work."
4. See chap. 2, n. 36, chap. 7, n. 55, and similar phrases occurring in the rulings of early and more recent halakhic authorities, as we shall see below.
5. Gedalya Allon, Studies in the History of Israel (in Hebrew) (Jerusalem, 1958), pt. 2, n. 25; and subsequently, Benjamin De Vries, The History of Talmudic Halakhah (in Hebrew) (Tel Aviv, 1962), 90–95; Yitzhak D. Gilat, "Of the Early Origin of Certain Sabbath Prohibitions" (in Hebrew), Bar-Ilan Annual 1 (1953): 119. There is an important contribution to the clarification of the problem in a recent article by Yitzhak D. Gilat, Of the Development of the Endeavors Prohibited on the Sabbath (in Hebrew), Proceedings of the American Academy for Jewish Research 49 (1982): 9–21.
6. Mekhilta de-Rabbi Ishmael, ed. Horowitz-Rabin (Frankfurt am Main, 1981), 30–31. Nahmanides, in his commentary on the Pentateuch (Exodus 12:16), and R. Isaiah of Trani, Responsa (Jerusalem, 1975), 217–218, refer to the interpretation of

At a later stage the accepted Sabbath prohibitions were reexamined, whether as a result of events such as the refusal of the pious to defend themselves at the time of the Hasmonean war[7] or as part of the evolution of a rationalistic school of halakhic thought that aspired to explain the prohibitions and define them by means of these explanations.[8] Not all prohibitions were found justified by the simplistic interpretation of biblical verses, and so there developed differentiations between what was to be considered an original Torah ruling and what would be defined as *mi-divrei soferim*, "of rabbinic origin." In this respect, a Gentile performing creative labor for a Jew was defined as belonging to the second category. In the original terminology (*Shabbat* 150a), "telling a Gentile [to perform creative labor for a Jew on the Sabbath]" is a rabbinic prohibition.[9]

The homily adduced by the Mekhilta linking this prohibition with a biblical verse does not appear in either the Babylonian or the Jerusalem Talmud. It reappears in halakhic discussion in the Middle Ages,[10] at which time it caused some confusion, for it seemed to contradict the accepted talmudic opinion that the prohibition of "telling a Gentile" had no roots in the Torah. The problem was generally resolved by means of the standard formula invoked in such cases, that the homily appearing

---

the Mekhilta. According to the reading and understanding of Nahmanides, the interpretation referring to the prohibition of the work done by a non-Jew for the benefit of a Jew reflects the opinions of both Mishnaic sages (tannaim) mentioned in the Mekhilta, R. Josiah and R. Jonathan. Nahmanides' conclusion is that this is merely an *asmakhta*, a nonobligatory mention. According to R. Isaiah of Trani, R. Jonathan differed with this interpretation. The accepted halakhah that "telling a non-Jew" is only a rabbinical prohibition is according to his view. See below in the text and n. 10.

7. This matter is dealt with in many studies and in great detail in M. D. Herr, "The Problem of Warfare on the Sabbath in the Periods of the Second Temple and the Period of the Mishnah and Talmud," *Tarbiz* 30 (1961): 242–256.

8. This aspect was emphasized by Yitzhak Baer, *Israel Among the Nations* (in Hebrew) (Jerusalem, 1955), 101–102; and see Hanoch Albeck, *Mishnah Moed*, 10.

9. The exact wording is applied only by talmudic sages (amoraim) (see parallel passages to *Shabbat* 150a), but the commentators use it to explain various tannaitic rulings. See *Encyclopedia Talmudit*, s.v. *amira le-mokhri shevut*. For the concept of *shevut*, see Albeck in the supplementary material to *Mishnah Betsah* 5:2 and the studies referred to there.

10. *Sefer Yereim ha-Shalem* 304 (168b); *Sefer Mitsvot Gadol*, negative injunctions 75 (Venice 1547), 24b.

in the tannaitic midrashim was only an *asmakhta*,[11] that is, a mere scriptural support for a rabbinic enactment. This explanation seems not to have satisfied everyone, for it was found necessary to make a distinction between "telling a Gentile" on the Sabbath itself and giving him the task before the commencement of the Sabbath[12] or between labor involving the Jew's possessions and that involving the Gentile's possessions.[13] The only practical conclusion drawn, however, from the remaining doubt—that it might indeed be completely biblical[14]—was that one must be especially careful not to violate the prohibition.[15]

Nevertheless, the detailed instructions determining what was permitted and what was prohibited were not derived from any general principle but rather from the rulings learned from the talmudic tradition, most of which were phrased casuistically and defined each case— whether permitted or prohibited—on an individual basis. It may be said at the very most that it was possible to deduce or guess the reason for the individual prohibition or permission and to reason analogically concerning other cases in which the specific reason applied or did not apply. In clarifying the reasoning behind various rulings, certain abstract rules were formulated, which could then be used to decide in doubtful cases. The concept *sekhar shabbat*, that is, that it was forbidden to benefit from an action performed on the Sabbath, even if the action was itself permissible, is just such an abstract rule. It itself served as the reason for prohibiting the renting of a tool to a non-Jew who will then use it

11. Without a doubt with Nahmanides (see n. 6), as well as *Sefer Yereim* and *Sefer Mitsvot Gadol*. R. Isaiah of Trani (*Responsa*) has no need of this explanation, for he holds that R. Jonathan disagreed with the interpretation and that the halakhah was ruled in his favor.

12. *Sefer Mitsvot Gadol*, according to one explanation. According to the other one, it is all of rabbinic origin and the verse a mere mention.

13. *Sefer Yereim. Sefer Yereim*, too, refers to two explanations, one of which holds that it is all of rabbinic origin.

14. According to *Sefer Mitsvot Gadol*.

15. *Levush, Orah Hayyim* 243, adduces the opinion of those holding that the interpretation has to be taken literally, adding: "Therefore one must act very strictly because of the severity of the Sabbath," meaning that one must observe the prohibitions fastidiously, but not that it is obligatory to rule strictly as with all cases of doubt in rulings of biblical origin. Some later authorities tended to rule strictly in matters of "telling a Gentile." They found a basis for their rulings in the words of the Mekhilta, claiming that certain types of "telling" are forbidden biblically. See R. Meir Eisenstadt, *Panim Meirot*, pt. 1 (Amsterdam, 1715), sec. 38; R. Amram Blum, *Responsa Beit Shearim* (Munkács, 1909), sec. 89.

in his labors on the Sabbath, though Jews are not under any obligation to keep their tools idle on the Sabbath.[16] On the other hand, not all tool rentals are prohibited. The details of what is permitted and what is forbidden require study based on the examples provided by the sources. Therefore, in this case as elsewhere in the world of halakhah, rulings are characteristically reached by grafting abstract formulas onto original casuistic elements, an act giving rise to *pilpul*, halakhic argumentation, in both its positive and negative aspects.[17] At any rate, the development of abstract rules in no way challenged the importance of casuistic elements. A scholar desirous of learning the roots of laws making up a halakhic ruling in any field of halakhic endeavor must become acquainted with the concrete examples that gave rise to the decision.

We shall thus open our discussion of the Sabbath Gentile with a presentation of examples relevant to this matter. We shall not classify them according to their halakhic weight, their strictness or leniency. Rather we shall classify them according to their practical significance in private and public life. There would appear to be seven relevant categories.

1. Satisfying Personal Needs

The classic example of this category is having a Gentile light a candle for the benefit of a Jew, something which is forbidden, in contrast to the permission given by halakhah to using the light of a candle lit by a Gentile for his own benefit (Mishnah *Shabbat* 16:8). A parallel example is that of a Gentile constructing a gangway to enable people to disembark from a boat. This is illustrated by a story involving R. Gamaliel and other sages who arrived in a boat, "when a non-Jew constructed a gangway to facilitate disembarkation, and R. Gamaliel and the sages used it to disembark." A third example appears in a *baraita* (*Shabbat* 122a): "[If a Gentile] has filled [a trough] with water for his animal to drink, a Jew may use the water for his own animal afterward; [if, however, the Gentile did so] to water the Jew's animal, it is forbidden

16. See *Tur Shulhan Arukh, Orah Hayyim* 246.
17. For the ambiguous use of this term, see Dov Rappel, *The Debate about Pilpul* (in Hebrew) (Jerusalem, 1980), 17.

[to exploit this]." In this case, however, a qualification is added: "When does this apply? When the Jew is not acquainted with that Gentile; if he is acquainted with him, it is forbidden." This means that when the two are acquainted, there is the suspicion that filling the trough with water is liable to have been for the purpose of the Jew. Accordingly, it seems that R. Gamaliel should have refrained from disembarking via the aforementioned gangway, for that episode is certainly a case of "being acquainted." The Talmud (*Shabbat* 122a) supplies two solutions to the problem: "Abbaye said: This [putting up the gangway] took place when [R. Gamaliel] was not present. Rava said: Even if it is assumed that [R. Gamaliel] was present, a candle for a single person is the same as a candle for a hundred people." If the act was performed when he was not present, it is certainly permitted; and if it was performed in his presence, Rava permits it, and his ruling is accepted in the case of a candle and a gangway since the action taken by the Gentile serves both his own interests and those of a Jew; this is not the case with respect to filling a trough with water or similar instances, in which the Jew's acquaintance with the Gentile or his presence when the act is performed arouses the suspicion that the Gentile does additional work for the sake of the Jew.

2. Employing a Gentile to Do the Jew's Work

The simplest example of this is where a Jew hands a Gentile materials before the commencement of the Sabbath to have them repaired or otherwise processed, such as animal hides for processing or items for laundering. In these cases, Beit Hillel, whose halakhic rulings are decisive, permits the transaction, even if the Jew knows that the Gentile will perform the work on the Sabbath (*Shabbat* 17b–18a). Similarly, it was permitted for a Jew to hand a non-Jewish emissary a letter which the Jew himself could not deliver, either because of the restriction on carrying objects from one domain to another or because of the prohibition of traveling outside boundary limits (*Shabbat* 19a). Such permission, however, is conditional, depending upon the interpretation of the said source. In the same way it was permitted for a Jew to hand over his field to a Gentile tenant; one opinion (that of R. Simeon ben Gamaliel) was that this permission was unconditional, while another (that of R. Simeon ben Eleazar) held that the Jew must make this transfer conditional upon the Gentile's agreeing to refrain from cultivation of the field on the Sabbath (*Avodah Zarah* 21b–22a). This permission applied to a field but not to a public bathhouse. The reason for the permission was, according to R. Simeon ben Gamaliel, with whom the halakhic ruling agrees, that the tenant cultivates the field in order to earn his portion of the crop. Such permission does not, however, apply to a public bathhouse, even if the Gentile desirous of renting it agrees to a tenantlike status granting him a percentage of the income, because tenancy is not usual in connection with bathhouses, and an observer would conclude that the Gentile is working for the Jew on a daily basis. Elsewhere (*Moed Katan* 12a), the amora Samuel differentiates *kibbolet*, work done on a contractual basis when the worker's wages are paid in proportion to output, just as in sharecropping; such is forbidden when performed within Sabbath limits and permitted outside Sabbath limits. This demonstrates that the impression gained by the Jewish public is what is decisive: If the labor is performed in a place inaccessible to local Jews—or to any Jew, according to an alternative version—it is permitted. The question of whether these rulings may be mutually resolved, or whether, having been stipulated in various times and places, they are mutually contradictory, is one we need not answer. It was of concern to halakhic authorities, who based their rulings upon these sources; they could not do so until after they clarified, in their own fashion, the relationship between these two sources.

3. Partnership

The example is where a field is accepted for cultivation by Jewish and Gentile partners, with the labor and the crop being divided equally between the two. This was permitted, on condition that it be stipulated that the Jew would work on a weekday to balance the work of the Gentile on the Sabbath; if this were carried out, not only would no creative labor be done for the Jew on the Sabbath, but he would not even benefit from such Sabbath labor (*Avodah Zarah* 22a). This example, of course, figured prominently in discussions involving partnership in businesses and factories.

4. Starting a Sea Vogage

The simple interpretation of the relevant *baraita* (*Shabbat* 19a) leads to the conclusion that it was forbidden to set out fewer than three days before the Sabbath, unless the journey was intended to facilitate compliance with a Torah precept. The opinions of R. Judah the Prince and R. Simeon ben Gamaliel differed over the question of whether it is necessary to have the captain agree before setting sail to cease working on the Sabbath. This indicates that it is a case of a ship that belonged to the Gentile,[18] and the prohibition was apparently linked to the problem of a Jew benefiting from the services of a Gentile. Other doubts arose concerning a voyage by ship, such as walking around on board ship and disembarking (*Eruvin* 41b–42a); but these are not relevant to the question of a Sabbath Gentile.

5. Saving Property

The stated example is putting out a fire on the Sabbath. If the Gentile comes to put out the fire of his own volition, he is not to be stopped (unlike a Jewish child, who is prevented from putting the fire out). Furthermore, it was permitted to announce "that anyone putting out the fire would not suffer [because of it]" (*Shabbat* 121a)—an anonymous promise to the potential fire fighter that he would be rewarded.

6. Medicine and Precept Observance

Not only is a Jew permitted to treat a person considered dangerously ill, but it is obligatory for him to do so. This is not the case if the life of the sick person is not considered in danger. "Telling a non-Jew" to treat the patient in this instance is permitted (*Shabbat* 129a). The same applies to the observance of a religious precept such as circumcision, when the required implements were inaccessible without desecrating the Sabbath. In such a case, it is permitted to employ the services of a Gentile (*Eruvin* 67b–68a).

---

18. Professor Saul Lieberman reconstructed an external Mishnah (*baraita*) in the Jerusalem Talmud relating a disagreement between Beit Shammai and Beit Hillel concerning a Jew setting sail in his own ship: Beit Shammai bans it altogether and Beit Hillel permits it three days before the Sabbath (*Ha-Yerushalmi Kifshuto* [Jerusalem, 1934], 58–59). This halakhah vanished together with Jewish sailors; for the common ruling concerns Jews setting sail in a ship belonging to a Gentile.

7. Caring for the Dead

The burial of a person who passed away on the Sabbath is deferred until after the Sabbath, although ways were found to permit a Jew to perform the necessary preburial rites. However, in the case of two consecutive days (such as the two festival days observed in the Diaspora), during which a Jew could not engage in creative labor, the burial could not be delayed until after the festival was over. The halakhic ruling was that "if death occurred on the first day, Gentiles could deal with it"; the second day was considered profane for the purposes of burial, and the obligation of burial fell to the Jew (*Betsah* 6a). This dependence upon the services of a Gentile was ruled out by the amora Levi (*Shabbat* 139a), who was asked for a ruling on the matter by the citizens of Bashkar. His reasoning, as explained by the Talmud, was based on the fact that those who approached him in this connection were "not learned in the Torah" (*Shabbat* 139b). In the days of Ravina, the last of the amoraim, this ruling was abrogated lest the contemporary Persians (Parsees) seize on it in order to compel Jews to engage in other labors on Jewish festival days (*Betsah* 6a).

2

Halakhic Theory and Practice in Geonic Times

The tradition of Sabbath and festival observance was undoubtedly passed down from one generation to the next through family and community institutions. Jews exiled from place to place reintroduced into their new homes the various institutions in their accustomed fashion, which outstandingly included Sabbath and festival observance. The new living conditions in which Jews found themselves did not necessarily match their previous situation, and the reconstruction of institutions could not therefore be complete without some shifting or change. Moreover, conditions of existence could change wherever Jews were living, which led to situations in which halakhic rulings adduced in the Talmud were no longer relevant as precedents. At any rate, these situations required solutions, which could come at one of two levels: the popular, spontaneous approach or the authoritative, scholarly one. It is occasionally evident that certain customs had already become entrenched in the community even before the question was presented to the halakhic authorities of the day. In such cases, halakhic authorities had to face a number of questions: First, could they confirm the accepted custom retroactively? If this was impossible, could they just ignore the violations of halakhah in accordance with the rule: "It is better that they err inadvertently than deliberately"? Or were they obliged to uproot the accepted custom?

The decision taken in these cases depended upon the severity of the specific violation, as understood by the halakhic authority consulted, and his judgment was likely to be dependent upon his system of learning and his mastery of the sources and interpretational boldness. The halakhic expert's own character and other personal traits, together with the degree of authority afforded him by the community, could influence his decisions. A historian is obliged to try to identify the factors active in each case, to whatever extent the sources reveal these attributes, and insofar as his critical-analytical ability permits. The sources sometimes make it clear that halakhic scholars first dealt with the relevant questions through the study and interpretation of the sources, without any specific concrete problem requiring their attention. In other cases the authority answers a question in a practical matter, accepting direct responsibility for the results of his ruling.

Three situations involving halakhic ruling are here presented as archetypes: one, in the face of accepted custom; another, purely theoretical; and the third, practical but a priori. There are cases where the sources leave no doubt which of the types is under discussion. In other cases, however, the factual background is obscure, thus leaving it to the historian to clarify to the best of his ability the precise nature of the case and the archetypes to which it refers. The halakhic authorities distinguished in their own way between rulings with practical effects and between theoretical decisions and the like, but the sources did not always preserve the conditions under which the various decisions were made. Later authorities state their conclusions dogmatically, sometimes reading "some forbid," "some allow," and the like. As far as halakhic experts are concerned, such anonymous generalizations do not detract from the authority of the source; in fact, they may even enhance it. The historian, on the other hand, can get the most out of a given source only if he succeeds first in conceiving of it in its authentic historical context. Only by viewing it in this way can he trace the formulas adopted by the evolving problems and their solution over the generations. This, then, as in any other field, is the aim of historical research in the field of the study of the halakhah: to describe chronological development. In the present case, the purpose is to trace the rise of new problems or new solutions relating to the employment of a Gentile in connection with the Sabbath observance of Jews, during various periods from the geonic era until modern times. The geonic era is the direct extension of the Mishnaic and talmudic period, at least with regard to the main area in which Jews conducted their lives. Changes of regime and religion affecting neighboring peoples led to changes in the lives of the Jews as well, in their language, their education, and their livelihoods, without upsetting the principles of faith upon which Jewish community life was based. Everyday individual and community conduct was shaped by a religious tradition inherited from previous generations, while new issues that arose were decided by contemporary halakhic authorities, the geonim, who referred to the Mishnah and Talmud, the literary sources to which they had ready access. This is why the question of the written halakhah adapting to changing circumstances is already apparent at this time, as our discussion of the Sabbath Gentile will clearly demonstrate.

The problems occupying halakhic authorities of the day were no different from the examples adduced in the Mishnah and in the Talmud with regard to the Sabbath-observant Jew requiring the assistance of a non-Jew in meeting his own personal needs. Such issues as "a Jew living among Gentiles on the Sabbath, with nothing to eat"[1] or "a Jew stranded on the Sabbath, be he on a long or short journey, with nothing to eat or drink"[2] seem to have been resolved in the aforementioned talmudic source. Accordingly, in a responsum referring to the first of these cases, the authority concerned reproves the Jew for having eaten with the Gentiles "warm bread and milk that they had milked that very day."[3] The Jew had justified his doing so by saying, "they had prepared [the food] for themselves, and [so] it was permitted." There were no grounds for permitting this here because "when one is acquainted with him it is forbidden, especially when one is accustomed to eating with them during the week." Moreover, this case does not resemble that of the candle or the gangway, where the rule is "a candle for one is a candle for a hundred people"; "rather, bread and milk eaten by a single person is not the same as when two partake of them." Where foodstuffs are concerned,

---

1. *Otsar ha-Geonim, Shabbat* 352.
2. Ibid., 353.
3. The entire passage referred to in *ibid.*, 352.

it may be assumed that the Gentile host will prepare more food for his Jewish guest. This is a typical example of permission being requested by the person involved on the superficial basis of what he had incidentally learned of the halakhic tradition. This is also an example of careful public supervision; representatives of the community asked the gaon whether that Jew "had spoken correctly . . . or whether or not he is legally liable to punishment and a fine." The gaon thus ends his responsum, saying: "He should be warned not to repeat this in his folly; but if he does it again, he is to be suitably chastised and punished."[4]

Not all halakhic authorities, however, reacted in the same way. One gaon, when asked—with no connection to a specific instance—whether a Jew might drink the water a Gentile had brought for his own needs, replied in the affirmative after examining the relevant sources in detail.[5] The difficulty in granting the permission stemmed from the stipulation that the Jew and Gentile must not be acquainted; otherwise it is to be assumed that the Gentile would bring more water for the Jew. In most actual cases, the Jew and the Gentile would be acquainted since the Jew has need of the Gentile's services. This gaon limited the stipulation: The familiarity the Talmud refers to, he explained, was one of extreme closeness between the Jew and non-Jew ("he feels affection for him, or he requires something of him"), "but in ordinary cases, though he may be acquainted with him, there is no need to worry and it seems to be all right."[6]

A third source, which considered the problem of a Jew who found himself on a journey at the onset of the Sabbath, granted him permission to avail himself of the services of a non-Jew for a reason not mentioned anywhere in the Talmud. Because the Sabbath began while the Jew was traveling, and he had neither food nor drink, he may accept from Gentiles what they had prepared for themselves. "Why so? Because of the verse [Isaiah 58:13], 'You shall call the Sabbath a delight'—you are to make the Sabbath a delight and not an affliction.'"[7] This gaon was of the opinion that the obligation to maintain a pleasant Sabbath overrides

---

4. Ibid.
5. Ibid., 355.
6. Ibid.
7. Ibid., 353. For the concept of *oneg shabbat*, see *Shabbat* 118b. Further on, the gaon rules that even a person normally careful not to eat the bread of Gentiles may do so, also for the reason of *oneg shabbat*.

the suspicion of instructing a Gentile (to work) as long as the perform-ance of creative labor is not done at the direct request of the Jew to the Gentile.

The straightforward interpretation of talmudic injunctions were not always in harmony with what occurred in practice. The accepted custom was sometimes more lenient, and at other times stricter. The reason for deviation occupied halakhic authorities, and is a most significant starting point for historical study. The question of setting out by ship demonstrates this amply.

The aforementioned baraita[8] asserts the prohibition on setting sail in a boat three days before the Sabbath. It means that a person who embarked on a ship three days before the Sabbath is permitted to remain on board during the Sabbath without any question. However, according to Rav Hai Gaon, "We have never learned, either from our forefathers or from the scholars of the two academies, of anyone who permitted an individual to stay on board a river boat on the Tigris or on the Euphrates or any other river; it is customarily forbidden."[9] Similarly, the Jew from Egypt who questioned Rav Hai Gaon testified that "the Jews living in the towns and villages of Egypt maintain a strict prohibition in respect to the use of their Nile, preferring to hurry off the boats on the eve of the Sabbath."[10] According to Rav Hai Gaon, exception was made only if it was dangerous to get off the ship on Sabbath eve ("where there are herds of beasts to endanger life if one sojourns in the wilderness"), but "great rabbis and the steadfast sages of Israel refrain even in such cases."[11]

This undoubtedly refers to an ancient local tradition, probably dat-ing from the talmudic period,[12] and it seems to contradict the literary tradition that did not forbid one from remaining on board ship if the journey did not begin close to the Sabbath. Hai Gaon resolved this con-tradiction by claiming that the baraita, which grants permission under the stipulated condition, was referring to starting out on a sea journey,

8. See chap. 1.
9. Otsar ha-Geonim, Shabbat 46.
10. Ibid.
11. Ibid.
12. There is no reason to assume that a ban would have become entrenched in an open, public matter of this kind had it not already existed in previous generations.

as indicated by its terminology:[13] "Sailing is what is prohibited." That Hebrew *haflagah* specifically indicates the sea voyage was stated also by other commentators.[14] These others, however, concluded, as we shall yet see, that the entire prohibition did not apply to rivers,[15] whereas Hai Gaon argued otherwise in view of the prohibition current in his country that there was no permissible way to remain on board ship on the rivers.

What reason is there for a prohibition that applies absolutely in respect of rivers but only conditionally in respect of the sea? Hai Gaon tells us nothing on this occasion, but other sources relate in his name that traveling by ship is included in the rabbinic prohibition that "one may not float upon the water," which appears in the Mishnah (*Betsah* [5:2]);[16] but he never claimed that the reason for this prohibition was also of traditional origin. This is even more apparent with later scholars who proposed other reasons for the prohibition. There is no doubt that they based their proposals upon guesses and hypotheses. Furthermore, not one of the proposed reasons can explain all relevant halakhic details, as we shall yet see. Hai Gaon's explanation, repeated by R. Isaac in the Tosafot commentary,[17] apparently as an original hypothesis, encounters difficulties, for if it is the real reason, what is the point in distinguishing between setting out three days before the Sabbath and after it?[18] The historically valid conclusion seems to be that one would do best to abandon the attempt to uncover the original reason for this prohibition on the basis of halakhic principles that crystallized over the course of time.[19] If in Babylonia and Egypt setting sail on rivers was strictly for-

---

13. *Otsar ha-Geonim, Shabbat* 46. Just as Rav Hai concluded, so did the gaon Samuel ben Eli in his debate with Maimonides, *Responsa of Maimonides*, ed. J. Blau (sec. 309), (p. 572). The matter will be considered in chap. 3.

14. See Rashi to *Shabbat* 19a, beginning with the word *mafligin*.

15. See chap. 3, n. 51.

16. *Otsar ha-Geonim, Eruvin* 93.

17. See chap. 3, n. 40.

18. The Meiri used strong words concerning this explanation (*Shabbat* 19a, beginning with the word *shemua* [*Beit ha-Behirah* to Tractate *Shabbat*, ed. J. S. Lange (Jerusalem, 1965), 78]): "For if so it will always be prohibited."

19. Professor Saul Lieberman (*Ha-Yerushalmi Kifshuto* [Jerusalem, 1934], 57) accepts the opinion of *Baal ha-Maor* (see chap. 3, n. 19): "that the main reason we do not set sail on the Great Sea three days before the Sabbath is the fear that one may be endangered and have to desecrate the Sabbath." But Professor Lieberman proves (ibid., 58–59) that Beit Shammai prohibited setting sail the entire week for

bidden, such that pious Jews adhered to the ban even during time of danger, we may assume that such an action was considered a desecration of the Sabbath, although not necessarily according to any formal halakhic definition. It was certainly not easy for a person to observe the Sabbath, with its restrictions, atmosphere, and ceremonies, while traveling from place to place; and so the traveler was ordered to interrupt his journey if such an arrangement was at all possible.

There is no way to be sure of the extent to which this prohibition actually limited the freedom of movement of the Jew. We learn from Maimonides that it compelled Jews to take the alternative of traveling by caravan along the banks of the rivers of Babylonia.[20] In Egypt the prohibition was breached already in the days of Hai Gaon. This was the reason that the inquiry was addressed to him from Egypt: "Someone had arrived and granted them permission."[21] If, in Hai Gaon's lifetime, there were still "some who honored the prohibition,"[22] by Maimonides' time, the prevalent custom was undoubtedly one of permission.[23] It was apparently knowledge of this permit that prevailed in Egypt with the acquiescence of Maimonides that prompted R. Abraham ha-Kohen of Baghdad to appeal to him with a question, in the hope that Maimonides' authority would suffice to have permission granted in Babylonia as well.[24] Maimonides' disputant, Samuel ben Eli, indeed declared "that no possibility was found to permit traveling by boat on the rivers, either in the rulings of the sages or in common practice,"[25] but this does not mean that people encumbered by the prohibition did not think of ways

---

the same reason—the fear of having to desecrate the Sabbath. Considering the tradition of an absolute ban regarding the rivers in Mesopotamia and Egypt, is it not more likely to assume that staying on board ship was itself considered a desecration of the Sabbath in early times? At any rate, limiting the ban to three days before the Sabbath appears to be a compromise with the original absolute ban.

20. *Responsa of Maimonides* 310 (p. 577).

21. See n. 9 above.

22. Ibid.

23. Maimonides (n. 20 above) does not mention Egyptian affairs, but it seems from the context that the question involved only Babylonia, whereas in his land the problem did not exist.

24. *Responsa of Maimonides* 308. Concerning the questioner, see Samuel Poznanski, *Babylonische Geonim im nachgeonäischen Zeitalter* (Berlin, 1914), 21–22, where there is also a description of the correspondence between Baghdad and Egypt, but with no analysis of the content.

25. *Responsa of Maimonides* 309 (p. 572).

to permit the act, especially since they had heard that in Egypt the ranking authorities had permitted it.

The other aspect of the prohibition, setting sail on the sea three days before the Sabbath, had been breached and perhaps even abrogated completely during the geonic period. Justification for the permission granted was provided in the name of Mar Jacob Gaon bar Mordecai.[26] He found a basis for this lenient ruling while elucidating in a surprising fashion the *baraita* from which the prohibition was derived: "One may not set sail in a boat less than three days prior to the Sabbath—but if for fulfilling a precept, it is in order." The text also adds: "And one must stipulate with the captain that it is on condition that he will rest on the Sabbath, and then he does not rest; this is Rabbi's view. R. Simeon ben Gamaliel says: It is unnecessary [to do so]." The simple interpretation of the latter part of the *baraita* is that, according to Rabbi, even during the first few days of the week, when it is permitted to set sail, one must stipulate with the ship's captain that he will rest on the Sabbath. But R. Simeon ben Gamaliel rules: "He need not." The gaon claimed that both Rabbi and R. Simeon ben Gamaliel were referring to the last days of the week: According to Rabbi it is permitted to set sail provided the stipulation is made, whereas R. Simeon ben Gamaliel's opinion is that he need not strike this agreement, and he may set sail without it.[27] Some have held that this permission was accepted by the author of *Halakhot Gedolot* as well, either for the reason supplied by Jacob Gaon or for another reason.[28] While there remains some doubt as

---

26. *Otsar ha-Geonim, Shabbat* 45.

27. See Saul Lieberman, *Tosefta Kifshuta, Shabbat*, p. 218. According to Lieberman, the gaon interpreted *u-fosek* (and he stipulates) as if it were *o posek* (or he stipulates), this being in his opinion (ibid., 217) a completely new reason for permitting a Jew to set sail in a boat. But see chap. 3, n. 37, where R. Abraham ben Nathan maintains this interpretation.

28. The person putting the question to the gaon (n. 26) raised the opinion of *Halakhot Gedolot* and asked if he might rely on it. The respondent maintained that the compiler of *Halakhot Gedolot* was merely copying Mar Jacob Gaon, and the interpretation of the latter is not acceptable. R. Abraham ben Nathan (sec. 60) cites the words of *Halakhot Gedolot*: "But *Halakhot Gedolot* grants permission even on Sabbath eve." Thus, he, too, interpreted this as meaning that the permission granted concerned setting sail on Friday. The interpretation of the *Tur Orah Hayyim* appears to be the same (sec. 248) because the entire section deals with the question of setting sail on Friday. The *Tur*'s commentators, the *Beit Yosef* and the *Bah*, however, reinterpreted the matter as if the *Halakhot Gedolot* were deliberating the question of

to whether the *Halakhot Gedolot* was referring to the permission to set sail or not, it is certain that Rabbenu Hananel upheld the lenient view. Contrary to Hai Gaon's explanation that the *baraita* was dealing with sea voyages and not with river sailing, Rabbenu Hananel restricts the prohibition to rivers, and this only "when the boat barely touches the bottom, the water being less than ten handbreadths deep, this ruling being derived from the rule of Sabbath travel limitations."[29] The boat takes its Jewish passenger beyond the Sabbath travel limit. According to tractate *Eruvin* (43a), however, the rule of boundary limitation does not apply over ten handbreadths above ground level; that is, if the boat moves ten handbreadths above ground level, the travel limitation rule is void a priori.[30] If the prohibition to set sail depends upon that of travel limitations, it can only apply to such a boat barely touching bottom; in other words, one moving just above the river bed. This explanation could produce a permissive ruling even regarding great rivers, and later scholars, who were interested in such a position, did base their decisions upon such reasoning.[31] It is not clear whether Rabbenu Hananel is to be considered one of these scholars, but he undoubtedly strove to justify permitting setting out on sea voyages, as we may deduce from the way he concluded his concise commentary: "For this reason, it is customary to journey on the Great Sea."[32] We may safely say that this explanation,

---

acquiring the right to spend the Sabbath where there was no ban on setting sail. And see R. Isaac Alfasi (*Shiltei ha-Gibborim, Shabbat* 7b), who adduces the words of the compiler of *Halakhot Gedolot*, adding: "Perhaps this is what present scholars rely on in doing so." Thus he too understood the source as permitting a Jew to board the boat, even on the Sabbath itself. Similarly, *Shibbolei ha-Leket ha-Shalem* 111. The modern editor, Azriel Hildesheimer (*Halakhot Gedolot* [Jerusalem, 1972], pt. 1, p. 161), makes use of both considerations: He notes the opinion of Mar Jacob Gaon (according to which setting sail is what is permitted), adding that the source of this ruling is in *Eruvin* 42b, i.e., that it refers to occupying space within the confines of the ship before the onset of the Sabbath.

29. The interpretation of Rabbenu Hananel to *Shabbat* 19a, cited by R. Isaac Alfasi and attributed to an anonymous source.

30. The question whether there are limitations above a height of ten handbreadths is not resolved in *Eruvin* 43a–b, and Rabbenu Hananel rules leniently.

31. This was Maimonides' opinion in his responsum to R. Samuel ben Eli, *Responsa* 310 (p. 575), but he did not agree with this reason. See the opinion of R. Samson of Sens, *Or Zarua* 2:3, which justifies the opinion of Rabbenu Hananel and which on that basis construes a permissive ruling concerning sailing on large rivers. See chap. 3, nn. 53–54.

32. N. 29 above.

though forced and utterly rejected by later commentators,[33] was produced only to resolve the apparent contradiction between prevalent custom and explicit talmudic halakhah.[34]

The examples appearing in the Talmud, whether permissive or prohibitive, served as a precedent for rulings in similar cases, although whenever the similarity between precedent and current case was less than complete, external considerations proved capable of deciding the matter in either direction. As we have already seen, renting a field to a Gentile was allowed, but a public bathhouse was not.[35] What, then, was the ruling concerning ovens, millstones, or oil presses—installations apparently more commonly in Jewish hands than were bathhouses during the geonic period? One authority who was asked these questions compared the three individual cases to that of ovens, in that such an enterprise "is known by the name of the Jew, so that when the Gentile performs work on the Sabbath, desecration of God's Name occurs."[36] This respondent grasped the problem from the viewpoint of a prohibition that seeks to prevent a contradiction between the Jew's resting from labor and work being done in an enterprise bearing the Jew's name— this is the meaning of "desecration of God's Name" in this context— and so he forbade the arrangement. Such a ruling, however, would have restricted the sources of Jewish livelihood, and while some authorities inclined to this view,[37] it did not become accepted halakhah in actual practice. Another geonic source testifies: "In Babylon, it is accepted practice for Jewish oil presses to be rented out to Gentiles, and the scholars do not object."[38] This sage affirms the custom and reasons: "We have seen that bathhouses are known by the name of their owner, but not oil presses or large baking ovens."[39] It is reasonable to assume that

33. See chap. 3, n. 12.
34. In the words of the *Tashbets* 1:21: "Others try to justify the custom, saying that only setting sail in a boat near ground was forbidden."
35. Chap. 1.
36. *Otsar ha-Geonim, Shabbat* 27.
37. Joseph Gaon also forbids the renting of a baking oven, *Kolbo* (Venice, 1567), 154a.
38. *Teshuvat ha-Geonim* (Lyck, 1864), sec. 64. The question was also asked about an inn, the gaon ruling as a matter of course that this was not forbidden, according to Mishnah *Avodah Zarah* 21a. Millstones are not mentioned in this responsum.
39. Ibid.

this distinction did not derive from an observation of existing circumstances, for there is no way to distinguish between installations of these
three kinds. The distinction must have been a formal one. The Talmud
mentions only the bathhouses, and so it can be claimed that the law
applies exclusively to a bathhouse and to nothing else.

Jews still engaged in agriculture in the geonic period—though exactly where and to what extent is unknown[40]—and some jobs could not
be postponed for a full day. Certain types of fruit in the orchard had to
be picked daily, otherwise they would spoil. Could it be picked by a
non-Jew? The way to permit such activity was by selling the fruit to a
Gentile on Friday for a fixed sum and having the buyer pick the fruit
he had acquired before the onset of the Sabbath. Support for this permissive ruling was deduced from the aforementioned discussion of the
question of partnership with a Gentile; if the non-Jew's work on the
Sabbath leads to no profit for the Jew, it is permitted. Here, too, "if the
price drops, the Gentile loses; if the price rises, the Gentile profits—
under these conditions, it is permitted."[41] Another case was that of
watering a field, where the locally enacted apportioning of water meant
that the field could be watered only on the Sabbath. The labor had to
be carried out by a (non-Jewish) tenant of the Jewish landowner; Sherira
Gaon ruled that this was forbidden. On the one hand, it would seem
that the handing over of the field to one's tenant was explicitly discussed
in the Gemara (*Avodah Zarah* 21b) and allowed. On the other hand, the
other source ruled in the name of Samuel that "it is forbidden to give
out work on a contract basis within Sabbath limits."[42] The gaon ignored
the source in *Avodah Zarah* and followed Samuel's ruling, drawing the
conclusion "that if Jews are to be found in these fields on Sabbaths and
festival days, the tenant may not water them . . . but if they are distant,
it is permitted."[43] The gaon suggested a solution to the problem: "If it

40. Omitting the place of origin of the questions in most of the geonic sources
prevents the phenomena from being located with any precision, but there have been
attempts on the part of historians to ascribe them, especially to North Africa. See C.
Z. Hirschberg, A. *History of the Jews in North Africa* (in Hebrew) (Jerusalem, 1965),
pt. 1, 196–198.
41. L. Ginsberg, *Geonica* (New York, 1909), 2:153.
42. See chap. 1.
43. *Otsar ha-Geonim, Shabbat* 26. The rewriting of the responsum is attributed
to Hai Gaon.

is possible to lead water to them before the onset of Sabbath, it is permissible, even within Sabbath limits";[44] that is, the work is begun on Friday by opening the irrigation pipe to the field—this being explicitly permitted in Tractate *Shabbat* (18a). It is not known if this suggestion actually provided a practical solution; at any rate, the desire of the ruling authority not to cut off the source of a Jew's livelihood comes through clearly.

It had always been clear that Sabbath observance required a Jew to forfeit some potential source of livelihood, and there is no doubt whatever that the restrictions dictated by Sabbath observance did actually limit the enterprise a Jew was prepared to pursue in order to make his living. No Jew inquired whether he could serve as the manager of a Gentile-owned farm or as a soldier in an army led by a non-Jewish general, as these positions would a priori have required him to desecrate the Sabbath. But the case of a Gentile working for a Jew, though in principle also prohibited, was a different matter.

The attitude of simple Jews seems to have been that as long as they were not involved physically in jobs performed on their farms or in their plants they were not considered Sabbath desecrators. Prevalent labor prohibitions became second nature to Jews who were the product of a traditional upbringing, just like any taboo that one recoils from violating. The very recoiling ensures its perpetuation. The fact that these prohibitions involve a taboo of temporary validity has no effect upon the nature of the taboo. The cyclical character of these weekly prohibitions and their links with characteristics generating a "Sabbath atmosphere" render them a time-linked taboo that, when operative, is as effective as any taboo that is independent of temporal considerations for its validity.

Sabbath prohibitions, however, according to their halakhic definition, affect even those deeds unconnected with the Jew in a physical sense—such as having a Gentile perform the work of the Jew. But these lack the built-in automatic reflex apparatus. The awareness of the existence of such a prohibition is acquired by means of intellectual study, but is not ingrained in one's personal consciousness. There is thus no inhibition against evading such a prohibition, especially when there are

44. Ibid.

economic or other considerations. Such evasive action encounters the formal rules of halakhah, but this factor naturally carries greater weight with the halakhic authorities who are entrusted with the community's Sabbath observance than with the people directly concerned with the action to be taken. Maneuvering between those pressuring to find a way to allow a certain action and the halakhic considerations blocking this process falls within the realm of the halakhic authority. His decision does not always meet the expectations of the party that is directly involved and who is required to observe it. In such a situation there develops the gap between the popular tendency and the ability of the scholars to take this tendency into consideration. This phenomenon appears again and again throughout this study, and it is amply demonstrated as early as the geonic era under discussion.

The owners of a flock handed their sheep over to a Gentile shepherd, a doubtful procedure, *inter alia*, because of Sabbath regulations. There were those authorities who feared that the shepherd might lead the sheep outside Sabbath limits, a forbidden step according to the Mishnah (*Betsah* 5:3), which rules: "Animals and utensils are like the owner's feet." Hai Gaon is actually said to have advised not to hand over one's domestic animal to a non-Jew, unless one is capable of ensuring that the animal remains within Sabbath limits.[45] Nahshon Gaon did not acknowledge this fear, ruling that the animal enters the possession of the shepherd when he pulls it after him, and from then on Sabbath limitations no longer apply.[46] However, retorted Hai Gaon, if this is so, then handing the animal over to the Gentile is itself prohibited, just like renting or lending an animal to a non-Jew.[47] Hai Gaon's father, Sherira Gaon, had already judged a similar ruling,[48] but in the case he considered an additional factor was present. The person who had put the question to the gaon described the situation as it was in his place. At any rate, people acted as if handing over their flocks to a Gentile was permissible, for the majority of the people were not able to manage

45. Ibid., 39–40.
46. Ibid., 41.
47. Ibid., 42. The prohibition of lending and leasing is explicit in *Avodah Zarah* 15a.
48. *Teshuvot Geonim Kadmonim* 92. Attributing the responsum to Sherira Gaon, *Teshuvot Geonim Kadmonim* 31b.

without the services of the shepherds.[49] The case apparently involved
a place in which Jews made their living from agriculture or in part from
agriculture. Thus the gaon ruled that one must not "prohibit something
needed by the many . . . It is better that Jews do something inadvertently
than deliberately."[50] This is a clear example of the sages admitting their
inability to enforce religion, that is, religious law in all its detail.

Jews required the services of Gentiles in a number of ways. Their
farms seem to have depended upon the labor of slaves of both sexes.
Such servants, whether they were duly circumcised, thus becoming a
kind of semi-Jew, or whether they were neither circumcised nor ritually
immersed, could not be forced to work on the Sabbath. However, it is
doubtful if simple people kept this precept carefully.[51] Nevertheless,
wherever people were aware of the halakhic stipulations or wherever
halakhic scholars were firmly in control, there existed a rule whereby
Sabbath observance was never forced on slaves, "for we have no option
but to allow them to rest and to inform them of the precepts of honoring
the Sabbath. If they observe the Sabbath, this is all for the good."[52]
Moreover, the work of a Jew was never imposed upon them either. This,
then, offers no solution to the problem of doing necessary labor on the
Sabbath.

An example of such labor was milking cows or goats. This is defined
in the Talmud (Shabbat 144b) as creative labor in its fullest sense. The
only permission that could be granted depended upon having the animals milked into a container already containing some foodstuff. Yet it
is unclear if this was the way the prohibition was circumvented in the
talmudic period. During the geonic period, at any rate, this was not

49. That the inquirer depicted the situation is evident from the respondent's
answer: "Since they conduct themselves permissibly . . . as you have mentioned in
your letter."

50. Ibid.

51. Rav Natronai was asked if it was permissible to say to a slave on the Sabbath:
"Collect figs and grapes for us, in order to bring them to us after dark." His answer
was: "It is forbidden . . . for one's slave is obliged to observe the Sabbath like
himself." Otsar Ha-Geonim, Shabbat 455. With regard to a person who died on the
first day of a festival on which the burial has to be performed by a Gentile, a warning
was issued that "slaves of a Jew are forbidden to bury the dead on the first day of the
festival . . . and if they do so, they should be warned and their owners reprimanded."
Ibid., Beiza, 8.

52. The words of Sherira Gaon. Otsar Ha-Geonim, Shabbat 456.

considered a solution; nor could the milking process itself be left until Saturday night because such a step was considered hazardous to the animal. Some milked the animals using a different vessel, thus hinting at the special nature of the day. Such permission was approved by several anonymous "rabbis," but was rejected by the known authorities: "those 'scholars' . . . who ruled contrary to the halakhah, improperly and unjustly," wrote Mattathias Gaon.[53] He advised using the services of a Gentile, under two conditions: that the Gentile be instructed before the onset of the Sabbath and that the milk be given to a Gentile. It would thus be permissible "because of the danger to the animal."[54] According to the testimony of Hai Gaon, "Here it is customary to make use of a Gentile, with Gentiles taking the milk for themselves."[55] Utilizing non-Jews was undoubtedly common. But forfeiting the milk would have been an economic burden, and it is hard to assume that everyone abided by it.[56]

Economic pressure created popular permission, the approval of which for halakhic authorities depended upon the ability of the latter to find justification for them on the grounds of dialection; but the readiness to do so was not dependent upon the severity of the prohibition according to halakhic categories. In some cases, the prohibitions could be logically circumvented, like the aforementioned legal stratagem whereby a Jew could sell his field or his portion in a farm or store to a Gentile partner on Sabbath eve, only to buy it back on Saturday night. The authority consulted on this point defined this device as a deceit, ruling that even if the sale is carried out according to all the rules of purchase, a person acting in such a fashion would be guilty of "deceiving both God and man, such an act involving a Sabbath prohibition . . . and a desecration of the Sabbath and the name of God in the eyes of both Jews and Gentiles."[57]

Similar situations in which evasive tactics were employed in Jewish

53. *Otsar Ha-Geonim, Shabbat* 444.
54. *Ibid.*
55. *Ibid.*, 442, the end of the responsum, p. 150.
56. For the explicit permission by the Ashkenazi sages, see below, chap. 5. See the note of B.M. Levine, *Otsar Ha-Geonim, Shabbat* 443. He understood that the permission given by the Haggahot Maimonides, chapter 8:7 (there erroneously, 10) relies on a Geonic source. The context does not allow this interpretation.
57. *Geonica* II, pp. 196–7.

life despite the protests of halakhic scholars are demonstrated by the following statement made by Joseph Gaon, here quoted in full:

> Our Rabbi Joseph Gaon of blessed memory was asked whether a Jew can enter into a partnership with a Gentile in a shop, with the Gentile sitting in the shop on the Sabbath, selling and buying in the shop on the Sabbath. In our opinion such a thing is forbidden for one may come to do bookkeeping and benefit from income generated on the Sabbath; people will then say that he makes a profit on the Sabbath, and this is forbidden. It is also forbidden for a Jew to enter into a partnership with a Gentile in ploughing, with the Gentile doing the ploughing on the Sabbath with animals belonging to the Jew, because a Jew is commanded to cease work on the Sabbath—he himself, his ox, his ass, and all his animals. A Jew is also forbidden to give his Gentile partner money for purposes of ploughing, so that the Gentile could buy oxen and other animals with that money and then plough with them on the Sabbath, because the Jew has a share in the oxen and other animals and so they are considered to be his own animals, and this is forbidden. It is also forbidden for a Jew to use evasive tactics with his Gentile partner with whom he ploughs and sell him the animal he ploughs with or the goods in his shop and then buy the animal back after the Sabbath—for it is deceitful and is forbidden unless he parts with the animal or the goods completely.[58]

The steps described here—the Gentile partner sitting in the shop on the Sabbath, the Jew participating in the purchase of animals and in their working on the Sabbath under the direction of the Gentile without selling them or with only a formal sale—are not mentioned in the talmudic sources. If the gaon found it necessary to mention them explicitly, he must have known that such deeds were actually performed.

Formal halakhic definitions did indeed serve as jumping-off points for halakhic rulings, but their boundaries were determined by a grasp of the essence of the Jewish Sabbath. The uneducated Jew tended to view his own abstention from creative labor as fundamental, whereas the scholars shouldering the responsibility for the community also took into consideration the impression that a particular step would create. It should not appear as if the Sabbath were being observed only outwardly. In this approach the halakhic authorities had talmudic examples to rely upon.

58. Kolbo (note 37).

3

Traveling by Sea and River in European Lands

The arrival of Jews in Europe signified a change in the physical conditions under which Jews lived, and many of the problems that had plagued earlier generations vanished almost automatically. Jews living in Europe no longer made a living by farming; we no longer hear of difficulties in irrigating fields or harvesting the fruits of the land on the Sabbath. Nevertheless, the kind of occupations typical of European Jewry involved contact with Gentiles, and these contacts gave rise to problems that did not always have a precedent in geonic tradition. Furthermore, the sages of these generations refused to recognize the absolute authority enjoyed by the geonim, preferring to refer to talmudic sources for acceptable solutions to questions they might have resolved in accordance with geonic instructions.

The integration of these two factors, the change in physical reality and the independent interpretation and ruling of scholars living outside Babylonia, is especially illustrated in the problem of traveling by boat on the Sabbath. In contrast to Babylonia, where traveling by river was considered forbidden, Maimonides testifies that the scholars of Spain used to sail along the Guadalquivir River and from there to Alexandria

by sea, without interrupting their journey on the Sabbath.[1] He mentions
six of the most renowned sages of the generations preceding himself,
the most recent of whom being R. Isaac Alfasi and his disciple, R. Isaac
Migash. In Germany we find R. Nathan ha-Makhiri on board ship during
the Sabbath together with his mentor, "our teacher, the Light of the
Exile," en route from Mainz to Worms.[2] R. Eliezer ben Nathan mentions
a custom accepted in his hometown, Mainz, "of boarding a boat on
Sabbath eve, just before sundown, to travel to Worms or Cologne";[3] and
R. Samson of Sens lists the three rivers, the Danube, Rhine, and Elbe,
on which one may embark as late as Friday with no fear of Sabbath
violation.[4] They were apparently unaware of the Babylonian tradition
forbidding travel by river; or if they knew of the ruling they simply
ignored it. They even interpreted the limited permission allowing em-
barkation during the first three days of the week as referring to travel
by sea only, as Rashi emphasizes. He has two interpretations for the
term *haflagah* used in the Talmud; according to both it refers to sea
journey exclusively.[5]

This limiting definition, however, did not explain why the prohibition of setting sail three days before the Sabbath should apply to sea
travel but not to rivers. Furthermore, the practiced tradition contradicted the teaching regarding sea travel as well, as stated by R. Menahem
ha-Meiri: "The commentators are all confused in connection with this
topic, especially since nobody has ever refrained from traveling by sea
even on Fridays, and they have not heard of anyone protesting this custom."[6] Indeed, we find no one attempting to restore the old prohibition,
as sometimes occurred when later scholars discovered that custom had
deviated from the halakhically obligatory ruling. It seems that the reason
for this is the practical difficulty involved, on the one hand, and the

1. *Responsa of Maimonides*, ed. J. Blau (Jerusalem, 1960), sec. 310 (p. 576).
2. Ephraim Kupfer, *Responsa and Decisions by Scholars of Ashkenaz and France* (in Hebrew) (Jerusalem, 1973), 112 n. 7. Kupfer identifies the rabbi as Rabbenu Ger-shom, the Light of the Exile, whereas Avraham Grossman, *The Early Sages of Ash-kenaz* (in Hebrew) (Jerusalem, 1981), 365 n. 24, identifies him as R. Isaac ben R. Judah.
3. R. Eliezer ben Nathan, *Even ha-Ezer* (Jerusalem, 1913), par. 60. Setting sail on a river seems to have been considered fully permitted. Eliezer ben Joel, *Sefer Ravia*, pt. 1, sec. 391.
4. *Or Zarua* 2:3.
5. *Shabbat* 19a, beginning with the word *mafligin*.
6. R. Menahem ha-Meiri's *Beit ha-Behirah, Shabbat* 19a, beginning with the word *shemua* (see chap. 2, n. 18).

lack of obvious connection between the prohibition itself and actual
Sabbath observance, on the other.

The practical difficulty is clearly demonstrated in R. Isaac ben
Sheshet's description of the Jews' "setting sail by sea and sometimes
having to arrive on the Sabbath in a boat, for the sailors do not want to
wait for them and the Jews worry too much about their goods to leave
them with them."[7] Refraining from setting out during the second half
of the week meant missing half of the opportunities to set out. There
is no doubt that this impediment was a central factor in rescinding the
prohibition as early as the geonic period. No less important, however,
is the second factor: Refraining from setting sail on the days preceding
the Sabbath caused no break in the set of restrictions and symbols determining the character of the Sabbath. The prohibition could be justified on formal grounds only, and the rule applied that the authority
that prohibited could equally permit it. It was shown in the preceding
chapter that, as early as the geonic period, there were scholars who
justified rescinding the prohibition, and once it was rescinded it was
never renewed.

It is true that the reason underlying this leniency as given by Mar
Jacob Gaon[8] was apparently unknown in Europe. It is not adduced by
a single halakhic authority as a basis for ruling and was discovered only
recently, with the disclosure of geonic sources unknown to previous
generations.[9] Rulings of the *Halakhot Gedolot* were known, and though
his phraseology is unclear and his reasoning not explained, they did at
times serve as a reference for permitting this activity.[10] Clear and explicit permission was of course included in Rabbenu Hananel's ruling,[11]
but its basis came under attack. R. Isaac Alfasi at first agreed with him
but later challenged his ruling.[12] It will be recalled that Rabbenu Hananel limited the prohibition to rivers shallower than ten handbreadths,

---

7. *Responsa of the Ribash* 152.
8. See chap. 2, nn. 26–28.
9. First printed in *Geonica*, edited by L. Ginsberg (New York, 1909) 2:85–86.
10. See chap. 2, n. 28.
11. See chap. 2, n. 29.
12. As R. Zerahiah ha-Levi (Baal ha-Maor) writes (to *Shabbat* 19a, beginning
with the words *veha deteno*): "R. Isaac Alfasi interpreted this in the laws pertaining
to a barge and afterward retracted it in a responsum." In the edition before us there
appears Alfasi's reservation concerning Rabbenu Hananel's interpretation in the halakhah (see next note), but this was not apparently so in the edition before the author
of the *Maor*.

to which the Sabbath distance limitations also applied. But Alfasi reasoned that if distance limitations were applicable here, how could it be permissible for a person who had set sail three days before the Sabbath?[13] R. Isaac Alfasi then suggested a new reason for the prohibition, namely, setting sail shortly before the Sabbath would make *oneg shabbat* (Sabbath enjoyment) impossible because of seasickness, which affects a person at the beginning of his sea voyage.[14] Accordingly, the prohibition would apply specifically to journey on the Great Sea, and consequently, Rabbenu Hananel's conclusion that "for this reason it has been customary to travel by sea" would be nullified; as the Meiri says, "According to this, [setting out] three [days] before the Sabbath for secular purposes [as opposed to religious ones] is forbidden."[15] The Meiri does add that a basis for granting permission can be found according to the following explanation: "for anyone accustomed to it or, perhaps, in our day for everyone, since the sailors are expert at it, etc."[16] (referring to improved sailing conditions as compared with those of the talmudic period). We cannot know whether he interpreted Alfasi's intent correctly or not. But the latter's silence in refraining from drawing the logical conclusion from his system—according to which the justification for the popular leniency is nullified—indicates that he had no desire to challenge it. Furthermore, Maimonides' testimony that Alfasi himself acted permissively is well known.[17] In accordance with Alfasi's understanding, Maimonides, too, explained the prohibition in his code and responsa,[18] but he made no particular effort to secure the prohibition in actual practice. On the contrary, in connection with traveling by river he mentioned "that by virtue of necessity it is required to permit certain things previously forbidden."[19] The prohibition was apparently to be reinstituted also according to a third reason proposed by Rav Zerahiah ha-Levi, who wrote that someone setting sail three days before the Sabbath—"all three days before Sabbath are called 'before Sabbath'—appears to be stip-

---

13. R. Isaac Alfasi, *Shabbat* 19a. Alfasi raises two other points as well, but this is the main one.
14. Ibid.
15. See n. 6 above.
16. Ibid.
17. See n. 1 above.
18. *Hilkhot Shabbat* 30:13. The responsum ibid.
19. *Responsa* 310 (p. 577).

ulating that the Sabbath be set aside,"[20] for the place was hazardous.
And where life was endangered, nothing was sacrosanct. This opinion
was expressed by way of interpretation, and there is no indication that
the writer sought to put an end to the permissive approach accepted by
the general public. On the contrary, according to the tradition expounded by Rabbenu Nissim ben Reuben Gerondi, Nahmanides based
his permissive ruling upon the reasoning of Rabbi Zerahiah ha-Levi. He
claimed that the prohibition originally applied only to a ship on which
the majority of passengers were Jewish, in which case, creative labor
performed on board by the ship's Gentile owners would be performed
for Jews. By contrast, "on board ship with a majority of Gentile passengers and only a few Jews"—a typical situation in the Middle Ages—
any work performed would be performed for the Gentiles, and a Jew
need not worry about benefiting from it.[21] Another tradition, reported
by the *Maggid Mishneh*, related that Nahmanides was not completely
satisfied with this permissive ruling, adding that "a sensitive person
will be disturbed by it [taking advantage of this permit]."[22] This is the
only indication that any halakhic authority had second thoughts about
the accepted permission, and ha-Meiri's statement that no one protested
against this permissive approach[23] is thus supported by the testimony
of the sources.

In contrast to the Sephardic halakhic authorities, as well as those
of southern France, who often made their halakhic rulings without taking into account whether they complied with accepted practice or not,
their Ashkenazic counterparts were always very sensitive to questions
of the correlation between halakhah and accepted custom. This Ashkenazic trait can be illustrated with reference to the two points under
consideration: traveling by river on the Sabbath and setting sail by sea
just before the Sabbath or even on the Sabbath itself.

The leniency on both accounts was enjoyed by Ashkenazic Jews,

20. See n. 12 above.
21. Rabbenu Nissim to Alfasi, *Shabbat* 19a. After adducing the opinion of the
Baal ha-Maor, he says: "And in this way Nahmanides permitted sailboats to enter
the sea on the Sabbath." The Baal ha-Maor is apparently referring to Sabbath desecration committed by the Jew when in danger, but it is also forbidden to use the
Gentile's labor during the regular voyage, if it is done for the Jew.
22. *Maggid Mishneh, Hilkhot Shabbat* 30:13.
23. See n. 6 above.

apparently from the earliest days. Evidence of this custom being approved by a halakhic authority comes to light in a tradition ascribed to R. Nathan ha-Makhiri and R. Samuel ben Meir, quoting Rashi, "that it is permissible to board a boat on the Sabbath, to travel past Sabbath limits, and to carry an object while on board. . . . In addition, it has been ruled that even if one did not board the ship before sunset, he may still set sail on the Sabbath itself."[24] The doubts to be resolved according to Rashi's ruling concerned secondary halakhic questions: whether it was permissible to carry while on board ship, whether this permit depended for its validity on whether the passenger was already on board ship when the Sabbath began,[25] and whether it was permitted to board the ship on the Sabbath itself. The fact that one was permitted to set sail just before the Sabbath—unlike the beraita's three-day limitation—appeared unproblematic in their eyes.

Permission was undoubtedly accepted not only for rivers but for sea travel as well, for R. Samuel ben Meir's ruling—admittedly with no connection to Rashi's tradition—has reached us in its original wording. He deals explicitly with the question of "why the sages permitted sailing in a boat on the sea."[26] The rulings of Rabbenu Hananel[27] and R. Isaac Alfasi[28] were apparently unknown to R. Samuel. In contrast to their opinion, he assumed that sailing by both river and sea involved a violation of the Sabbath limits prohibition[29] but that one should differentiate nevertheless between "a person walking by foot on dry land . . . which is extremely troublesome, whereas a person on board a moving ship seems to be stationary, and he may make use of the ship like he makes use of his house; moreover, once the ship has moved it is as if he is unable to stop it, since it is in the hands of its captain who steers

24. *Shibbolei ha-Leket ha-Shalem* 111 (p. 82).
25. Carrying meant walking outside the four cubits considered the space required by any person, a question dealt with in *Eruvin* 42b–43a. See also Kupfer, *Responsa and Decisions by Scholars of Ashkenaz and France* 112–113, esp. n. 7.
26. *Or Zarua* 2:146 (p. 78). In summarized form, the words of R. Samuel ben Meir also appear in Tosafot *Eruvin* 43a, beginning with the words *halakhah ke-Rabban Gamliel bi-sefinah.*
27. See chap. 2, nn. 29–30.
28. See n. 13 above.
29. Proved by the wording of his question: "And if you ask why the sages allowed one to set off in a boat at sea since he is then putting himself into a situation where he will have no choice but to violate Sabbath limits" (n. 26 above).

it; he is a Gentile, and it is in his power to anchor it or let it travel."[30] These phrases express the feeling of the Jewish traveler that he is not physically violating any of the Sabbath regulations, which, R. Samuel assumed, was why "the rabbis were not so strict with boats."[31] If this permit appears to contradict the words of the *baraita*, which rules that "we do not set sail, etc.," R. Samuel neutralized this source by ascribing the *baraita* to Beit Shammai, who ruled strictly concerning other labors as well, saying that they had to be finished before the inception of the Sabbath.[32]

The fact that we are dealing with a widely accepted custom for which the support of the traditional literature was belatedly sought is proved by virtue of Rabbenu Tam's having proposed a halakhic justification different from that suggested by his brother R. Samuel. The *baraita* (*Shabbat* 19a) forbidding setting sail less than three days before the Sabbath adds: "In what case is this valid? When [the goal of the voyage] is optional, but when it is obligatory [*mitsvah*], it seems to be all right." Rabbenu Tam's contribution was his definition of *devar ha-reshut*, something optional," as being like "someone going for a walk," whereas a person traveling on "business is considered something obligatory"[33] because according to talmudic tradition (Kiddushin 30b, Bava Metsia 30b), it is obligatory (*mitsvah*) for a person to make a living from some craft. Furthermore, even a person "going to visit a friend is considered something obligatory."[34] In actual practice, therefore, the prohibition against setting sail just before the Sabbath was in effect abrogated, while the permission to do so was extended to include setting out on the Sabbath itself.

30. Ibid.
31. Ibid.
32. Ibid.
33. *Mordekhai, Shabbat* 258. This reasoning is found in R. Eliezer ben Nathan, sec. 60, as well: "And I have found," without mentioning the source. Ephraim E. Urbach, *Baalei ha-Tosafot* (Jerusalem, 1980), 174–175, notes a case where R. Eliezer ben Nathan disagrees with a ruling by Rabbenu Tam without mentioning his name. In the matter under consideration here, too, R. Eliezer disagrees with Rabbenu Tam. He considers it obligatory (*mitsvah*) only "to supervise public enterprises as well as anything involving a danger to life, but trade is merely something allowed, for if one does not set out for the journey one day, he does so the next day." We shall see below how R. Eliezer ben Nathan resolves the matter.
34. *Mordekhai, Shabbat* 258.

The contradiction between the accepted practice and the simple interpretation of the halakhic sources continued to trouble the scholars of the generations after R. Samuel ben Meir and Rabbenu Tam as well. The responsa of the latter did not satisfy everyone. Their contemporary, R. Eliezer ben Nathan, already challenged Rabbenu Tam's definition of the concept "obligatory," for, in the opinion of the former, setting out "on business is optional";[35] and R. Samuel's responsum was challenged as soon as notice was taken of the relevant *baraita* as it appears in the Jerusalem Talmud. This version demonstrates that the *baraita* was accepted by all schools of thought, including that of Beit Hillel, the prohibition against setting out just before the Sabbath not being limited to Beit Shammai at all.[36] Nevertheless, the examination of the reasons underlying the permissive ruling did not touch upon the ruling itself. R. Eliezer ben Nathan did not doubt that the accepted permission had its origins not in people's nonchalance, but rather in a ruling laid down by the early Ashkenazic sages, the *rishonim*, although the *aharonim*, the scholars of a more recent generation, extended this permission beyond the limits intended by their predecessors.[37] Even so, however, "it is not recommended to prohibit that which is customary, for it is better for the people to transgress inadvertently than to do so deliberately, as it is stated in a number of places."[38]

One generation after R. Eliezer's, R. Isaac introduced another source into the debate, the anecdote related in *Shabbat* 139b concerning a young scholar who wanted to cross the river on the Sabbath, and to this end spent Friday night in a boat. The Talmud defines such behavior as circumvention normally not justifiable. At any rate, it is clear that

35. See n. 33.
36. *Or Zarua* 2:146 (p. 78).
37. R. Eliezer ben Nathan draws the contrast between the *rishonim*, the first generations of scholars in Ashkenaz, and the *aharonim*, in connection with his hypothesis that the *rishonim* ruled that one must stipulate with the seaman to interrupt the journey, in which case the matter is permissible, whereas the *aharonim* neglected this condition. This shows that R. Eliezer thought of Mar Jacob Gaon's interpretation (see chap. 2, n. 27).
38. In addition to this assumed explanation, adduced in the previous note, R. Eliezer raises the idea that there is no prohibition in the case of rivers because one is not far from shore and "it is not obvious he will not rest on the Sabbath" as there is in setting off by sea, if one does so just before the Sabbath. Third, he assumes that they relied on R. Samuel ben Meir's explanation that the *baraita* follows Beit Shammai, although in the end he rejects this explanation.

boarding a boat on the Sabbath was considered forbidden, a prohibition valid even within Sabbath limits as in the case of the journey of that youthful scholar.[39] Consequently R. Isaac devised a new reason: "It resembles floating in a river on the Sabbath . . . where there is room for fear lest one steer the boat, in which case it falls into the category of one leading the boat four cubits" in a restricted area.[40] Hai Gaon preceded R. Isaac with the main element of this explanation, as we have already noted,[41] but the gaon had retained the original talmudic ruling that permission is to be granted only three days before the Sabbath, whereas R. Isaac acquiesced in the practice common in Ashkenaz that it is permitted to set out even on the Sabbath itself but that "he who wanted to fix his Sabbath stay on board at twilight must be on board for the entire twilight period, embarking before the beginning of the period and staying there. After the end of the period he may go home and eat and return after dinner, either at night or on the morrow, by day."[42] The reasoning behind this permission is that "he who has fixed his Sabbath stay in a certain place from twilight has a distinguishing marker and need not be anxious about desecrating the Sabbath."[43] This is a surprising explanation, for the concept of "fixing one's Sabbath stay" appears only in connection with Sabbath limits and is unknown as a distinguishing marker to dispel doubts about performing labor.

R. Isaac's statement must apparently be understood from its continuation: "Some people prepare for a Sabbath meal aboard ship from before the Sabbath and light candles there, so as to be considered as 'fixing one's Sabbath stay' there; then they rely on this in boarding the ship on the Sabbath and setting sail."[44] R. Isaac continues: "They are mistaken because preparing a meal and lighting candles have no effect on fixing one's Sabbath stay, unless they stay on board for the entire

---

39. *Or Zarua* 2:146 (p. 78). Tosafot *Eruvin* 43a, without mentioning R. Isaac's name.
40. *Or Zarua* 2:146 (p. 78). The Tosafot there attribute this idea to R. Isaac ben Abraham (Rizba).
41. See chap. 2, n. 16.
42. *Or Zarua* 2:146 (p. 78). This ending is missing in the aforementioned (n. 39) Tosafot, which is why later halakhic authorities came to the logical conclusion that R. Isaac banned setting sail on the Sabbath; see *Tur Orah Hayyim* 248.
43. *Or Zarua* 2:146 (p. 78).
44. Ibid.

twilight period, as I have explained."[45] R. Isaac seems to have assumed the existence of a tradition permitting the boarding of a ship on the Sabbath to a person having fixed his Sabbath stay there, whereas more recent generations confused "fixing one's Sabbath stay" at twilight with fulfilling the ceremony of lighting candles and preparing a meal to be eaten the following day. At any rate, R. Isaac felt he was on safe ground in permitting a person who had been aboard ship during the entire period of twilight to board the ship on the Sabbath.

In the parallel source (Tosafot *Eruvin* 43a), which contains a paraphrase of R. Isaac's ruling, mention is made of "people who light candles on board ship on Friday eve and dine there and then rely on this to permit their setting off in the boat on the Sabbath."[46] Halakhic authorities challenged this custom, that is, dining and the sanctification (*kiddush*), even if they took place at twilight, have no effect whatever.[47] Some tried to find some halakhic significance for it. Their opinion was that the custom was not intended to permit setting sail on the Sabbath but rather to permit movement aboard the entire ship or disembarking from it at a port to be entered on the Sabbath.[48] The forced nature of these explanations reveals their source: the contradiction between the popular understanding concerning Sabbath observance and the halakhically precise definition of this same term. The custom stemmed from a belief of Sabbath observers celebrating a central ritual of inaugurating the Sabbath on board the boat—candlelighting or even the sanctification (*kiddush*) and the Sabbath dinner—the passenger ensured his observance of the sacred day despite the change in his location. This is reminiscent of the feeling expressed by R. Samuel ben Meir, who wrote that "a person setting sail in a boat . . . seems to be stationary, and he may make use of it like he makes use of his house."[49] The fact is that the custom

45. Ibid.
46. Tosafot *Eruvin* 43a.
47. It was Rabbenu Asher, *Eruvin* 4, 3, who mentions this opinion and rejects it saying, "It is completely useless." See also the *Responsa of R. Asher* 22:12; and see the *New Responsa of Ribash* (Jerusalem, 1960), 22: "Great scholars went into the matter but found nothing whatever"; see the discussion of the *Beit Yosef, Orah Hayyim* 248.
48. Rabbenu Nissim dealing with R. Isaac Alfasi to *Shabbat* 19a, beginning with the word *u-lefikhakh*; and see *Beit Yosef, Orah Hayyim* 248; *Responsa of Benjamin Zeev* (Jerusalem, 1959), 220 (p. 43).
49. See n. 30 above.

persisted, just as permission to set sail persisted, despite the many doubts and hesitations it created.[50] Scholars of Ashkenaz were especially interested in the question of river travel, and many proposals were made in order to justify and perpetuate the actual permissive practice. R. Eliezer ben Joel ha-Levi of Bonn and R. Eleazar ben Judah of Worms (the author of *Sefer ha-Rokeah*) differentiate "the Great Sea with its smelly waters and troublesome waves, but on rivers it is permitted, for there is no trouble and no stench";[51] and each adds an additional reason for this permit, namely, Rabbenu Tam's definition of traveling for business reasons as "obligatory" (*mitsvah*).[52] An apparent challenge of such permission may be discerned in the ruling of R. Hananel, which was already known to R. Eliezer ben Nathan. His opinion was that the prohibition was relevant to rivers only, but R. Eliezer questioned and rejected this reasoning.[53] Deciding otherwise, R. Samson of Sens upheld Rabbenu Hananel's ruling but restricted the prohibition derived from it to rivers that are "not ten handbreaths deep; one is, however, permitted to set sail on big rivers like the Danube, the Rhine, and the Elbe, which are very deep, even more than ten, even on Fridays as long as the sun is high."[54] Concerning sailing on the sea, the practical question was "to cross the sea of the island called 'Iglitari'" (i.e., England). The solution according to the writer of *Sefer ha-Terumah* was that "it was normal to cross in a single day when they enjoyed a good wind, and it was permitted to embark on Friday, even if not for an obligatory purpose."[55] He was apparently recording the custom accepted by French Jewry, not just his personal

---

50. Benjamin Zeev (n. 48) considers the matter as a practical problem. R. Moses Isserles, *Orah Hayyim* 248:3, says: "That is the custom in some places." More explicit is the *Levush* (*Orah Hayyim* 248:3): "Some perform the sanctification ritual (*kiddush*) on board ship and return to their homes . . . even if it has not yet become dark, and in some places this custom is considered completely acceptable and no protest is to be made against them." R. Azriel Dienna, *Responsa*, ed. Jacob Buksenbaum (Tel Aviv, 1977), sec. 25, does not accept the common permissive ruling but declares that there is no chance of having it abrogated, so it is better for people to act inadvertently, etc.
51. *Ha-Rokeah* 197; and similar wording is to be found in *Rabiah* 1:385 (p. 416).
52. Ibid.
53. R. Eliezer ben Nathan (n. 3 above).
54. *Or Zarua* 2:3.
55. *Sefer ha-Terumah*, p. 225, and consequently, with a slight change in wording, *Sefer Mitsvot Gadol*, negative injunctions 68 (Venice, 1547) 154 (17b).

opinion.[56] Theoretically they upheld the prohibition concerning setting out by sea less than three days prior to the Sabbath, but they solved the practical problem of crossing the English Channel by virtue of the fact that under favorable weather conditions one could reach the English coast within a single day, and so England could be considered "close by," that is, a place to which one could travel on Fridays.[57]

In connection with a number of regulations concerning the conduct of a passenger boarding the ship, remaining on board, and disembarking, dissenting opinions and contradictory customs remained in force.[58] Certain strict rulings, like the one prohibiting a passenger from disembarking at his port of destination unless forced to do so by the Gentile captain,[59] were likely to make life difficult for the passenger but not to prevent use of this vital means of transportation. Had the prohibition on setting out and traveling on the Sabbath been enforced, there would have been created a formidable barrier preventing Jews from exploiting the means of livelihood open to them. Rabbenu Tam's definition of going out on business as obligatory (mitsvah) reflects external pressures that, in this case, cleared the way for a permissive ruling couched in halakhic terms of one kind or another. It would, however, be incorrect to attribute the existence of this permissive ruling solely to the degree of pressure; it came about to an equal degree by virtue of the flexibility of the Sabbath, that it could be observed even on a journey, albeit imperfectly. The convergence of these two conditions—economic pressure and Sabbath resilience—led halakhic formality to overcome formal difficulties: "The mouth that had framed the prohibition is the one that now framed the permit."

To demonstrate the truth of this thesis it is sufficient to apply ourselves to the apparently parallel problem of departure in a caravan. R.

56. Concerning the connection between the compiler of Sefer ha-Terumah, R. Baruch ben R. Isaac of Worms, and the doctrine of the French sages, see Urbach, Baalei ha-Tosafot, 349–350.

57. The reference in Shabbat 19a, "and from Tyre to Sidon it is permitted, even on Friday," is adduced explicitly in Sefer Mitsvot Gadol (n. 55 above).

58. R. Samson of Sens (n. 54 above) allowed one to enter the boat only on Friday, not like R. Samuel ben Meir (n. 24 above) and R. Isaac (n. 42 above).

59. In this connection, too, Maimonides was asked (in Responsa 308) and forbade it unless the boat entered the area of the port before twilight, whereas Nahmanides to Eruvin 43a (beginning with va-ani) mentions this custom, wanting to abrogate it. See Responsa of Maharam Alashkar 108.

Simeon Duran[60] and R. Isaac ben Sheshet[61] were asked about this. They replied that if the caravan leaves three days before the Sabbath, one may join it even knowing in advance that a Jewish traveler would be unable to leave the caravan on the Sabbath because of the dangers involved and thus would certainly have to desecrate the Sabbath. These two scholars found this permissive ruling made explicit in the writings of Baal ha-Maor, who explained the reasoning behind the distinction between setting sail three days before the Sabbath and doing so earlier. In the first instance, he appears to "be stipulating the overriding of the Sabbath because nothing can withstand the requirement of preserving human life,"[62] that is, it applies to the case of a boat piloted by a Jew or by a Gentile for mainly Jewish passengers. Baal ha-Maor concludes by saying: "This also applies to going out into the wilderness or any dangerous place where a person is going to desecrate the Sabbath."[63] This is a logical conclusion, but its validity in actual practice was dependent upon whether the Baal ha-Maor's explanation of the rule of sailing was the only one possible, so that it could in turn become the basis for further permissive rulings. It remained for R. Simeon Duran to demonstrate the compelling nature of this explanation, for only in this way could there be a resolution to the accepted custom of setting sail in a Gentile vessel even on Friday, as long as the Jewish travelers were a minority.[64] R. Isaac ben Sheshet, for his part, held that Baal ha-Maor's conclusion concerning departure in a caravan was accepted by R. Isaac Alfasi as well, though he made no mention of Baal ha-Maor's explanation of the reasoning concerning sailing.[65] At any rate, here was a permissive ruling given by two great halakhic authorities concerning departure in a caravan during the first three days of the week. Furthermore when one departed for a purpose in fulfillment of a *mitsvah* such as emigrating to Palestine—this was the subject of a halakhic question—one may do so even on the Sabbath eve.[66]

This permissive ruling, however, did not take root. The two great

---

60. *Tashbets* 1:21.
61. *Responsa of Isaac ben Sheshet (Ribash)* 17–18, 101.
62. See n. 20 above.
63. Ibid.
64. *Tashbets* 1:21; and see n. 21 above.
65. *Responsa of the Ribash* 17–18, 101.
66. Ibid., and *Tashbets* 1:21.

halakhic authorities of the sixteenth century, R. David ben Zimra[67] and R. Joseph ben David ben Lev,[68] rejected it. The former even noted that the Jews of Palestine refrain from joining caravans leaving Gaza for Egypt, that is, even during the first few days of the week—unless it is guaranteed that they will arrive at their destination before the Sabbath.[69] R. Joseph ben Lev explains his rejection by noting the halakhic basis for R. Isaac's ruling. This equates departing in a caravan with setting out in a boat piloted by Jews, which is also permitted by Rabbi Zerahiah ha-Levi. This sailing, however, even when started during the first few days of the week, need not lead to certain Sabbath desecration. "They might stop over on the Sabbath in some port or other and thus will have no cause to desecrate the Sabbath . . . whereas Jews traveling through the desert in Arab caravans or the like will surely have to desecrate the Sabbath because of the dangers."[70] In fact, of course, the contrast was between sailing in a Gentile vessel, where a Jew could refrain from personally desecrating the Sabbath, and traveling in a caravan, where this was impossible. The permissive ruling of R. Simeon Duran and R. Isaac ben Sheshet, based on logic—according to which, labor a Jew was compelled to perform because of danger to his life was not considered a desecration of the Sabbath[71]—could not stand up to the instinctive sense that, let the scholars say what they will, performing physical labor by a Jew was indeed a desecration of the holy day. The popular understanding of halakhah followed strictness and not leniency.

67. *Responsa of David ibn abi Zima* (*Radbaz*) 4:77.
68. *Responsa of Mahari ben Lev* 2:53.
69. *Responsa of Radbaz* 4:77.
70. *Responsa of Mahari ben Lev* 2:53.
71. R. Shem Tov ha-Levi, the friend and colleague of Ribash, protested this permissive ruling of Ribash while the latter was still alive (*Responsa of Ribash* 101), claiming that in a caravan the very body of the traveler actually commits a desecration of the Sabbath. Ribash replied that according to the explanation given by the compiler of the *Maor* one was permitted to set sail in a boat during the first three days of the week, even if the sailors are Jewish and they, too, would desecrate the Sabbath themselves, but this is not considered a desecration.

4

Household Needs in European Jewish Communities

The Jewish household in European countries, at least in the well-to-do class, was undoubtedly dependent upon "slaves and handmaids" to perform the major household tasks. The quotation marks framing the expression "slaves and handmaids" are necessary because their legal status includes a number of categories: bought slaves who were in every respect their owner's property, some having been circumcised and ritually immersed in water and others who remained uncircumcised and without such immersion. The term "slaves and handmaids," however, is also applied to servants merely hired for their work either for a fixed period of time or with no such limit. The meaning of the expression is not always clear, and it may be the case historically as well that the boundaries between these groups were also unclear and that the involved parties themselves were unaware of the precise status of certain male and female servants. The important point is that their place was in the household and they fulfilled their assigned roles within it.

It would seem that for halakhic reasons a clarification of their precise status was necessary because the definition of the status of a male or female servant had practical halakhic implications for various matters, including the requirement that they work on the Sabbath and on other festive days.

According to talmudic tradition, reiterated in geonic teachings, a maidservant acquired by a Jew had to be ritually immersed by her master; a manservant similarly acquired had to be circumcised as well. These ceremonies resulted in the servants being semi-Jewish and thus obliged the female servants to observe those commandments incumbent upon Jewish women. As early as the talmudic period, however, a way was found to permit one to retain male and female servants without circumcision and immersion.[1] In this way there was created an intermediate category, that of "the uncircumcised servant," which apparently became the most common variety especially in Christian lands, for ritual immersion and circumcision, which constitute a kind of semiconversion to Judaism, were banned by their governments. The halakhic status of the uncircumcised servant involved exemption from the commandments of Judaism, including that of Sabbath observance, but his master was forbidden halakhically from making him work on the Sabbath. This prohibition is not because "telling a Gentile [to work on the Sabbath] is forbidden"; it is stricter yet, being a positive commandment: "[your bondman and the stranger shall rest"] (Exod. 23:12).[2] Avoiding the rites of circumcision and immersion was thus an ineffective means of facilitating the work of servants on the Sabbath—some other way would have to be found to circumvent the ban.

We first hear of such circumvention from Nahmanides and from R. Yom Tov ben Abraham Ishbili, in the name of his teacher, R. Aaron ha-Levi of Barcelona. The prohibition on the labors of the uncircumcised slave emanate from his subordination to his Jewish master. If the latter announces on Friday that he terminates this relationship by saying, "Go! Let your labors feed you on the Sabbath!" then the servant's master is

---

1. *Yevamot* 48b; Maimonides, *Hilkhot Issurei Biah* 14:9, and *Hilkhot Milah* 1:6. The condition postulated by Maimonides, that the servant has to accept the seven Noachide precepts, is uniquely his. See the reservations expressed by R. Abraham ben David in both places. A ruling permitting the ownership of uncircumcised slaves for unlimited periods of time was handed down as early as the geonic period; see *Otsar ha-Geonim, Yevamot* 276–277. Nahmanides uses the talmudic expression *eved arel*, uncircumcised servant; see *Hiddushim al Yevamot* on *Yevamot* 48b, and his *Torat ha-Adam: The Writings of Nahmanides*, ed. C. D. Chavel (Jerusalem, 1964), 2:113, and included under this heading are the servants customary in his day.

2. Implicit in the Talmud, *Yevamot* 48b, as explained in the geonic sources, *Otsar ha-Geonim, Yevamot* 276–277; and see Maimonides, *Hilkhot Shabbat* 20:14; R. Solomon ben Abraham Adret, *Responsa* 1:59, 68.

no longer under obligation to feed him, and the servant is no longer obligated to work for his master. And thus "the work he does is for himself and not for a Jew."[3] Nahmanides adds, "and such was the custom."[4] R. Yom Tov ben Abraham, quoting his teacher, stipulates a precondition for such permission: "On condition that it be private, in a way that does not arouse the suspicion of viewers."[5] This meant that the work was not to be done publicly, for a casual viewer could not know whether the stipulation of freeing the servant from his master's control for the Sabbath had indeed been met.

But the circumcised servant, to the extent that such existed, was considered on his way to becoming a Jew, for he was obliged to observe some of the commandments, and upon his emancipation he would be obliged to observe them all. In contrast, the uncircumcised servant remained a Gentile and the ban on having him work on the Sabbath was a formality, which was why no inhibitions were felt in circumventing it. In the opinion of Nahmanides, the suggestion was raised that the entire prohibition on forcing the slave to work on the Sabbath be considered valid only if he undertook to observe at least the seven Noachide laws, thus becoming a kind of *ger toshav*,[6] a Gentile entitled to reside in Palestine. Nahmanides, however, refrained from drawing practical conclusions from this proposal. He left this to a later scholar, the author of *Maggid Mishneh*, who supported Nahmanides' suggestion, claiming that this was Maimonides' opinion as well.[7] It thus turned out that the typical uncircumcised slave enjoyed the status of a simple Gentile, whose work on the Sabbath was limited only by the rule of "telling a Gentile is forbidden." The acquisition of male and female servants of Muslim origin was common in wealthy Spanish Jewish homes. Conversion to Judaism by the process of circumcision, immersion, and manumission was undoubtedly rare. As long as they remained Gentiles, they

3. Nahmanides, *Hiddushim al Yevamot* 48b.
4. Ibid.
5. R. Yom Tov ben Abraham Ishbili, *Yevamot* 48b, beginning with the word *veha-ger;* adduced in his name, too, in the *Nimmukei Yosef* commentary on R. Isaac Alfasi, *Yevamot* 48b.
6. Nahmanides, *Torat ha-Adam;* R. Solomon ben Abraham Adret disagreed with him in *Responsa* 1:68.
7. *Maggid Mishneh*, *Hilkhot Shabbat* 20:14. The rulings of the *rishonim* in this matter are laid out clearly in *Yam shel Shelomoh*, *Yevamot* 4:53.

were set apart from the Jewish family, despite their close physical relationship, and were not prevented from serving as "Sabbath Gentiles."[8]

Things were different in Ashkenaz. There is clear evidence[9] that Jews possessed slaves during the early period of the establishment of Jewish communities there. These slaves had been brought from abroad, from the Slavic tribes of eastern Europe. They had been bought by their masters, some having been circumcised and ritually immersed as Jewish law required, others having already been freed and assimilated into the community.[10] At any rate, bought slaves were unlikely ever to have been the sole mainstay of the Jewish household in central Europe. Alongside them were hired servants from the immediate surroundings. These, too, were termed "men- and maidservants" in Jewish sources and indeed fulfilled the function of slaves, for they were attached to the household in which they lived, which was their means of support, and all their labors were performed for its benefit. As time passed, this kind of servant almost completely supplanted the bought slave. Most of the discussion in Ashkenazic halakhic literature concerning the position of male and female servants in matters of the dietary laws, Sabbath regulations, and so forth dealt with this type of servant.[11] The status of bought slaves is considered only rarely and then only for theoretical purposes or in borderline cases.[12] Laws pertaining to slaves in the original, full sense of the term were no longer relevant and could not even be used as a source for the definition of the status of a servant of the new type.

---

8. See Abraham A. Neuman, The Jews in Spain (Philadelphia, 1942), 2:208–210; Yitzhak Baer, The History of the Jews in Christian Spain (in Hebrew) (Tel Aviv, 1959), 495–496 n. 3. The Maggid Mishneh writes in the conclusion to his discussion of the permissive ruling based on Nahmanides: "And because this is quite common I treated it at length" (Hilkhot Shabbat 20:14). Neuman, relying on the words of R. Solomon ben Abraham Adret (n. 2 above), described the status of the uncircumcised servant as that of a person belonging to the Jewish family. But even according to R. Solomon, the prohibition applying to the work of the servant does not affect him personally, and it does not remove the religious gap between him and his master.

9. See Avraham Grossman, The Early Sages of Ashkenaz (in Hebrew) (Jerusalem, 1981), 66 n. 131, 84 n. 26.

10. Simha Assaf, "Jewish Slaves and Slave Trade in the Middle Ages" (in Hebrew), in Be-Oholei Yaakov (Jerusalem, 1943), 236–237; and see Grossman, The Early Sages of Ashkenaz, 66 n. 131, 84 n. 26.

11. Examples of Sabbath matters in the sources are adduced below. Concerning dietary laws, see Jacob Katz, Exclusiveness and Tolerance (Oxford, 1961), 41–43.

12. See n. 14 below.

We do encounter a thirteenth-century case of someone inquiring of R. Avigdor-Kohen Tsedek whether the ban of "the son of your maid-servant shall rest," that is, the uncircumcised slave, applied to a Gentile hired by a Jew for his work for a limited period of time as well. "He replied that this certainly included a Gentile whose person was bought, like the case of those who buy slaves outright, but those who are hired for a period of a year, or more or less, are not owned by a Jew, who may therefore neither force him nor prevent him from performing work."[13] The question occupied the earliest tosafists, R. Eliezer of Metz, R. Eliezer ben Joel ha-Levi of Bonn, and the author of *Sefer ha-Terumah*, who reached the same conclusion as R. Avigdor, that is, that the hired Gentile is not included among those whom a Jew is commanded to have rest on the Sabbath,[14] It may be, however, that this distinction became clear only as time went on, once the hiring of male and female servants of the new kind became a regular phenomenon.

Rabbenu Simhah related a tradition that the "ancients had a custom according to which the maidservants were not allowed to perform their labors in a Jewish home,"[15] and he strove to enforce this ban for reasons to be discussed below, even though these hired female servants were excluded from the definition of slaves. For this reason he forbade the kindling of "fires lit by the Gentile women on the Sabbath in their masters' homes."[16] As we shall see, this prohibition, despite the difficulty in maintaining it, was enforced in scholarly circles at the same time that the permissive ruling spread throughout the community. The

13. *Shibbolei ha-Leket ha-Shalem* 113.
14. R. Eliezer of Metz, *Sefer Yereim ha-Shalem* 226 (pp. 200–201), excludes hired servants from the obligation to have one's servant rest. He raises the possibility "that the Jewish employer can well be an owner" but rejects this conclusion. R. Eliezer ben Joel ha-Levi of Bonn *Ravyah* (257) considers the status of "a Gentile man- or maidservant hired for a year or less." He concludes his discussion saying, "All this explanation of mine applies specifically to an uncircumcised Gentile whose body is not owned, but if his body is owned, then he falls under the category of 'your servants and resident strangers shall rest.'" *Sefer ha-Terumah* 222 (according to the corrected version in *Haggahot Maimoniyot, Shabbat* 6:6) writes: "A Jew is permitted to allow his man- and maidservant to do work when the work is their own and not the Jew's, in which case he does not violate 'so that your servant shall rest' except when dealing with a Canaanite slave who is obliged to keep some of the Commandments."
15. *Haggahot Maimoniyot* 6:6; *Haggahot Mordekhai, Shabbat* 452; the first version is the more accurate one.
16. Ibid.

author of *Shibbolei ha-Leket* learned from his mentor "that he had seen
a case in Ashkenaz where even a Gentile maidservant refrained from
sewing her own garment on the Sabbath";[17] that is, the maidservant
was forbidden to do any work even with her own personal belongings,
just like the tradition to which Rabbenu Simhah of earlier days had
subscribed. It seems well-founded that the early generations in Ashkenazic communities were very strict in their interpretations of anything related to "telling a Gentile," as will be seen in the next chapter.
The strict ruling concerning the female servant is difficult to explain
halakhically.[18] Possibly it stemmed from the habit of regarding servants
as potential converts to Judaism, for they were to be circumcised and
ritually immersed. At any rate, when bought slaves gave way to hired
servants, all grounds for such strict rulings no longer existed, and they
were gradually rejected by most halakhic authorities.

The status of a hired servant was thus the same as that of ordinary
Gentiles,[19] and the rule of "telling a Gentile is forbidden" applied in all
its details and served as the starting point for relevant halakhic rulings.
It appears that many questions concerning the work done by a Gentile
in the service of a Jew arose in actual practice in connection with the
household servants. The answers to these questions depended upon the
halakhic authority's ability to find an analogous case for either a permissive or a restrictive ruling in the talmudic sources. "A man- or maidservant drawing water from a well . . . and conveying it across public
domain for a Jew and especially if he drew it from the river" was permitted by Rabbenu Tam.[20] The Mishnah states (*Shabbat* 122a): "If he
drew water to offer his animal . . . but if for a Jew, it is forbidden."
Rabbenu Tam concluded that the Mishnah had banned the act only
when it was done for an animal but not for a human being, and he found
a logical reason for distinguishing between them.[21] But as regards a fire
prepared by a Gentile to provide warmth, the need for which is no less
than the need for water, Rabbenu Tam found no grounds for a permissive
ruling and could only concede that "if they were seated [on the Sabbath]
and the Gentile made [a fire], of which they [Jews] availed themselves,

17. *Shibbolei ha-Leket ha-Shalem* 113.
18. Concerning the claims of Rabbenu Simhah, see nn. 27–28 below.
19. The wording of R. Eliezer ben Joel ha-Levi is adduced in n. 14 above.
20. *Mordekhai, Shabbat* 404.
21. Ibid., and in the parallel passages adduced in n. 23 below.

they have no need to leave their seats on account of it."[22] The rule concerning the drawing of water was rephrased in later sources to refer to any Gentile,[23] and the question of warming the house was considered in other sources as referring to the household maidservant.[24] Rabbenu Simhah was alone in his struggle to maintain the ancient tradition prohibiting household maidservants from doing any work.[25] He claimed that all rulings that permitted Gentiles to do work for Jews concerned situations outside the Jewish home, where it is at least likely that the Gentile is doing work of his own accord; the work therefore is not thought of as being Jewish.[26] This is not so inside a Jewish home. In his opinion, too, it was not the workers being "men- and maidservants" that was decisive but rather where the work was done—in a Jewish household.[27] All other halakhic authorities refrained from making this distinction, as R. Eliezer ben Joel ha-Levi, Rabbenu Simhah's contemporary and friend, put it: "Gentile male or female servants hired for a year or less also work of their own accord for their own profit."[28] This seems to have been composed in order to reject R. Simhah's point, and so anything that can be done by a Gentile, such as administering medicine to a sick person not in danger of his life, "can be done by them . . . just as by any other Gentile."[29] Elsewhere, R. Eliezer ben Joel ha-Levi relies on the conclusion drawn by one of his teachers, "There is no need to protest against Gentile maidservants doing their work in Jewish homes, but it is forbidden for them to do our work, and if they do, this must be protested."[30]

22. *Sefer ha-Yashar le-Rabbenu Tam*, ed. Shimon Schlesinger (Jerusalem, 1959), 286.

23. See Tosafot *Shabbat* 122a, beginning with the word *mashkeh*; R. Eliezer ben Joel ha-Levi adduced in n. 14 above.

24. See below in the text.

25. See passage adduced in n. 15 above.

26. These concepts appear in connection with renting out factories and handing over the jobs of a Jew; see chaps. 1, 5. For the reason of "being known by his name," Rabbenu Simhah prohibited a maidservant, known to belong to Jews "and that everything she does during the week is for Jews," from being told on Friday to make purchases; see *Responsa et decisiones*, ed. Ephraim Kupfer (Jerusalem, 1973), sec. 67.

27. Rabbenu Simhah brings evidence from the Jerusalem Talmud as well to the effect that a Jew brooks no work by Gentiles in his home on the Sabbath.

28. See n. 14 above.

29. Ibid.

30. Meir of Rothenburg, *Responsa* (Prague-Budapest, 1895), 559: "My upright teacher approves." Who is he?

Even since a Gentile, unfettered by the ban on productive labor, lived among Sabbath observers, the temptation to enjoy his services—if not directly, then at least indirectly—was of course unavoidable. The maidservant was permitted to prepare a fire for herself, and, as we have seen, Rabbenu Tam ruled that if a Jew benefited from this, he did not have to move away. What if the Gentile left the vicinity of the fire and it subsequently appeared as if he had made the fire to meet the needs of his master, or if there was "reason to fear that he had increased the fire for the Jew"? In such cases R. Eliezer of Metz and R. Eliezer ben Joel ha-Levi ruled against permitting it.[31] But from the wording of their rulings it is clear that they were aware of the difficulty in maintaining a boundary line between the permissible and the prohibited. Not for nothing did they supplement their rulings with the admonition: "In all such cases the Torah states, 'You shall fear your God,' and one must avoid any circumvention in this respect"[32]—a talmudic expression (Bava Metsia 58b) used in matters of conscience with no human supervision.

Great halakhic authorities found it difficult at times to extricate themselves from embarrassing situations. The son of R. Isaac Or Zarua, R. Hayyim, relates "that they once heated our winter house on the Sabbath and my late sainted father did not want to eat there, and so he dined outside; my teacher R. Avigdor Kohen Tsedek did the same."[33] A similar story is told by R. Meir of Rothenburg about himself: He had warned the household maidservant not to warm the winter house, and when he sensed that she continued to do so privately, he made a lock for the furnace. "Every Friday I lock it and leave it locked until Saturday night."[34] These scholars continued the tradition of the ancients, attested to by Rabbenu Simhah, at least in connection with this important matter of heating the house during winter. We cannot know how the first two sages explained the ruling of the ancients, but R. Meir of Rothenburg viewed this custom as mere "rigorism and asceticism." He upheld it,

31. Haggahot Mordekhai, Shabbat 461, R. Eliezer ben Joel ha-Levi (see n. 14 above). R. Eliezer attributes the warning to R. Shalom. For his identity, see editor's n. 21.
32. Ibid.
33. R. Hayyim Or Zarua, Responsa 199.
34. Maharam, Responsa (Prague-Budapest, 1895), 92; and idem, Responsa (Cremona, 1557) 3:5. The version quoted is made up of both sources.

as he says, because when others ban permitted actions one is not allowed to give permission to do them in their presence (*Pesahim* 50b).[35] But this does not mean that the general public upheld this ban until his time. He mentions that in France, to which he moved as a youth in order to study the Torah, they ruled leniently on this subject. He heard from his teacher that R. Jacob of Orleans "even permitted a Jew to tell a Gentile to stoke the fire."[36] The reason for this lenient ruling, which we shall yet deal with, seems to have been acceptable to him.

There is reason to believe that this lenient approach had already begun to spread through Germany as well. Rabbenu Simhah's aforementioned discussion was maintained in the context of "fires lit by Gentile women in the homes of their masters on the Sabbath,"[37] and his decision to forbid this was a reaction to this custom. From what had been related concerning the above-mentioned three scholars, their strict observance of the ban seems not to have been in accord with the custom rife in their vicinity. R. Meir of Rothenburg's two disciples, R. Menahem ben R. David and R. Hillel ben R. Azriel, to whose question he replied, phrased their problem as follows: "Concerning the winter houses heated by Gentile women on the Sabbath without having been instructed to do so, on their own—does this involve a transgression or can one be silent and let them do as they please?"[38] A third disciple, R. Meir ha-Kohen, the author of *Haggahot Maimoniyot*, approved of the French leniency, interpreting his mentor's ban—in contrast to its simple meaning—to be a personal ban applying only to himself.[39] He also claimed that his teacher was inconsistent in this matter and related a case "in the tower of Wassenburg when, on Friday, we made a fire to heat us at night; while we were still sitting there until it nearly went out, the servants came and rebuilt it, saying explicitly that they were doing so for our benefit; they sat there and we with them, and we were very happy at this."[40] Be that as it may, R. Meir's definition of the matter

35. Ibid.
36. Ibid.
37. Nn. 15, 26, 27 above.
38. N. 34 above.
39. *Haggahot Maimoniyot, Shabbat* 6:6. "He himself acted as if it were forbidden," which means that he did not prohibit it to others. However, from his reply to his disciples it seems that R. Meir did not want to rule permissively.
40. Ibid.

as one "in which others acted strictly in banning it" is not, it seems, to be taken literally. There was a tradition of a prohibition and scholars who still upheld it, and he did not think he had the right to uproot it. In fact, this ban was gradually uprooted by itself under the pressure of circumstances and the influence of the French lenient ruling, which itself had developed only recently and was then in the process of winning adherents.

That the French ruling permitting the warming of the home by means of a Gentile was not itself an ancient tradition may be deduced from Rabbenu Tam's reservation, permitting a Jew to warm himself at the fire only if he was already seated and the Gentile presented him with a *fait accompli*.[41] Clearer testimony comes from the source from which we learn of the lenient ruling, R. Yom Tov of Joigny. He opens his responsum with the words, "Ever since I was a boy I have wondered at those who forbid us to warm ourselves at a fire made by a Gentile for a Jew."[42] The reason for his wonder was that he had seen his "father, his teacher, as well as the late Rabbi Meshullam, both men scrupulously observant, warming themselves—and also other great rabbis."[43] Two opposing camps, the lenient perspective and the strict interpretation, confronted one another, the lenient camp being the innovators. This is not surprising, as this camp was of the French school with Rabbenu Meshullam of Melun its outstanding representative. It held that one should not be deterred from making practical changes in accepted custom provided that sufficient grounds for innovation could be found in talmudic sources.[44] The reasoning underlying their permissive ruling was based on a complex of three elements, the most innovative and most important being the statement that dwelling in the cold is equivalent to illness that does not endanger life, for which "telling a Gentile" had been allowed. A second element was the decision that there was no need for an individual examination to determine if a person could withstand the cold, for there was a similar situation connected with

41. N. 22 above.
42. Four versions of Rabbenu Yom Tov's statement are extant: Maharam (Prague), 478; *Haggahot Maimoniyot, Shabbat* 6:6; *Mordekhai, Shabbat* 250; *Haggahot Mordekhai, Shabbat* 452.
43. Ibid.
44. See my article, "Maariv bi-zmano-u-maariv she-lo bi-zmano," *Zion* 35 (1970): 46–47. Reprinted in *Halakhah and Kabbalah* (Jerusalem, 1984), 185–187.

"preventive medicine"—one is permitted to warm water for the needs of a newly circumcised infant, for regarding circumcision, all such are considered to be unwell (*Pesahim* 68a). Here, "with regard to cold, all are considered unwell." And if the person concerned is not actually unwell, he is certainly discomforted, and a person suffering discomfort was permitted to violate a rabbinic ban (*Yevamot* 114a) if he could thereby be relieved of his discomfort.[45]

Climatic conditions made it difficult to maintain the strict ancient tradition; and not everyone managed to do so. When news of the permissive ruling handed down by recognized authorities became common knowledge, it spread throughout the community. The behavior of the latter, however, did not match the reasoning underlying such permission. If, with regard to cold, everyone was considered to be unwell, it should be permissible to tell a Gentile to light a fire with no hesitation whatever; as a result, those scholars who practiced consistency were not afraid to rule accordingly, as we have seen.[46] The public, however, settled for what was felt to be compelling. The author of *Haggahot Maimoniyot* relies on the teachings of Rabbenu Yom Tov but applies them only to situations he saw: "Where winter homes are heated for children or for male and female servants who do not want to dwell in the cold, adults are permitted to enter and enjoy the warmth."[47] R. Hayyim Or Zarua relates of the Jews in his community, apparently Cologne, that "here in our town, most rely on [R. Yom Tov's] ruling and remain in winter homes heated by Gentiles on the Sabbath. They do not, however, tell them to heat the houses; and it is best to keep silent about it."[48]

The pattern of community behavior was stricter than that required by formal halakhic ruling. In other cases it was more lenient. During

---

45. From the version of Rabbenu Yom Tov's discussion in *Haggahot Mordekhai*, *Shabbat* 452, and in *Mordekhai*, he seems to be the innovator of this reasoning—"for the reason mentioned above." However, in the *Responsa* of Maharam, the version reads, "and they gave their reason"; this is undoubtedly the original. Rabbenu Yom Tov thus had a reasoned responsum written by those who ruled permissively. In *Haggahot Maimoniyot* we find, "and he wrote the reason down," which, from the context, seems to refer to his father.

46. See n. 36 above. R. Hayyim Or Zarua, *Responsa* 199, says explicitly that "according to [Rabbenu Yom Tov], it is permissible even to tell a Gentile to heat something up."

47. N. 39 above.

48. N. 33 above.

the days of R. Jacob ben Moses Moellin, the permissive ruling was already completely accepted: "No one at all accepts the ban; on the contrary, anyone doing so is considered snobbish and peculiar."[49] He and other contemporary scholars withdrew their reservations, "it being my custom to heat the house whenever the cold becomes oppressive."[50] The public, on the other hand, was not careful and heated its houses even "when it was not so cold and when they had no children to suffer discomfort." However, according to the ruling that "everyone is unwell with regard to cold," when the cold could be borne, there was "a strong ban, but I do not have the ability to stop it, and I refrain from stating so publicly, for it is better for them to sin unknowingly than to do so deliberately."[51]

The conclusion we drew is thus vindicated: The community developed its own behavioral patterns not necessarily according to the logic of formal halakhah. A direct appeal to a Gentile to perform this labor on the Sabbath, though formally acceptable according to the definition of "weakness not endangering life," was met with psychological inhibition. Making such an appeal is, after all, a kind of act that transcends the limits of resting from all labor on the Sabbath,[52] whereas benefiting from something done by a Gentile more or less of his own accord was something else entirely. On the other hand, once it became accepted to make use of the services of a Gentile in this particular labor, not everyone was capable of making precise differentiations and deciding if the cold had reached that degree justifying the permissive ruling from a formal point of view. A "Sabbath Gentile" for heating homes

---

49. R. Jacob ben Moses Moellin, *Responsa* 196.

50. Ibid. Concerning his teacher he reports that he would not agree to the proposal made by a friend that they settle for heating the winter house "on Friday since they used to heat it only once every twenty-four hours, but he did not want to listen, for it was pleasurable to have it warm on the Sabbath morning" (ibid.). R. Jacob ben Moses Moellin's disciple, R. Jacob Weil, *Responsa* 46, uses the permissive ruling concerning the heating of the winter house as the basis for another permissive ruling—having the Gentiles cook for babies: "Any baby is considered ill as far as eating is concerned, and this is like our permitting the heating of the winter house on the Sabbath, in that a permissive ruling has become common throughout Ashkenaz."

51. N. 49 above.

52. Rashi, *Avodah Zarah* 15a, links the ban on telling a Gentile with the talmudic ruling based on (Isaiah 58:13) that "one's speech on Sabbath should be different from one's speech during the week" (*Shabbat* 113a–b). See *Encyclopedia Talmudit,* s.v. *amira le-nokhri shevut.*

became a permanent institution, and only halakhic experts were likely to limit its use in accordance with halakhic criteria.

From attempts made to limit the ban on "telling the Gentile" to the Sabbath day itself but allowing a Jew to do so before the Sabbath, we learn that "telling the Gentile" on the Sabbath day was felt to be a greater violation of its sanctity than were its results—the work done by a Gentile for the Jew and the Jew's benefiting from this work. "Some feel that 'telling the Gentile is forbidden' applies specifically when the 'telling' takes place on the Sabbath, but when it precedes the Sabbath, though the Jew is commanding the Gentile to do work on the Sabbath, it is permitted—but this is a mistake."[53] This means that what is involved is not the ruling of halakhic authorities but rather a commonly held opinion. It is easy for the writer of this responsum to reject this supposition. All the halakhic limitations applying to giving work to a Gentile or hiring out implements before the Sabbath prove that a direct order to perform the labor of a Jew is prohibited, even if given prior to the Sabbath. The writer adds: "Even with no evidence of a ban, we are not to make a distinction between 'telling the Gentile' on the Sabbath and doing so before the Sabbath, with regard to the rule that 'telling the Gentile is forbidden.'"[54] Such a ruling was given by the scholars repeatedly,[55] but it never managed to become an absolute, uncontested prohibition. R. Isaac Or Zarua, though familiar with the view of the strict school of thought, expressed his doubts: "Telling a Gentile on Sabbath eve that he should work on the Sabbath—I'm not sure if this is forbidden or not."[56] R. Isaac does not cite any talmudic evidence but argues on the basis of the reasoning behind the ban, which, in his opinion (as in Maimonides'),[57] is "lest he put himself in a position where he might do it, but on Sabbath eve, there is no point in such a fear."[58] In

---

53. Maharam, *Responsa* (Jerusalem, 1957), 202 (ed. Cahana), 2, *responsa* 66.
54. Ibid.
55. Maharam, *Responsa* (Prague), 559. The halakhic authority in this case is Rabbenu Joseph. In Dr. Avraham Grossman's opinion this refers to Rabbenu Tam's disciple, R. Joseph ben Moses. Concerning him, see Ephraim E. Urbach, *Baalei ha-Tosafot* (Jerusalem, 1980), 114–116. R. Baruch ben R. Isaac, the author of *Sefer ha-Terumah*, and his strict ruling are cited in *Or Zarua* 2:84, sec. 25.
56. *Or Zarua* 2:84, sec. 25.
57. Maimonides, *Hilkhot Shabbat* 6:1. See *Encyclopedia Talmudit*, s.v. *amira le-nokhri shevut*.
58. *Or Zarua* 2:84, sec. 25.

a gloss to a responsum that adhered to the prohibitive ruling, there appears an alternative opinion, obviously of recognized halakhic authorities, according to which "before Sabbath it is permitted to say 'do such and such on the Sabbath.'"[59] It stands to reason that "telling the Gentile" on a weekday, though it had consequences on the Sabbath itself, was unlikely to be considered forbidden to the same extent as "telling" on the Sabbath itself. We have already encountered similar situations in connection with embarking on a ship, where the prohibition three days prior to the Sabbath was easily dislodged.[60] The popular tendency to circumvent the banning of "telling a Gentile" by doing so before the Sabbath had its effect upon the mood of the scholars as well. Recognized halakhic authorities also took part in the search for ways to circumvent the banning of "telling a Gentile." The author of Sefer ha-Terumah, who forbade "telling a Gentile" before the Sabbath, adds: "However, after the Sabbath, one may ask one's male or female servant, 'Why didn't you light the fire or the candle last Sabbath?'—though it may appear to be a ruse aimed at the following Sabbath."[61] This ruling was repeated by the author of the Sefer Mitsvot Gadol[62] and is ascribed to R. Meir of Rothenburg as well.[63] Some even permitted money to be given to a Gentile before the Sabbath, "as long as the Gentile is not explicitly told, 'Buy on the Sabbath.'"[64] An even more sophisticated circumvention was to tell the Gentile to buy for his own purposes and that the Jew would buy it from him at his convenience.[65]

Even on the Sabbath day itself, ways were found to benefit in ha-

59. Maharam (n. 55 above).
60. See chap. 3.
61. Or Zarua 2:84, sec. 25.
62. Sefer Mitsvot Gadol, negative injunctions 65 (Venice, 1547), 19b.
63. In the aforementioned gloss (n. 59 above).
64. Adduced in the Mordekhai, Shabbat 249 in the name of Sefer Mitsvot Gadol. But in the version of the Sefer Mitsvot Gadol (21b) that we have there is only a ruling permitting the giving "of money to a Gentile to do business with them; although the Gentile does business on the Sabbath, he splits the profits with him equally, which is the way all the geonim ruled." This case is one in which the Gentile is responsible for the money. The way described in the Mordekhai was banned by Saadiah Gaon, Rabbenu Asher, Bava Metsia 7:6.
65. Haggahot Maimoniyot, Shabbat 6:2, quoting R. Samuel ben Baruch. He rejects the permissive ruling ascribed to Sefer Mitsvot Gadol.

lakhically acceptable fashion from the services of the household servant. Rabbenu Tam ruled that it was permitted "for a Gentile to walk alongside a Jew on the Sabbath with a lighted candle in his hand to any place, whether to draw wine or deliver bread,"[66] just as he ruled that it was permissible to benefit from the water brought by the servant from the well.[67] R. Eliezer of Metz is reported to "have had a maidservant called Hydron. On Sabbath nights, when the rabbi desired to go to sleep, he would say to his servant: Go and take off Samuel's shoes, and she understood and took the candle and accompanied him so as to illuminate the way."[68]

Halakhic authorities, adept at suggesting delicate distinctions upon which depended the differentation between fit and unfit foods, between innocent and guilty, and between permitted and forbidden activities, viewed these rulings as nothing else but the consistent application of the rules of talmudic study. Rabbenu Tam, who permitted drawing water and carrying a candle by a maidservant for the benefit of a Jew, forbade his disciple, R. Isaac ben R. Mordecai, "to eat bread baked by a Gentile on the Sabbath."[69] The difference is that in respect to drawing water or using a candle, the Jew can achieve his ends, if necessary, without the intercession of the Gentile, which is not the case in the eating of bread.[70] R. Eliezer ben Joel ha-Levi vigorously upheld this ban,[71] as we shall yet see, whereas Rabbenu Tam's two disciples, R. Isaac ben R. Baruch and R. Samuel Mordan, "permitted the purchase of bread baked by a Gentile on the Sabbath in an emergency."[72] Thus, they did not follow the distinction drawn by Rabbenu Tam. It is told of R. Eliezer

66. Maharam, *Responsa* (Prague), 222.
67. See n. 21 above.
68. Maharam, *Responsa* (Prague), 558.
69. In *Sefer ha-Terumah* 247, we find: "He forbade R. Isaac"; but in *Or Zarua* 2:358 there appears "and R. Isaac ben R. Mordecai of blessed memory has already asked if one may eat bread baked by a Gentile on the Sabbath and Rabbenu Tam forbade this."
70. Rabbenu Tam's reasoning is given explicitly where mentioned in nn. 21–23 above.
71. *Or Zarua* 2:84, sec. 25; and see n. 87 below.
72. *Or Zarua* 2:84, sec. 25, as corrected by Urbach, *Baalei ha-Tosafot*, p. 153 n. 5, according to *Haggahot ha-Rosh, Betsah* 3:17.

of Metz, that he "ate fish that a servant broiled for herself,"[73] even though the fact that she was a household servant provided an extra reason for prohibiting his action. R. Isaac, who apparently tended to rule leniently in cases involving a Gentile in general,[74] held "that in everyone's opinion if the servant of a Jew cooks or bakes on the Sabbath, his master may not eat of it even if the servant prepared the dish for himself" because "if he is his acquaintance, it is forbidden, for by eating it he trains the servant to do it again on another Sabbath."[75]

Of course, the use of analogy cannot rely upon objective criteria. The two instances recorded in the Talmud (Eruvin 67b–68a), which show that certain labors performed by a Gentile for the purpose of circumcision were permitted, served the halakhic authorities as examples facilitating the granting of permission for other mitsvot. "In a certain community five miles away from Bonn," the community etrog (citron for Sukkot) "broke into pieces, whereupon they sent us a messenger immediately, on the day before the festival, for another etrog. He arrived in the middle of the night, whereupon we discussed the matter and concluded that as long as they had not been negligent and what had happened to them was accidental, it was permissible to tell the Gentile to take the etrog of his own accord, just as in the case of circumcision ... for if a mitsvah is involved, 'telling the Gentile' is permitted."[76] This ruling was handed down by R. Joel, the father of R. Eliezer ben Joel ha-Levi of Bonn, in reply to Rabbi Judah ben R. Kalonymus of Speyer. The reason for the latter's inquiry was that about a year after the occurrence referred to in the question, one of the individuals who had taken part in the discussion in Bonn, R. Ephraim ben R. Jacob, handed down a decision in the same kind of affair, ruling permissively even where no accident was involved. The questioner wanted to know if R. Joel agreed with this ruling.[77] R. Joel's answer implied a kind of reproof

73. Tosafot Betsah 3b, beginning with the word gezerah, as corrected by the Bah, according to the version of Haggahot ha-Rosh, Betsah 1:1. In Sefer ha-Neyar, ed. G. Appel (New York, 1961), 16, this was ascribed to "R. Yitshak ha-Zaken" (old Rabbenu Isaac), but he forbade such things; Or Zarua 2:84, sec. 25.

74. Related one of his disciples; Or Zarua 2:84, sec. 25.

75. Ibid., at the end of the responsum.

76. R. Eliezer ben Joel ha-Levi, Ravyah (407), adduced also by Or Zarua 2:84, sec. 25.

77. This results explicitly from the beginning and conclusion of the responsum. See Ravyah, p. 463 n. 26.

aimed at R. Ephraim, "for, had he not been one of us I would have kept silent."[78] His opinion was that a permissive ruling is possible only when the need has arisen completely by accident, as in the talmudic example (in which the water was spilled out before the circumcision), "whereas, if there has been no accident, permission would be rejected by all Israel."[79]

R. Ephraim was, however, not the only one to draw an analogy from the case involving the circumcision and to expand the lenient ruling to include any obligatory act (mitsvah). "Some wish to be permissive . . . in telling a Gentile to bring a book through the public domain on the Sabbath in order to study from it."[80] Similarly the author of the 'Ittur maintained "that lighting a candle on the Sabbath is obligatory at dinner, and so it is lit by a Gentile on the Sabbath."[81] R. Isaac ben R. Samuel, however, upset the basis of the analogy. As he put it, making use of a Gentile was allowed "specifically in connection with circumcision, which itself supersedes the Sabbath . . . but in respect to other mitsvot . . . we do not tell a Gentile and have him do it."[82] Had R. Joel and his disciples accepted this limitation, they could not have permitted the dispatch of the etrog.

It does indeed seem as if the halakhic authorities themselves found it difficult to determine the extent to which Jews should refrain from using the help of their household servants or just any Gentile. No wonder this was the case with simple people who violated these, in contrast to other Sabbath regulations, with no pangs of guilt. The halakhic scholars were well aware of this situation, a fact that found expression in the

---

78. Ibid., at the beginning of the responsum.
79. Ibid., at the end of the responsum. A question regarding "an etrog possessed by a certain community while another community had none, whether they may send it over on the festival day . . . by a Gentile" was put to R. Isaiah of Trani, Responsa, ed. A. J. Wertheimer (Jerusalem, 1975), 88. The editor thought that the case under discussion was the one dealt with here, and that the responsum was aimed at R. Isaac Or Zarua, with whom R. Isaiah was in contact. This case, however, took place a generation before Or Zarua, who merely copied the words of R. Joel. R. Ephraim had a reason to turn to other halakhic authorities to have his ruling confirmed, and R. Isaiah's responsum does match his own opinion; the permissive ruling was given unrestrictedly, but chronologically it seems difficult to identify the questioner with R. Ephraim.
80. Or Zarua 2:85, sec. 25 (p. 43).
81. Baal ha-Ittur, Hilkhot Milah 3:1.
82. Or Zarua 2:85, sec. 25.

reason offered for the distinction between those who desecrate the Sabbath by inadvertently performing some labor and those for whom the labor is performed by a Gentile. "A person who cooks inadvertently on the Sabbath may eat the food," and we do not fear he may then do it deliberately, "for, on the contrary, he is sure to repent."[83] This is not so in the case of a Gentile doing the work, for if we permit him to benefit from what the Gentile has done for him, he will then command the Gentile to do as he instructs him. This means that having a Gentile perform creative work would not be considered by the Jew to be real Sabbath desecration.

Permission was indeed granted increasingly in cases of this kind, as we have already seen, and all limitations were sometimes overridden completely. R. Hayyim ha-Kohen, a disciple of Rabbenu Tam, describes the situation as it was in French communities: "Are there no judges in Israel? Why do the Jews make a point of acting arbitrarily, sending their servants to fetch bread and beer at their will, so that it is almost fitting to term them people who do not observe the Sabbath in public?"[84] The rabbi went on to list the prohibitions violated by those who act as described, for what was involved was telling servants explicitly to perform labors for the benefit of their masters.[85] R. Hayyim was apparently of the opinion that the community leaders were obligated to impose discipline in this area, whereas in actual practice they treated the matter as if no transgressions were involved. We do not know just how common this phenomenon was in France or if it was limited to a single community or to certain communities.[86] In Germany we find that R. Eliezer ben Joel ha-Levi "chastised people who had eaten bread baked by Gentiles on the Sabbath," as reported by R. Isaac Or Zarua, who witnessed this himself.[87] This means that R. Eliezer had no hesitation about en-

---

83. *Shibbolei ha-Leket ha-Shalem* 113 (43b). Similar is the responsum of the writer of *Sefer ha-Terumah* 247: "One who cooks by mistake on the Sabbath may eat . . . for there is no need to rule in accordance with 'lest he cook deliberately' for we are not dealing with evil people. But in the case of Gentiles who cooked for themselves, if one permits this for a Jew to eat, there is room to fear lest he tell the Gentile to cook for him."

84. *Sefer ha-Neyar*, 16.

85. Ibid.; in addition to telling a Gentile "there is a transgression on account of negotiating and mentioning the sum of the deal and expenses."

86. R. Hayyim lived in Paris. See Urbach, *Baalei ha-Tosafot*, 124.

87. *Or Zarua* 2:358 (p. 150, end of the second column).

forcing religious law in accordance with his strict interpretation, even in matters about which there was disagreement. It seems that he relied upon a tradition from the earliest generations of Ashkenazic Jewry, who used to chastise a desecrator of the Sabbath without regard for the severity of the transgression according to its halakhic definition.[88]

88. See the *siddur* of Rabbenu Solomon of Worms, ed. Moshe Hershler (Jerusalem, 1972), 257–258, sec. 116 (ed. n. 2), 269, par. 33.

5

Problems Linked with Means of Livelihood

With regard to the maintenance of Jewish households new problems arose in French and German communities resulting from the dependence of those households upon the services of "men- and maidservants." Yet, concerning the means of Jewish livelihood, we discern a reduction in the difficulties stemming from cooperation with non-Jews. Once Jews ceased to engage in agriculture, they were no longer concerned with problems relating to the leasing of fields or the handing over of flocks to a Gentile shepherd. Nevertheless, the use of animals in the Jewish household remained an everyday occurrence, amply demonstrated by the numerous discussions regarding the question of the sanctity of the firstborn animal.[1]

The problem of milking animals on the Sabbath required a solution. There seemed no way to avoid the definition of milking as creative labor in the fullest sense of the word, and the only solution involved the services of a Gentile. This was common and had been permitted since the geonic period, which is apparently why no reference to the question

1. See, e.g., *Or Zarua* 1:480, 500; Maharam, *Responsa* (Prague), 3, 14, 78.

is found until the days of R. Meir of Rothenburg.[2] R. Meir strengthened the permissive ruling of the geonim with new proofs based on the argument that the fear of causing cruelty to animals overrides the ban on "telling a Gentile." The problem is that the geonic source cited by R. Meir stipulates that the lenient ruling applies when the Jew "says to the Gentile: Milk [the animal] and take the milk for yourself,"[3] a stipulation that was not acceptable to R. Meir of Rothenburg, according to the testimony of his disciples. The compiler of *Haggahot Maimoniyot* says: "My teacher says that even the milk may be drunk by a Jew."[4] In the *Mordekhai* we find: "The milk must be purchased from the Gentile, for then he will have been laboring at his own possession,"[5] whereas in the *Orhot Hayyim* the version is as follows: "The Jew shall purchase it from her [the Gentile woman] at a small price, like an apple or anything he wants, even if it is worth less than a *peruta*, and then one may partake of it."[6] We do not know if R. Meir of Rothenburg himself used one of the expressions adduced above, but it is certain that they reflect accepted custom, according to which the Jew avoided the loss of milk by circumventing the prohibition or even without any such circumvention.

Although agriculture was not a common occupation of the Jews of Europe, nevertheless contact with it was not completely lost. Practical questions concerning the possibility of Gentiles using Jewish beasts of burden for their agricultural pursuits were considered from Rashi's day up until the end of the tosafist era, and echoes of the relevant halakhic problems are revealed in the halakhic deliberations of those generations.

Extremely significant is the responsum written by R. Isaac ben Menahem of Orleans to his disciple, R. Eliezer bar Judah of the town of Kablon (apparently Chalon-sur-Saône),[7] and Rashi's reference to this responsum as well. R. Eliezer ruled permissively concerning "oxen pulling a plough on the Sabbath . . . since a Gentile accepted the responsibility

2. Maharam, *Responsa* (Prague), 49.
3. Ibid.
4. *Haggahot Maimoniyot*, Shabbat 8:7.
5. *Mordekhai*, Shabbat 448.
6. *Orhot Hayyim* (Florence 1750; photo ed., Jerusalem, 1956), 100.
7. Joel Mueller, *Responses faites par de célèbres rabins français et lorrains*, (Vienna, 1881), 17. For the two individuals and their places, see Henni Gross, *Gallia Judaica* (Paris, 1897), p. 591.

for it."[8] The oxen belonged to a Jew, whose obligation to give his animals rest on the Sabbath would apparently not be satisfied by hiring them out to a Gentile. However, once the Gentile had accepted responsibility for the animals, that is, that should they be lost he undertakes to pay for them, R. Eliezer felt that the animals had essentially left the possession of the Jew, who was thus no longer responsible for their resting on the Sabbath. R. Isaac, his teacher, adds that if this is the basis for the permissive ruling, then the Gentile must be held responsible for the full price of the ox in cases of *onsa* (when the ox dies in circumstances completely out of the Gentile's control) and also of *zola* (when its value on the open market drops), for under such circumstances the ox can be considered the property of the Gentile. However, says R. Isaac, "despite all this, the capital (represented by the ox) belongs to the Jew; I am uneasy about this permissive ruling."[9] Though the Gentile has accepted full responsibility for the animal, it is still considered the property of the Jew.

R. Isaac thereupon set out in search of an alternative way to rule permissively. He suggested that the Jew and the Gentile establish joint ownership of the oxen, at which time the explicit rule of joint ownership of a field (*Avodah Zarah* 22a) would apply: They are permitted to come to an arrangement whereby "on Friday the Jew takes all the profits for himself, and the Gentile acts similarly on the Sabbath."[10] Such would be the case if the Jew and the Gentile had each invested his own money in this enterprise; but in fact, it is the Jew alone who invests the money, whereas the Gentile does the work. The proposal made thus says that "if the Gentile has no money, the Jew lends him money for his portion."[11] By virtue of the loan, the Gentile became a partner, and, as a partner, he set aside the labors of the Sabbath for himself alone. This is doubly fictitious, and the writer himself sensed the weakness of this invention, for he added: "I should prefer not to be asked questions of this sort, for the Jews should be left alone in this matter. It is better for them to transgress inadvertently than to do it deliberately. . . . Thus, if they come to ask your advice, explain the truth to them precisely, but

8. Mueller, *Responses*, 17.
9. Ibid.
10. Ibid.
11. Ibid.

if they do not come for advice, it is best to keep silent."[12] It is thus evident that deals of the type under consideration were common both in Orleans and in the hometown of the writer of the question, apparently Chalon-sur-Saône;[13] the local sages either allowed them with not a little difficulty or simply ignored their existence.

Rashi's reply to R. Isaac ben Menahem's responsum shows that this phenomenon was not restricted to these places. According to the version available to us, Rashi rejected this problematic ruling out of hand: "He was vexed by it and dismissed it,"[14] doing so even if the Jew and the Gentile were actual co-owners of the oxen, since the talmudic rules of partnership were applied to the ownership of a field and not of an animal. The difference between the two is substantial:[15] "For in the case of the stipulated partnership the Jew has no part of it [the field], whereas, in the case of an animal, the part belonging to the Jew is actually being worked, the stipulation being invalid, for as long as the Gentile is not allowed to sell the animal on that Sabbath . . . the animal is still considered 'your' [i.e., Jewish] property, and the Jew is forbidden to allow it to labor."[16] Rashi would not confirm such doubtfully permissive rulings handed down by the two other scholars: "And when a lenient perspective is suggested to our Rabbi [Rashi], he will have nothing to do with it."[17] This shows that the practical problem was troublesome in Rashi's surroundings as well, and since he could not find a way to rule permissively, he preferred to close his eyes to it.

The details of this discussion have been preserved in halakhic literature. The author of *Sefer ha-Terumah* was aware that "in the lifetime of the late R. Solomon, this question was raised, and there were some

12. Ibid.

13. See n. 7 above.

14. At the beginning of the responsum (Mueller, *Responses*).

15. "They are as far from one another as East is from West" (Mueller, *Responses*).

16. See Mueller, *Responses*. In the case of the talmudic example: The partnership is between a Jew and a Gentile in the receipt of the work, but the field does not belong to them. Even if the field were theirs, however, it would make no difference, for the Jew is not commanded to leave his land idle on the Sabbath. The main point in Rashi's reasoning is thus not the fact that the Jew does not own any part of the field but rather the fact that he is commanded to leave his animal idle on the Sabbath. See R. Levi ben Habib adduced in n. 24 below.

17. See Mueller, *Responses*.

PROBLEMS LINKED WITH MEANS OF LIVELIHOOD   73

authorities who ruled permissively . . . while others banned it."[18] It was
forgotten that Rashi himself was the authority who banned it and that
he did so absolutely. On the contrary, *Sefer ha-Terumah* concludes his
comments on this subject saying, "A way to permit this should be
found,"[19] that is, a permissive ruling was considered a matter of public
urgency.

That such was the case may be deduced from the question brought
before R. Isaac ben Abraham, whose father "had gone into partnership
with a Gentile, joining his own fields and oxen together with the Gentile's fields and oxen."[20] The case involved an entire farm, with a Jew
as a partner and the actual labor performed by a Gentile. As far as the
fields were concerned, R. Isaac found no fault in hiring them out, and
in connection with the oxen he made the same kind of proposal suggested by the disciple of R. Isaac ben Menahem, "that he sell them to
the Gentile tenant or lend them to him under conditions allowing the
Gentile to use them without asking permission . . . [or] turns the value
of the ox into a loan and the latter submits it to the Jew as collateral."[21]
The purpose of all this was to remove the animal from the ownership
of the Jew, so that the latter would not be obligated to rest his animal
on the Sabbath. A generation or two later, R. Avigdor Kohen Tsedek
was asked by R. Benjamin, the brother of the author of *Shibbolei ha-
Leket*: "What remedy does a Jew have who acquired oxen and went into
partnership with a Gentile for a few years, letting the Gentile plow with
them both on Sabbaths and on weekdays?"[22] The questioner assumes
a priori that a solution to the problem exists and is merely inquiring as

18. *Shibbolei ha-Leket ha-Shalem* 111. See Israel Elfenbein, *The Responsa of
Rashi* (New York, 1943), 95, who, surprisingly, prints statements made by Rashi's
contemporaries, according to later sources, instead of what Rashi said as cited in
Mueller, *Responses.*
19. According to the version in *Orhot Hayyim* 1:120. In *Shibbolei ha-Leket ha-
Shalem* 113, the wording is "and points for permission must be found."
20. Maharam, *Responsa* (Prague), 452 and (Lvov), 401. *Or Zarua, Avodah Zarah*
141, but the wording is imperfect.
21. Ibid. The proposal made by R. Isaac ben Abraham might have satisfied Rashi
as well, for the oxen were no longer the responsibility of the Jew.
22. *Shibbolei ha-Leket ha-Shalem* 113. The replacement of *arisut* by *shutafut*,
"partnership," is necessary. If *arisut* were the correct term, meaning that the Gentile
worked with the animals the entire week, the responsum would be incomprehensible.

to the nature of the solution. And indeed R. Avigdor did reply permissively, saying "that a stipulation must be made with the Gentile in advance concerning 'the days the oxen are to be brought to me,' such as on Monday or Tuesday only, as the Gemara rules; if this stipulation is made in advance, then the partnership is permissible."[23] R. Avigdor thus applies to the oxen the permission granted in the case of a field, an analogy rejected outright by Rashi.[24]

These three cases concern the practical question of animals resting on the Sabbath. The difficulty in maintaining the halakhah in this matter is reflected in the mainstream of halakhic discussion. The talmudic conclusion reached in *Avodah Zarah* 15a is that the animal remains in the possession of the Jew and must be allowed to rest, even if it is temporarily in the possession of a Gentile by virtue of being borrowed or hired out. The conclusion, as phrased by R. Samuel ben Meir,[25] is that "it is forbidden to lend or hire one's animal to a Gentile, even if stipulating explicitly that you do not want him to work the animal on the Sabbath," unless the condition is made clear "that the animal be returned before the Sabbath"[26]—a very difficult condition to honor. Indeed, R. Samuel left a loophole by which the prohibition might be circumvented, saying, "My teacher told me that if the Jew says to the Gentile that his [= my] animal is your property, then it is permitted."[27] "My teacher" is apparently Rashi himself, his advice here matching his teachings to the effect that only a complete transference of ownership to the Gentile frees the Jew from the obligation to have his animal rest. On the other hand, an explicit statement to the Gentile that the animal now belonged to him could not have been very pleasant to Jewish ears. A solution to this dilemma was proposed in the days of the early tosafists: a formal cancellation of Jewish ownership of the animal by de-

---

23. Ibid.
24. R. Levi ben Habib (*Responsa* 106) considers the problems of the partnership without mentioning the opinions of his predecessors and finds a reason to rule permissively, "for since they made this stipulation at first when purchasing the animal, it is as if the animal is owned by the Gentile on the Sabbath." Urbach's question (*Baalei ha-Tosafot* [Jerusalem, 1980], 268) as to whether the phenomenon reflected in R. Isaac ben Abraham's responsum is unique is answered right there: It is very common.
25. His commentary on *Avodah Zarah*, adduced in *Or Zarua* 2:2 (p. 5).
26. Under this condition, R. Isaac Or Zarua tends to rule permissively (ibid.).
27. Ibid.

claring it ownerless,[28] some going so far as to state that this declaration was automatic "for we can legally presume that the owner would declare it to be ownerless."[29]

The sources do not reveal how this permissive ruling came about. Rabbenu Asher quotes Rabbenu Samson as saying that "if he loaned it to the Gentile and failed to take it back before the Sabbath, he can declare it ownerless, even without any witnesses."[30] It may be that this ruling, originally intended for emergencies, was then applied more generally and eventually accepted by those seeking to rule permissively. Those authorities preferring a stricter ruling, however, could retort that a declaration of lack of ownership is invalid when not witnessed.[31] Nevertheless, the general public eagerly accepted this and other solutions,[32] and even halakhic authorities ceased to protest the custom of renting animals to Gentiles. The author of *Sefer Mitsvot Katan* made his permissive ruling conditional upon the animals being declared ownerless;[33] others followed the rule that it is better to let people sin unintentionally than to have them do so deliberately.[34]

Formally, ignoring the ban on renting animals was more serious than disregarding the rule that one was forbidden to give a Gentile instructions on the Sabbath, for the latter was considered a rabbinic ban, whereas the commandment to rest one's animals on the Sabbath was a positive injunction explicitly stated in the Torah. The two matters were similar in that in neither case was a Jew personally involved in creative

28. This opinion is adduced, albeit with reservations, in Tosafot, *Shabbat* 18b, beginning with the word *demaphkere.*

29. *Or Zarua* 2:2 (p. 5), here, too, with reservations.

30. Rabbenu Asher, *Nedarim* 4:11.

31. Ibid.; *Or Zarua* 2:2 (p. 5) adduces indirect evidence to the effect that this permissive ruling was not authorized.

32. See Meiri, *Avodah Zarah* 15b, ed. A. Sofer (Jerusalem, 1944), 38.

33. *Sefer Mitsvot Katan,* negative injunctions 281.

34. "Some disagree with all of them, yet they, too, rely on the rule of 'Let the Jews, etc.,'" Meiri (n. 32 above). Raising animals at home but refraining from selling them to Gentiles, as the Mishnah requires (*Avodah Zarah* 14b), was admitted by R. Isaac to be impossible: "For the ban on selling an impure animal was certainly aimed specifically for those days when there were a lot of Jews together, so that if a Jew had an animal he did not need he could sell it to another Jew and would not take a loss; but now, what can a person do but take a loss if he cannot find anyone to sell it to." Tosafot *Avodah Zarah* 15a, the passage beginning *emor* (see my *Exclusiveness and Tolerance* [Oxford, 1961], 30–31). The difficulty in refraining from renting the animal out was no less great.

labor, and this was decisive in eliciting a response to the practical needs involved. Riding a horse belonging to a Jew was considered a mere rabbinic ban,[35] but no one thought of having the Jew circumvent this ban in any way. This reconfirms the rule explicated above that neither the severity of the ban nor the economic pressure involved was decisive but rather the kind of act concerned and its position in the set of rules delineating the ritual nature of the Sabbath.

The forms of livelihood generally engaged in by Jews in the Middle Ages, trade and moneylending, did not usually generate any employer-employee relationship between Jews and Gentiles, such a relationship being the source of most of the problems that made it difficult to observe the Sabbath in previous generations and that would create additional difficulties in the future. Whereas the renting of fields, workshops, and domesticated animals and the handing over of objects and materials for processing were restricted in such a way as would prevent the Gentile from appearing as if he were performing the labors of the Jew, lending money was unrestricted in any way, as long as it was performed before the Sabbath. Furthermore, even if the money is handed over in the framework of a business deal in which a portion of the money remains under Jewish ownership, "even though the Gentile engages in his business on the Sabbath, the Jew may take an even share of the profits"[36]—an accepted custom during the geonic period and one unchallenged by any authority. The impersonal, abstract nature of money seems to have resulted in "the source of the deal not being identifiable," as *Ha-Rav ha-Maggid* put it.[37]

It is nevertheless true that problems of Sabbath observance did arise

---

35. Mishnah *Betsah* 5:2.

36. Maimonides, *Hilkhot Shabbat* 6:18. He writes: "All the geonim ruled this way"; and a ruling by an anonymous gaon supporting this is adduced in *Responsa of the Geonim* (Jerusalem, 1960), 43, and attributed to Rav Sherira, in *Geonic Responsa* (Lyck, 1863–1864), 68.

37. His wording is merely a summary of the reasoning of the geonim in the aforementioned sources. They distinguish between handing money over to another and goods sold at a shop, which is forbidden because the shop is known by the name of a Jew. He supplies another reason: "For this work is not for the Jew to do"; and the Kolbo explains (Venice, 1567), 31a: "For that profit is merely the profit of his own money, which is like renting tools, which is not forbidden to us." However, accordingly, *iska* involving goods traded by a Gentile for a share of the profit should have been included in the permissive ruling; but the anonymity of money was surely decisive here.

in connection with the lender-borrower relationship as well. There was a case in the days of Rabbenu Tam and R. Isaac ben Samuel in which "a Jew took possession of half an oven in repayment of a debt owed him by a certain Gentile, while another Gentile, the baker, owned the other portion."[38] By virtue of collecting a debt owed him, the Jew unavoidably became a partner of the Gentile baker, who understandably had no desire to give up the use of the oven on the Sabbath. The Jew could rent his portion of the oven to his partner, and so the question—already considered during the geonic period[39]—arose as to whether an oven resembled a field and as such could halakhically be rented out or whether it resembled a bathhouse, in which case such a deal would be forbidden. R. Isaac was originally of the first opinion and Rabbenu Tam of the second, with the disciple eventually accepting his teacher's line. Rabbenu Tam suggested a solution whereby the Jew would first return the oven to his debtor; then, before re-collecting his due, he would first arrange with his future partner that the Gentile would take the oven for himself on the Sabbath and he, the Jew, would do so on a weekday. In this way the partnership became permissive, as explained in the *baraita* in *Avodah Zarah* 22a.[40] There were cases where the oven functioned as collateral for a loan, with the Jew receiving the income from the use of the oven as interest. Such an arrangement was not considered halakhically faulty with regard to Sabbath observance, for the oven remained under Gentile ownership, the Jew merely being entitled to the usufruct.[41]

Whenever the collateral was portable, the borrower was liable to come on the Sabbath to redeem his property or to replace it, and if it had already been redeemed before the Sabbath—even to take it with him on the Sabbath. Early halakhic authorities dealt only with the last instance. They do not seem to have considered the possibility of the Gentile wanting to redeem the collateral on the Sabbath, a step involv-

38. *Or Zarua, Avodah Zarah* 142. In Tosafot *Avodah Zarah* 22a, beginning *lo yomar*, the matter is described somewhat differently. In this version the Jew received the entire stove and the baker had the right to use it "a certain number of days."

39. See chap. 2, nn. 36–39. The case is also discussed by Nahmanides, *Hiddushei Avodah Zarah* 21b, as a current matter, and also by Rabbenu Asher, *Avodah Zarah* 1, 25.

40. *Or Zarua, Avodah Zarah* 142; and Tosafot *Avodah Zarah* 22a.

41. Ibid.

ing calculations and paying his debt, and of the Jew agreeing to such a step. The Gentiles were of course aware that Jews refrained from conducting business deals on the Sabbath, and they even respected the Jews' religious customs. But it was difficult to prevent the removal of collateral that had already been redeemed, and the halakhic authorities themselves did not find it easy to prohibit this. Rabbenu Joel found a basis for such a ban in a ruling discussed in a *baraita* (*Shabbat* 19a): "Foodstuffs are placed before the Gentile in the yard"; this ruling was interpreted narrowly, that only foodstuffs, but no other portable objects, could be so treated.[42] However, his son, R. Eliezer ben Joel ha-Levi of Bonn, is reported to have ruled that it is permissible if a place was set aside for them before the onset of the Sabbath, that is, "already beyond the jurisdiction of the Jew." He used as a basis for his ruling the halakhah concerning the Gentile's leaven (on Passover) in Tractate *Pesahim* (6a), according to which, if a place had been set aside for it, it counted as belonging to the Gentile and there was no need to destroy it.[43] Rabbi Isaac Or Zarua had no tradition concerning this matter, and in a case that occurred in Regensburg, where a Gentile "came to reclaim his collateral from a Jew on a festival, with the collateral already redeemed the day before," he forbade it—apparently only because the collateral itself was *muktseh* (not usable on Sabbaths or festivals). But another scholar disagreed and permitted it.[44] "So I inquired of my teacher, R. Simhah," and he replied: "We do not allow collateral to be returned because it looks like business, unless it is in an emergency and involves a violent person."[45] The term "we do not allow" indicates that the tradition accepted in his hometown, Speyer, was being attested to. He considered the reason for the ban to be an opinion that was accepted by others, that the return of the collateral was part of the business deal, from which a Jew should refrain on the Sabbath as much as possible. The ban was lifted in the case of a violent owner of the collateral.

Concerning the replacement of the collateral by its owner, we learn from Rabbenu Yeruham, who writes: "The custom was to allow this

---

42. *Mordekhai, Shabbat* 253.
43. Ibid. The disagreement concerning the interpretation of the *baraita* is expounded fully in *Raviah* 198 (p. 260), but without linking the matter with the return of the collateral.
44. *Or Zarua* 2:53.
45. Ibid.

. . . because it is not business."[46] In the days of R. Alexander Suslin ha-Kohen of Frankfurt, in the fourteenth century, the problem seems to have assumed new dimensions. He accepted the ruling that one was permitted to give in to the demands of a violent Gentile, saying: "I have also seen my own teachers do so."[47] And he added: "When I was asked a number of times [for a ruling], they told me that the Gentiles are violent [that is, as a general rule] and sometimes brought them to me," apparently meaning that the Jews brought the Gentile owners of the collateral to the rabbi, to pressure him into allowing the collateral to be returned.[48] The collateral involved here had not previously been redeemed before the Sabbath, and the entire redeeming process had to take place on the Sabbath. In his distress, the rabbi instructed them to act in a way with which he was apparently unhappy: "I eventually used to tell those inquiring of me: If you are willing to fast on the day after the Sabbath or the festival, then let the Gentile take his collateral himself and replace it with some other collateral or with money of corresponding value, so that the Jew does not touch either of the items of collateral; nor does he involve himself in their calculation."[49] What had changed since the earlier days? Had the Gentiles become less tolerant of the Jews, or were the Jews less willing to observe the Sabbath fastidiously? Or perhaps there were special circumstances of this case, the Sabbath being market day, which was when the owners of the collateral came to town to take care of their business with the Jews. We have no way of knowing. R. Alexander Suslin of Frankfurt tells of yet another lenient ruling common in his time, in which previous generations were not likely to have acquiesced: "I have also seen Gentiles in debt bringing wagonloads of grain on the Sabbath, the Jew giving them the key to his warehouse, and they unloading, measuring, and counting."[50] The rabbi makes no protest in this case. On the contrary, he says: "I have not seen any of my teachers protesting this because the grain belongs to the Gentile as long as the Jew has not taken part in the calculations."[51]

46. Rabbenu Yeruham, pt. 12.
47. *Hiddushei Agaddah*, an appendix to Y. Weil, *Responsa* (Jerusalem, 1959), 162.
48. Ibid.
49. Ibid.
50. Ibid.
51. Ibid.

It was also difficult to maintain a complete disengagement of Jew from Gentile on the Sabbath in trade relations. If the market day fell on the Sabbath, the Jew would miss major business opportunities unless he entrusted a Gentile with the job of buying the goods he sought on his behalf. There certainly were Jews who did so. R. Meir of Rothenburg reports that "some hold that 'telling a Gentile is prohibited' only when one does so on the Sabbath but that it is permitted to do so before the Sabbath even though one tells the Gentile to perform his duty on the Sabbath—but they are mistaken."[52] He is not talking of a scholar ruling in this way, but of simple people, who did not feel that in telling the Gentile before the Sabbath day itself they were in any way desecrating it. However, a certain ruling is attributed to R. Moses of Coucy to the effect that "one is allowed to give the Gentile money before the Sabbath to make a purchase for him on the Sabbath provided one does not actually tell him to buy with it on the Sabbath."[53] Yet anyone not accepting this lenient ruling could always "tell the Gentile: Take this money and buy yourself such and such with it, and if I need it I'll take it from you . . ."[54]; if it was the Jew who wanted to sell his goods, the author of the Sefer Mitsvot Katan allowed him to give the goods to a Gentile before the Sabbath and sell them on condition that they agreed on the price."[55] There were certainly permissive rulings that were very difficult to justify, even a posteriori. In the glossaries to the Rosh, Or Zarua is reported to have ruled that "one may purchase houses from Gentiles on the Sabbath. How is the Jew to act? He shows him his pouch [full] of dinars, and the Gentile signs and takes it to court."[56] R. Joseph Caro understood this ruling as referring to the purchase of a house in the Land of Israel;[57] in that case telling the Gentile directly was permitted.[58] At any rate, it is inconceivable that any Ashkenazic halakhic authority in the Middle Ages would so describe the purchase of a house, were it intended to apply to the Land of Israel alone. It seems likely that purchasing a house was sometimes considered mandatory even else-

52. Maharam, Responsa ed. Kahana (Jerusalem, 1957), pt. 1, 66.
53. Mordekhai, Shabbat 249.
54. Haggahot Maimoniyot, Shabbat 6:2.
55. Sefer Mitsvot Katan (Cremona, 1557), 281, ed. Kapost (1820), 580.
56. Haggahot Asheri Moed Katan 2:18.
57. Beit Yosef, Orah Hayyim 306, at the end of the section.
58. Gittin 8b. For the limits of the permissive ruling, see Or Zarua 2:85, p. 25.

where, such as a Gentile's house in a Jewish neighborhood.[59] At such a time, the restrictions on telling the Gentile and trading, which are merely rabbinic prohibitions, were set aside.

Alongside the common sources of livelihood, the Jews of the Middle Ages encountered additional possible sources of income, such as partnerships in the exploitation of salt mines, minting coins for the monarch, and leasing customs collection. The activities involved in these occupations could not cease on the Sabbath, and if the Jew himself took no part in them, his Gentile partner or representative acted as was customary on weekdays. It is doubtful if the Jews concerned always applied for halakhic sanction. The halakhic authorities refer to these matters as common phenomena in need of assessment as to whether they were being performed halakhically.

Rabbenu Tam is the earliest authority we find dealing with the minting of coins. He handed down an unambiguously lenient ruling, as quoted in his name, "that a Jewish minter may hire a non-Jew to mint his portion on the Sabbath, since he is working at his own job; this is what he allowed and taught in actual practice."[60] The context makes it clear that Rabbenu Tam was referring to a Gentile working under contract. And this is one of the conclusions to be drawn from Rabbenu Tam's ruling: He held that all kinds of contracted labor, and not just agriculture, were permissible on the Sabbath. According to Rabbenu Tam, Samuel's opinion (*Moed Katan* 12a) banning contracting within Sabbath limits relates to the rules of mourning but not to those of Shabbat. Rabbenu Tam was well aware of the fact that in his ruling he deviated from accepted tradition. The early sages of Ashkenaz, including Rashi's own teacher, R. Isaac ben R. Judah, banned contracting in construction work. They interpreted Samuel's opinion as relating to Sabbath matters, thus limiting the contracting permit to agriculture only.[61] The scholar Simeon (or Samuel) ben R. David is said to have contracted with Gentiles to build his house but not to have allowed them to work

59. The desire to keep Gentiles away from Jewish neighborhoods is expressed in the regulations concerning the priority option of neighbors, *Bava Metsia* 108b. See Rabbenu Asher, *Haggahot Asheri, Moed Katan* 9:28. Maharam, *Responsa* (Prague), 970, 1011.

60. *Or Zarua* 2:2A.

61. The prayer book of Rabbenu Solomon ben R. Simeon of Worms, ed. Moshe Herschler (Jerusalem, 1972), 261–262.

on the Sabbath. It so happened that workmen prepared "two stones as a doorframe outside city limits" for the house. When the sage heard of this, he broke up those stones in full view of the Gentiles; his contemporaries viewed this as a sanctification of the name of God, and they "all congratulated him and blessed him."[62]

Rabbenu Tam's ruling was elaborated upon in a letter to his brother, R. Samuel ben Meir.[63] The immediate reason for this correspondence between the two brothers is unclear. The introduction and conclusion of the letter seem to indicate that the discussion was a general one of principle: "I am very troubled to have to disagree with my teachers but . . . it is permissible for a Jew to allow a Gentile, working under contract, to do his work on Sabbaths and festivals."[64] He concludes saying: "Were such a case to happen to me, I would permit myself [to act accordingly]."[65] Does this mean that he had already instructed another Jew to act in this way? Or was the entire discussion still theoretical? Sooner or later, at any rate, he actually ruled according to his opinion in connection with minting.[66] There is also a tradition that "he permitted a Jew who had contracted to have his house built to have work done on it even on the Sabbath."[67] According to this tradition, as far as his own person was concerned, he never did as he had proclaimed himself willing to do. "For Rabbenu Tam, though ruling leniently in matters of contracting, was strict in respect of himself, and when he built his own house he did not allow non-Jews to build on Sabbath, even though they were working under contract."[68] Now, if this testimony is not a deliberate attempt to narrow the gap between Rabbenu Tam and those dissenting from his opinion, then we must assume that Rabbenu Tam fi-

---

62. Ibid., p. 262. See editor's note concerning the uncertainty in the name.
63. *Sefer ha-Yashar le-Rabbenu Tam* (Berlin, 1898), 6.
64. Ibid.
65. Ibid.
66. N. 60 above.
67. Tosafot *Avodah Zarah* 21b, beginning with the word *arisa*. In *Or Zarua, Avodah Zarah* 139, we find: "The wording of my teacher, Rabbenu Judah bar Isaac, called Sir Leon, whence Rabbenu Tam ruled permissively for a Jew who was building on a festival day by means of Gentiles under contract." In all the later literature, Rabbenu Tam's ruling is adduced in connection with the building of a house.
68. Tosafot *Avodah Zarah* 21b. This is also according to evidence provided by R. Judah Sir Leon, *Or Zarua, Avodah Zarah* 140: "Rabbenu Tam, too, when he built his house, did not rely on this."

nally took his disputants' opinion into account, for both his contemporaries and his disciples[69] disagreed with him. And the ruling permitting contracted labor of all kinds, even in public, remained a solitary opinion. Nevertheless, concerning minting, Rabbenu Tam was not the only authority to search out a *modus vivendi* for those who engaged in it.

His contemporary, R. Isaac of Corbeil, is said to have "permitted silver to be given to a Gentile to mint coins even on the Sabbath, wherever a Jew was in charge of the minting, as this is not a case of people imputing the work to a Jew; and there is no need to be cautious because the Gentile is working for a fixed wage."[70] This ruling is based on uncertain halakhic grounds,[71] although its practical intent is clear. The situation is similar to that of a tradition attributed to Rabbenu Judah Sir Leon of Paris by the Or Zarua, which deals with a partnership between Jew and Gentile in minting coins and rules that they may split the profits "if the Jew works on a weekday and the Gentile on the Sabbath."[72] And even if this was not agreed upon in advance, the Jew could still "hire the Gentiles to do his portion of the work on the Sabbath, for they are working on their own jobs, and this is permitted."[73] Here, too, although the legal basis for this ruling is unclear,[74] its practical purpose is obvious.

69. See in the aforementioned places.

70. *Haggahot Maimoniyot, Shabbat* 6:40.

71. This ruling was not considered by later authorities but is hinted at by R. Moses Isserles, sec. 244, par. 6: "A Jew in charge of the royal mint is to be equated with one in charge of the customs even though sound is made on the Sabbath by striking the coins." This ruling is based, as he says, on a contractual arrangement, and this seems likely. The words "since this is not a case of hearing a sound belonging to a Jew" mean that the work is not known by the name of the Jew, as is the case in public baths. R. Moses Isserles, however, explains (perhaps he had a different version before him) that [it means] despite the fact that the factory emits a noise, as does a mill (Shabbat 18a). However, there is a disagreement as to whether the generating of the sound is to be taken into consideration. Rabbenu Tam holds that the rule is not to take it into account and thus shows (n. 63 above) that contracting, too, is permissible openly. However, according to his opponent's view, it should have been forbidden because of the sound.

72. *Or Zarua, Avodah Zarah* 142.

73. Ibid.

74. *Beit Yosef* 245 realized that the Jewish partner would rent his part to the non-Jew, whereas the *Magen Avraham* 244:18 claims that the matter is one of delivery under contract.

From R. Meir of Rothenburg we learn about drying salt and renting the customs: "R. Meir ruled that where salt is dried, a Jew may rent out his pan to a Gentile for the Sabbath, and the Gentile gives his pan to the Jew on Sunday."[75] R. Meir based his ruling upon a similar finding appearing in the *Tosefta, Moed Katan* (1:2), according to which a Jew whose turn at distributing water for irrigation purposes falls on the Sabbath may exchange his turn for that of a Gentile that falls on Saturday night, after the conclusion of the Sabbath. This ruling contains no fundamental innovation; its basis rests upon the leasing of one's work implements to a Gentile over the Sabbath, a subject already considered by the authorities on the basis of directly relevant sources.[76] Thus, this ruling left no traces in the historical development of the halakhah. The second ruling of R. Meir, however, concerning the renting of customs was to reverberate for centuries.

The description of the matter "concerns Jews purchasing customs rights [and hiring] a non-Jew to take over the customs on the Sabbath; if this is done by contracting, it seems permissible. . . . What is meant by the customs contracting?" For example, if they hired the person stipulating that "when you collect 100 *libras* I'll pay you such and such."[77] This ruling permitting contracting is explicit in both the Babylonian and Jerusalem Talmuds, and R. Meir incorporates their rulings in his presentation. The question, however, was whether the concept of contracting was applicable in this context. The essence of contracting is that he who carries out the piece of work receives payment on the basis of output; he may do the work whenever he wants. The first stipulation is met, for the customs collector's wages are determined according to whatever he manages to collect. But this does not hold true for the second stipulation, for in contracting "the Jew does not determine that the Gentile do his work only on the Sabbath, and in this connection . . ., he does tell him to collect customs duties on the Sabbath."[78] The very role of the non-Jew is to take the Jew's place on the Sabbath. Thus this is not real contracting. "At any rate, there seems to be reason to rule permissively," the reason being adduced from an entirely different

75. Maharam, *Pesakim and Minhagim*, ed. Kahana (Jerusalem, 1957) 1:194.
76. See Maimonides, *Hilkhot Shabbat* 6:16 and the reservation of R. Abraham ben David, *Tur Shulhan Arukh* 246.
77. Maharam, *Pesakim and Minhagim*, vol. 1, n. 24.
78. Ibid.

context, from a rule appearing in the last chapter of Tractate *Shabbat* (153a): "If a person is traveling on the road when darkness falls (when the Sabbath begins) he should hand over his pouch to a Gentile." This violates the ban on "telling a Gentile," but, as the Talmud there explains, "It was permitted by the sages because of the loss involved, for had they not allowed this, the Jew would likely have carried [the pouch] four cubits in the public domain; the present case is not different."[79] This means that here, too, if the customs duty collector is not allowed to make use of a Gentile, he is himself liable to engage in the collecting. There is, however, a distinct difference between the two cases, for in the example adduced in Tractate *Shabbat* the situation was one in which the Jew found himself involuntarily, in that the traveler was late in reaching his destination, whereas in leasing the customs a person deliberately involves himself in the situation thus created. R. Meir himself sensed the weakness of the analogy he drew, for he added a second explanation: "This is even more applicable in a case of saving one's financial situation from Gentile hands, for, were we not to permit this, he would lose his entire debt sooner or later."[80] This seems to mean that once one acquired customs rights one had to collect duties on the Sabbath as well and could not put off the collecting until after the Sabbath; to do so would be to lose all that he had paid in leasing the customs rights. The concept of "saving . . . from Gentile hands" appears in Tractate *Avodah Zarah* (6b) in connection with collecting a debt on a pagan festival, all contact with pagans being apparently prohibited on such an occasion. However, if such contact were necessary to save Jewish money from Gentile hands, it was permitted. R. Meir makes no mention of this ruling, but he was clearly very much conscious of it.[81] At any rate, he was here responsible for a new halakhic ruling, for the fear of a financial loss now overruled the prohibition of "telling a Gentile," at least in such cases similar to those concerning the customs. According to the reasoning supplied, the permissive ruling should have been limited to a person who had already leased customs rights, for concerning a person deliberately putting himself into a position of involuntary loss, R. Meir's

79. Ibid.
80. Ibid.
81. This is how it was interpreted by *Magen Avraham* (244:17; see *mahatsit ha-shekel*).

reasoning is unprecedented.[82] His intent was, however, undoubtedly to justify this source of income, as shown by the single limitation he lists at the conclusion of his ruling: "But it is forbidden to spend the Sabbath with the Gentile who collects the customs duties."[83] The Jew's physical separation from the place where the money was collected was probably the psychological basis for popular allowance of this mode of customs collection, and this same physical separation was what eventually rendered this conduct acceptable by halakhic authorities as well.

82. Joseph Caro, in *Beit Yosef* 244, raises this question but finds a way to rule permissively without restriction.
83. Maharam, *Pesakim and Minhagim* 1:194.

6

The Economic Involvement of Polish Jewry

During both the last few centuries of the Middle Ages and the early part of the modern period, when tradition was still predominant in Jewish social life, there developed no new problems pertinent to our subject that could not be solved through the halakhic precedents of previous generations. The major rulings of these problems had already been summarized in the Sabbath and festival regulations codified in the *Tur Orah Hayyim*, and in greater detail in R. Joseph Caro's *Beit Yosef*. More or less unambiguous decisions were cited in the *Shulhan Arukh* and in the accompanying rulings appended by R. Moses Isserles. On the basis of these summaries, any rabbi could instruct the general public concerning desirable everyday conduct. Jews who participated in the development of new kinds of industry or integrated into economic fields in which they were not previously found would appeal for counsel to the outstanding halakhic authorities of the day.

R. David ben Zimra was asked about a Jew who "had to buy oxen to process sugar; if the processing were not carried out on the Sabbaths and festivals, everything would be lost."[1] A scholar in Constantinople

1. R. David ben Zimra, *Responsa* (Venice, 1749) 1:13.

in the seventeenth century considered the rule applicable "to the glass industry because everyone knows they have to work by means of Gentiles on the Sabbath; otherwise, the work spoils."[2] Residents of Tiberias asked R. Yom Tov Zahalon "about the bees called *dabur* in Arabic, which come and kill the wasps in their hives, the remedy being to smoke the place out so that the *dabur* are chased away or die in the smoke. . . . Is a Jew permitted to tell a Gentile on the Sabbath to make smoke or not?"[3] People who ask these questions expect the talmudic scholar to arrive at a decision permitting the employment of Gentiles in the plant from which they make their living,[4] and it is in general not beyond the capacity of the scholar to do so.[5]

At the same time, halakhic authorities continue to supervise the public lest halakhically confirmed permissive rulings be overstepped. In R. Elijah Mizrahi's time, "teachers" ruled in "Jewish communities," apparently in Constantinople, "that all storekeepers can tell Gentiles: Run my store on the Sabbath and I will run it on a weekday; you keep the Sabbath's profits and I will keep those of the weekday."[6] R. Elijah terms those who ruled according to this lenient approach "ignoramuses," although reading his words between the lines reveals that he was actually referring to "those scholars who rely on their own judgment and hand down decisions as they see fit,"[7] that is, the rabbis of one of the groups comprising the greater Jewish community of Constantinople. R. Elijah discredits the lenient ruling, insisting that one must rule

2. R. Eliezer Shangi, *Dat va-Din* (sermons with 19 *responsa*) (Constantinople, 1726), 6.

3. R. Yom Tov Zahalon, *Responsa* (Venice, 1694), 244.

4. The question addressed to R. David ben Zimra (n. 1 above) ends as follows: "How could this be remedied?" This resembles the wording of the question put to R. Eliezer Shangi (n. 2 above). The question put by the people of Tiberias (n. 3 above) is phrased as an open question, but another one put to R. Yom Tov Zahalon (sec. 76) has the following: "As for a Jew who gives a Gentile oxen and wheat to sow in a field as a tenant . . . what must such a Jew do so that his actions be permitted despite the Sabbath?"

5. R. David ben Zimra (n. 1 above) proposes "four ways" for a permissive ruling, and he lists them starting with the simplest. The other authorities to whom the questions were put also answer positively. In Ben Zimra, *Responsa*, ed. N. H. Sofer (Benei-Berak, 1975), 8:38, he is asked: "As for a Jew who sends merchandise to the land of Kush by camel, what must he do so as not to violate 'so that your ox and donkey rest, etc.'?" Here, too, Ben Zimra suggests three ways to rule permissively.

6. R. Elijah Mizrahi, *Responsa* 85.

7. Ibid.

strictly especially in his days, "since to our regret sinning has resulted
in a depreciation of Torah and piety amongst Jews, and any permissive
ruling is adopted as a starting point for further leniency, a trend that
could lead to a complete disappearance of the Sabbath."[8]

One generation later, R. Moses Alashkar was asked "about a Jew
giving his animal to a Gentile who works with it on the Sabbath. . . .
Some people rule leniently in this matter . . . and they take the permission for granted"[9]—the questioner himself being shocked at what
he beholds. R. Moses agrees that one should be shocked, for "such a
thing should not even be considered, let alone carried out . . . the biblical
verse reading 'so that your ox, etc. may rest.'"[10] We have no idea who
asked the question; Alashkar lived in Tunis, Greece and Egypt, and he
had already clarified the regulations applying to the matter under consideration in a responsum to the Jews of the island of Djerba. He explained the three kinds of permissive rulings developed by halakhic authorities: "by renouncing ownership or by having the Gentile accept
responsibility or by sale."[11] But he did not approve of them: "I don't
feel this is what a Jew should do; at any rate, if in certain areas people
are accustomed to lending or hiring out in one of these three ways . . .
and they rely on those who rule permissively and reject stricter rulings,
let them . . . but a careful Jew should restrain himself."[12] Djerba, of
course, was an old established community, and its scholars may have
been able to supervise the people and ensure that individual deals were
carried out in accordance with authorized procedures, but the unknown
place under discussion was representative of the general public, whose
Sabbath observance merely meant refraining from working themselves,
whereas what Gentiles did with their property, and even with their
livestock, they regarded as permissible.

8. Had R. Elijah tried to find a way to rule permissively, he could have advised
the shop owners to stipulate the breakdown of the days with their Gentile partner,
in which case he admits there is nothing wrong. Such advice was given to business-
men by halakhic authorities in recent times; see chap. 11, n. 7. He, however, wanted
to see the shops belonging to Jews closed, as was accepted practice.

9. R. Moses Alashkar, *Responsa* (Jerusalem, 1959), 42. This section is made up
of two responsa: The first is addressed to the community of Djerba and is discussed
below. The second, in the middle of the passage "and I found," is where this sentence
is found.

10. Ibid.

11. Ibid.

12. Ibid.

The Jews of eastern Europe—of Poland and Lithuania—became extremely involved in the economic life of their surroundings in the sixteenth and seventeenth centuries.[13] This involvement generated problems of Sabbath and Jewish ritual observance that were not easily solved. Jews engaged in the manufacture and sale of strong drink—brandy and beer—sometimes on the open market and on their own initiative but occasionally under franchise to the landowner, who would obligate the villagers subject to him to make exclusive use of the services of the Jew. A Jew might also rent a mill under franchise, so that the entire populace would make use of the service he offered in return for a percentage of the milled flour. The division of the Polish-Lithuanian state into a vast number of political subentities gave the local authorities, irrespective of their relative importance, an opportunity to levy customs duties of various kinds. The collection of these duties could be leased to anyone able to pay the rent to the ruler in advance; in this way customs collection became a common Jewish livelihood. Last but not least, Jews would rent entire villages, together with their accompanying tools and serfs, from the landowners.[14] Some of these sources of livelihood were also available to the Jews of Bohemia and Moravia.[15]

The workshops and farms involved would, of course, operate on the Sabbath—the workers' day of rest was Sunday—and the question that arose was how to avoid damaging the profitability of these workshops and farms, at the same time observing the limitations imposed on their

13. The economic life of Polish Jewry has often been described. See Yitzhaq Schipper, "The Economic History of the Jews of Poland and Lithuania from Early Times up until the Division of the Country," in The Jews in Poland (in Hebrew), ed. Israel Halperin (Jerusalem, 1948), 1:155–215; Raphael Mahler, The History of the Jews in Poland (in Hebrew) (Merhavia, 1946), 95–142.

14. All these features will be found below, reflected in the discussions concerning Sabbath observance.

15. Concerning Moravia, see Helmut Teufel, "Zur politischen und sozialen Geschichte der Juden in Mähren vom Antritt der Habsburger bis zur Schlacht am Weissen Berg, 1526–1620" (Diss., Erlangen-Nuremberg, 1971); concerning Bohemia, see the two excellent articles by Ruth Kestenberg-Gladstein, "A Census of the Jews of Bohemia Outside of Prague in 1742" (in Hebrew), Zion 9 (1944):1–26; idem, "An Economic History of the Jews of Bohemia outside of Prague in the Seventeenth and Eighteenth Centuries" (in Hebrew), Zion 12 (1947):49–65, 160–189. In Moravia the role of Jews in leasing tax-collecting rights is prominent and is also reflected in the Takanot medinat merin ed. Israel Halperin (Jerusalem, 1952), indexes. In Bohemia the major Jewish activity involving problems of Sabbath observance was in the manufacture of brandy, beer, and potash.

activity while in Jewish hands. A study of the responsa literature of the period and of the contemporary commentaries of the *Shulhan Arukh*, by R. Joel Sirkes (the Bah), David ben Samuel ha-Levi (the Taz), and the *Magen Avraham*, reveals only a very few traces of such problems.

In an important responsum, R. Solomon ben Jehiel Luria, referring to the drying of salt, rules in the case of a Jew acquiring the appropriate franchise and hiring "Gentile workers by contract for a year or for a month . . . where it is known that if the worker produces a certain amount of salt, the Jew pays him a certain sum, the implements belonging to the Jew."[16] The questioner wondered if the stipulations of the agreement met the requirements of contracting, by which the Jew has nothing to gain from the Gentile's working on the Sabbath, since in this case "if he refrains from working on the Sabbath, the Jew loses the profits accruing on that day."[17] However, the questioner believed that a precedent for just such a case was to be found in the permissive ruling maintained by R. Meir of Rothenburg concerning leaving the customs duty collection in the hands of a Gentile on the Sabbath in return for a percentage of the intake in order "to avoid a loss."[18] R. Solomon replied that if the crucial factor was one of loss, the case under consideration would not require a permissive ruling: "It would seem to be complete loss that is important here, but actually it is the mere withholding of profit in whatever is not done today. . . . This does not apply to customs duties, where one really loses, for others have already become liable to pay him."[19] From another point of view R. Solomon found the salt drying more analogous to contracting, in that the worker receives a real portion of the fruit of his labors, similar to contracting throughout the week, in contrast to customs duty collection. Contracting for salt drying is thus permitted even where there is no loss involved but rather mere withholding of profit.

This responsum of R. Solomon thus contributed to the precise definition of contracting and especially to the concept of loss, insofar as it distinguished between loss and withholding of profit. From this period on, anyone attempting to exploit the idea of loss in getting a permissive

16. R. Solomon Luria, *Responsa* 100.
17. Ibid.
18. Ibid.
19. Ibid.

ruling of any kind—following R. Meir of Rothenburg—would have to clarify the question of loss versus withholding of profit. This question arose repeatedly, apparently, in scholarly discussions of subsequent generations.

Another responsum of importance in its day and of great influence in the future was composed by R. Menahem Mendel Krochmal, the author of *Tsemah Tsedek*, the rabbi of Nikolsburg, and chief rabbi of Moravia:

> I was approached by residents of the Jewish community of Nikolsburg who make their living by owning horses and wagons and transporting cargoes over distances and who have Gentiles hired by the day or the week or the month engaged in transporting the freight. They asked me to consider their halakhic position and find a way to allow them to send their horses and loaded wagons on the Sabbath using the Gentiles by a procedure that avoids the ban on working their animals. They say that they have seen many people acting that way, having found a means of doing so by giving up the ownership of the animals or by selling them to Gentiles before the Sabbath.[20]

The presentation of the problem in this manner clearly shows that this kind of hauling enterprise was not new and that the permissive ruling they sought was common and accepted. Continuing his responsum, R. Menahem Mendel describes the habits of freight haulers: Their convoys would stop traveling on Sabbath eve; the Jewish owners would spend the Sabbath at an inn. "On the night of the Sabbath they make use of their own belongings and garments, and on the morrow, on the Sabbath, they hand everything over to the wagon drivers to take with them," and after the Sabbath is over, "they hurry after the wagons."[21] The owners made use of methods of transport faster than the freight wagons and so managed to catch up with the convoy. Here is another case of careful Sabbath observance by the Jew himself, who, simultaneously and with no pangs of guilty conscience, has Gentiles do the work. The problem of the formal ban on having one's beast of burden work on the Sabbath is solved, not by ignoring it but rather by circumventing the dilemma, that is, by the sale of the animals or by renunciation of ownership. This

20. Menahem Mendel Krochmal, *Tsemah Tsedek Responsa* (Amsterdam, 1675), 35.

21. Ibid., 42a.

system seems to have had its share of halakhic authorization, for it had some support in halakhic tradition, as R. Menahem Mendel Krochmal himself admits in the discussion contained in his responsum. It is thus likely that "the residents of Nikolsburg" did not suddenly, of their own initiative, question what they had always done under the assumption that it was permitted; rather their rabbi, upon assuming his position in the community,[22] examined the customs of his new constituency and found them wanting in this respect.

This is not surprising, for we have already found circumvention of the ban on working one's animals in the aforementioned manner to be common, even though halakhic approval was very difficult to substantiate.[23] Therefore, it was not difficult for anyone interested in maintaining halakhic strictness to find support for the position that there were really no grounds for circumventing the ban. The case of the inhabitants of Nikolsburg was even more problematic because the contradiction between the formal renunciation of Jewish ownership of the animals and their actual maintenance was so blatant: "Since the Jew constantly accompanies the animals he is responsible for feeding them, whereas the Gentile is merely hired by the day or week or month. Thus the whole enterprise is considered Jewish, and the matter of appearances is significant."[24]

According to the ruling given by R. Menahem Mendel, the haulers of cargoes had to halt the traveling of the entire convoy for the Sabbath. There is no way of knowing whether he was obeyed and whether the haulers reconciled themselves to the loss that this entailed, especially since they could always retort that "they have seen many people acting" as they did and doing so "with permission." It is, however, clear that R. Menahem Mendel's unambiguous stand had its effect upon later halakhic authorities whenever they were called upon to consider a similar problem.[25]

Most of our knowledge of the issues that concerned religious leaders does not come from responsa literature, but rather from regulations legislated by public bodies such as the Council of the Principal Commun-

22. Rabbi Krochmal was appointed rabbi of the community and of the state in 1650 and served in these posts until his death in 1661.
23. See chap. 5, nn. 7ff.
24. Krochmal, *Tsemah Tsedek* 42a.
25. Ibid., at the beginning of the responsum.

ities of the Province of Lithuania. We have detailed knowledge of three sets of regulations concerning mainly Sabbath observance: one from the Cracow community, a second enacted by the leaders of the Ladmir communities, and a third—actually an adjustment of the first group to the conditions that prevailed after the persecutions of 1648–1649.[26]

The archetype of all these regulations is the first series of rules, dating from 1590, attributed to R. Meshullam Phoebus of Cracow, which may have been approved by the Council of the Four Lands.[27] We can detect traces of the problems referred to in these regulations from the warnings sounded by preachers who criticized the lax behavior of their contemporaries regarding the Sabbath Gentile.[28]

The Jews of this generation were not suspected of desecrating the Sabbath in their personal lives. On the contrary, the regulations of concern to them reflect their desire to protect their economic interests by making Gentiles do any actual labor involved while the Jews themselves stood aside and observed. A person engaged in the sale of "beer, honey, and brandy" would sell them [on the Sabbath] "as they are sold on weekdays, by precise measurement and fixed prices"[29]—selling drinks on credit to Jews was also common—being careful not to handle any money.[30] For his part, the Gentile buying them would put the money

26. The Cracow arrangement is included in the *Records of the Councils of the Four Lands*, ed. Israel Halperin (Jerusalem, 1945), 483–487, where there is a discussion of the relationship of the council to the regulations. The other two sets of regulations will be adduced below according to H. H. Ben-Sasson, "The Sabbath Violation Regulations of Poland and Their Social and Economic Significance" (in Hebrew), *Zion* 21 (1956):183–206. The regulations of Vladimir were first published there. Ben-Sasson touches on the halakhic side as well in his precise discussion of the details of the regulations. Ben-Sasson (ibid., 184 n. 8) tends, on strong grounds, to believe that the earliest regulation did not have the approval of the council. At any rate, the matter is still doubtful, but from the point of view of the document's historical significance this is not too important. "Matters of Sabbath violation" in connection with "leasing, and millstones and tax collecting and breweries" were considered by the halakhic authorities of the Council of the Four Lands in 1507, as well, but their conclusions were not published, *inter alia*, for the reason "of incomplete agreement among us in connection with ruling permissively before the journeys taken by the heads of the academies from here after the fair," as it was put by R. Joshua Falk in *Records*, 22.

27. See previous note.

28. See below, at the end of the chapter.

29. *Records*, 484.

30. "Nor are they careful except for handling the money," *Records* 484. See Ben-Sasson, "Sabbath Violation Regulations," 199; and see below, at the end of the chapter, the opinion of the writer of *Korban Shabbat*.

in the Jew's till at his own initiative. It was even simpler to have domestic male and female servants handle the sale of drinks on the Sabbath.[31] The Jew in charge of collecting the customs duty would have a Gentile substitute for him on the Sabbath, although he or his Jewish assistant would keep an eye on the Gentile lest he appropriate some of the money collected.[32] In a similar fashion, a flour mill run by a Jew would be operated by an expert Gentile miller on the Sabbath in the same way it was operated on weekdays. The farmers, bringing their grain to the mill for grinding, set aside a certain percentage of the flour for the miller and the owner of the mill. The Jew or his aide would watch the procedure carefully, lest his share of the market be lost.[33]

Halakhic authorities found no fault with this kind of division of labor but wanted to ensure that the job would be entrusted to the Gentile according to halakhic requirements. Selling drinks in the home of a Jew, either by means of "household servants" or without them, was not permissible. Authorities wanted to obligate the innkeeper or bartender to remove the sign that "they hang all week long at the entrance to their house, informing the public that beer and honey are sold in this house."[34] The Jew who desired to ensure the satisfaction of his customers on the Sabbath as well had to sell some of his merchandise to a Gentile—but not to his household servants—before the onset of the Sabbath. He would then serve the customers in his own house, "being entirely responsible for all profit or loss, and the Jew having no part of it at all."[35] The authors of these enactments admitted, however, that it was not always feasible to insist that merchandise be removed from a Jew's home. If the owner of the bar was "in possession of a lease prohibiting the sale of brandy by anyone in town except the lessor,"[36] the terms of the concession obligated him to sell the brandy on the Sabbath in his own home. In such a case, he was permitted to have the merchandise sold on the Sabbath in his own house on condition that a Gen-

31. Ben-Sasson, "Sabbath Violation Regulations," 201.
32. Records, 485; Ben-Sasson, "Sabbath Violation Regulations," 202.
33. Records, 485; Ben-Sasson, "Sabbath Violation Regulations," 203–204.
34. Records, 484; similarly, Ben-Sasson, "Sabbath Violation Regulations," 199.
35. Ibid.
36. Records, 484–485; Ben-Sasson, "Sabbath Violation Regulations," 200. The last regulations make an exception of the sale to "the real servants of the squire."

tile actually do so in the following manner: The Gentile was to purchase the drinks before the Sabbath and sell them at his own initiative.[37]

It is doubtful if the authorities believed that their ruling would be put into effect. As they put it, "Most of the public is guilty of this transgression."[38] The difficulty in executing the ruling is clearly reflected in the regulations of the Lithuanian council: Decisions dating from 1639 recommend following R. Meshullam Phoebus's ruling forbidding any innkeeper but permitting one enjoying a lease (of the kind mentioned above), on condition that he sell the drinks to a Gentile before the Sabbath.[39] In 1662, the council demanded supervision by the leaders of the community together with the head of the local *beit din* (Jewish court), for "a number of barmen in our communities are guilty of desecrating the Sabbath."[40] However, fourteen years later (in 1676), the permit was broadened to apply to persons without leases as well, on condition that the sale not take place "in the house in which he lives with his family, unless it is in a special room that he never enters on the Sabbath."[41] Nevertheless, the admonitions concerning the observance of instructions did not cease.[42] The public continued to settle for those "protective fences" considered necessary for Sabbath observance as it understood the term.

Pouring drinks, that is, bartending, was a common way of making a living for the Jews of Poland and Lithuania, and this seems to explain the problems of Sabbath observance and the arousal of special concern. The same was also true of various levels of customs duty collection, a common Jewish livelihood, by Jewish capitalists, who leased customs rights from states and towns, and by Jews of limited means, who collected road and bridge tolls.[43] Collecting duties on the Sabbath personally was undoubtedly considered a desecration of the Sabbath. At the same time, we learn of "the villagers who collect duties without any

37. Ibid.
38. *Records*, 485, and 484, for similar expressions; Ben-Sasson, "Sabbath Violation Regulations," 199.
39. Simon Dubnow, *Pinkas ha-Medinah* (Berlin, 1925), sec. 358.
40. Ibid., sec. 530.
41. Ibid., sec. 713.
42. See ibid., secs. 740, 775, 912, 966.
43. See Mahler, *The History of the Jews in Poland*, 110–117.

Gentile."[44] It may be assumed that this was done without actually touching the money and certainly without writing.[45] Others had Gentiles actually collecting the money (but kept an eye on their representatives lest they appropriate any of it) and they were involved in "the calculations or in determining the sums to be paid."[46] The authorities phrasing the regulations confirm the right to employ a Gentile but make this conditional upon the work being performed under contract, that is, the Gentile must receive a certain percentage of the collected sum, "so that he works at his own initiative."[47] This stipulation had been acceptable from the days of R. Meir of Rothenburg.[48] Another condition for permission was that the Jew oversee the work done by the Gentile without being involved in negotiations with those who paid the duty.[49] R. Meshullam Phoebus's ruling recommends that the actual collecting on the Sabbath be done outside the home of the Jew.[50] Such an arrangement was clearly not considered to be practical, however,[51] and the other two sets of regulations do not include this recommendation.[52] All these regulations treat the collection of customs duties more leniently than selling drinks, for the reason, apparently, that the former had been per-

44. Only in the most recent regulations, Ben-Sasson, "Sabbath Violation Regulations," 202.

45. R. David ben Samuel ha-Levi notes that "in most small towns, the tax collectors do not write out tax receipts"; *Orah Hayyim* 244:6. See Ben-Sasson, "Sabbath Violation Regulations," 184, n. 6. The person putting the question to R. Solomon Luria (*Responsa* 16) simply says, "Any receiving of taxes involves writing," and was undoubtedly referring to the large-scale border tax collecting.

46. "He just must not help him accept the tax or make calculations or fix the amount, as many trip up on these things," *Records* 485; Ben-Sasson, "Sabbath Violation Regulations," 202.

47. Ibid.

48. See chap. 5, nn. 76ff.

49. R. Meir of Rothenburg ruled that "sitting beside the Gentile receiving the taxes is forbidden" (ed. Kahana, *Pesakim and Minhagim* 7:194), and R. Moses Isserles ruled accordingly (*Orah Hayyim* 244:6), whereas R. David ben Samuel ha-Levi (*Orah Hayyim* 244:7) found a basis for "the custom of those who have milling rights from the landlord to have a Jew sitting there even on the Sabbath, as long as they are careful not to talk about the business."

50. *Records*, 485.

51. Ibid.: "And if it is possible for the Gentile to receive the taxes outside the home of the Jew, it is better."

52. Ben-Sasson, "Sabbath Violation Regulations."

mitted ever since the Middle Ages. Not collecting the duties was considered a loss—as R. Meshullam Phoebus put it, a "great loss" to the lessee of the rights.[53]

A solution to the halakhic problem involved in milling flour was found by dividing roles between the Jewish lessee of the mill and the miller. According to the earliest regulations, the custom was for the two to lease the mill from the landowner, the miller, too, "having a franchise from the nobleman granting him a certain percentage, such as a tenth, a third, or a quarter."[54] The Jew invests his own money, of course, in the leasing of the millstones, and the miller contributes his expertise. They share the income, which is a certain percentage of the flour ground. The presence of the Jew is necessary only to ensure that his share does not suffer, and this can be performed by him personally or by his aide on the Sabbath as well.[55] The Jew is not permitted to rent the mill by himself and afterward hire a miller at his own expense. "Thus one must be careful . . . that no Jew leases millstones unless he does so in partnership with a Gentile miller"[56]—as was customary.

A Sabbath observer who actually owned a workshop or factory, such as a plant for brewing brandy or beer, encountered a more serious difficulty. Such a plant seems to have been rented out "to others, each person brewing [the beer or brandy] on his own specific day."[57] The economic exploitation of this plant would require that its Jewish owner be able to rent it out to Gentiles on the Sabbath or to operate it under his own responsibility by means of Gentile workers. However, even though the Jew did no actual work himself, this was considered Sabbath desecration because the plant "was known by a Jew's name."[58] It stands to reason that the compilers of the relevant regulation did not fear that their contemporaries would actually operate their plant on the Sabbath. Rather, they worried about the possibility of labor being performed in

53. *Records*, 485. R. Meshullam Phoebus's uses the expression "a heavy loss" figuratively. Halakhically speaking, the size of the loss is immaterial. The relevant distinction is between loss and withholding of profit. See R. Solomon Luria, *Responsa* 100.

54. *Records*, 485.

55. Ibid.; Ben-Sasson, "Sabbath Violation Regulations," 203–204; and also 202.

56. Ben-Sasson, "Sabbath Violation Regulations," 204.

57. *Records*, 483.

58. Ibid.

the plant, incidental to acts that were permitted, such as soaking "the grain before the Sabbath, the grain thus continuing to be soaked throughout the Sabbath."[59]

The difficulties already considered are negligible in comparison with the problem that arose whenever Jews rented entire farms together with their vassals, the villagers, who were obligated to perform the landowner's work. It is doubtful that it was economically feasible to place the farm under the limitations imposed by Jewish law: a ban on all work on Sabbath and festivals, a ban on pig raising and on feeding the workers food that was unfit for consumption by Jewish law, and so on.[60]

This, however, was precisely what the authorities wished to impose on the lessees. In the opinion of R. Meshullam Phoebus, a complete cessation of vassal labor on the Sabbath is an absolute requirement. These vassals "are employed by the day . . . and the villagers cannot care less if the work in the fields is completed or not. They are under no obligation to complete it and just work the number of days they are allotted, whether in the fields or at any other work their masters set them to. . . . This is well known to all."[61] R. Meshullam Phoebus tried to make the lessees (together, perhaps, with those halakhic authorities who defended them) realize that the vassals were certainly not to be considered "laborers under contract to plow, sow, and reap the fields."[62] His halakhic opponents wanted to view the vassals as workers with a defined job before them—cultivation of the fields—in which case they could be considered as working under contract, and this, under certain

59. Ibid., par. B; Ben-Sasson, "Sabbath Violation Regulations," 195–196. The compilers of the regulations give advice on how to avoid losses incurred by closing the factories: "The Jew should rent it out . . . to a Gentile for three or four years, stipulating that he refrain from . . . labor on the Sabbath and on festivals, so that even if he violates this condition, no sin is ascribed to the Jew." But did such advice have any practical meaning from an economic point of view? See *Records*, 483–484; Ben-Sasson, 197–198. The last two sets of regulations also describe a situation in which the distillery belongs to the landlord and the lessor has to operate it according to the conditions of the lease. In such a case, they allow the plant to be operated the same way they permit tax collecting.

60. The regulations also touch on these matters (*Records*, 486–487; Ben-Sasson, "Sabbath Violation Regulations," 205–206), but they digress from the present topic. See Ben-Sasson, 192–193; and the present author, *Tradition and Crisis* (in Hebrew) (Jerusalem, 1958), 79, 82, and esp. n. 13.

61. *Records*, 486; Ben-Sasson, "Sabbath Violation Regulations," 204–205.

62. *Records*, 486.

conditions, was permissible.[63] R. Meshullam Phoebus rejects this definition as fictitious and inherently lacking in credibility. The vassals' work obligation is defined in temporal terms, so many days, and not in terms of completing a defined task. Proof of this is to be found in the fact that the vassals do not engage solely in agriculture. Within the time framework laid out for them, they perform whatever work their masters impose on them.

His conclusion was: "It is forbidden for a Jew to let the villagers do their labor on Sabbaths and festivals, and this includes plowing, sowing, reaping, or any other labor";[64] that is, neither work apparently included in the limits of the contract nor any other kind of work. The halakhic authorities were unable to help the lessee by revealing a loophole in the law, and so they approached him with practical advice, on the one hand, and religious reproof, on the other. What was the nature of the practical advice? "If the lessee is alert, he will make sure upon signing the lease to include the stipulations that his legal obligation be discharged on weekdays and that he be freed from them on the Sabbaths and festivals."[65] In other words, the labor will cease on the Sabbath, but the vassals' workdays will not be wasted, for they will be relocated in advance to other days of the week. This, of course, was worthy of consideration only if "the villagers are under no obligation to perform their labors every day of the week,"[66] as the regulations of Vladimir have it. In fact, there is no certainty that this advice would have helped even with vassals whose work obligation was limited, for the farm would in any case cease working on the Sabbath because of the demands of the Jewish religion and on the morrow, Sunday, because of the Christian faith. It is doubtful if such a farm could survive this economically. R. Meshullam Phoebus's wording does read, in general terms, "and if this is impossible for him, then let him concede Sabbaths and festivals to them in their entirety."[67] The halakhic authorities realized that such a concession would entail a severe economic loss. That is why they resort to religious reproof, recalling the sons of Jacob who went down to Egypt

63. See chap. 5, for the discussion of Rabbenu Tam's ruling (nn. 63ff) and for R. Meir of Rothenburg's permissive ruling concerning tax collecting (nn. 77ff).
64. *Records*, 486.
65. Ibid.
66. Ben-Sasson, "Sabbath Violation Regulations," 205.
67. *Records*, 486.

and observed the Sabbath there, even under conditions of servitude: "How much more is this applicable when the Gentile is subservient to them. The instructions of the Torah and the sages must be carried out, for in this way will God be sanctified by them and not desecrated, God forbid."[68]

Whether the relevant parties hearkened to this reproof may well be doubtful. The regulations of Lithuania dating from 1632 also advise that if the work requirement of the vassals is for a number of days each week, "the Jew must be careful to exchange the Sabbath day for another day . . . and not have them work on the Sabbath."[69] What, however, is to be done if the work obligation of the villagers "is constant, all week long without interruption?" The authorities of Lithuania demand no compromise, preferring to have the lessee "go to the nearest rabbinic court and receive instructions as to how to proceed and how to behave."[70] Their assumption is, then, that the court will be able to help the lessee ensure that work on the farm is not stopped, while he will not be considered a desecrator of the Sabbath. Explicit evidence has indeed survived, cited by R. Joel Sirkes, that on leased farms "the Gentiles plow and sow on Sabbaths and festivals, lest the squire lose money; all the labors for the squire that have to be performed are actually carried out."[71] This statement is made in connection with financial rulings in support of the conclusion that the lessee "is a surrogate for the squire landowner," and just as the latter would be exempt from paying duties to the enfranchised Jewish duty collector, so would the lessee of his estate be similarly exempt. The lessee of the estate has not bought it outright "but rather the resultant reward,"[72] that is, only the crop of the farm.

R. Joel Sirkes seems to have inserted into this definition a kind of ruling that permitted with no restrictions whatever the work of vassals on an estate leased by a Jew.[73] If that really was his intention, he dis-

68. *Records*, 486; Ben-Sasson, "Sabbath Violation Regulations," 205.
69. *Pinkas ha-Medinah* 261.
70. Ibid. See Ben-Sasson ("Sabbath Violation Regulations," 191 n. 41), who discusses the difference between the other regulations and those of Lithuania.
71. R. Joel Sirkes, *Old Responsa* (Frankfurt, 1698), 27; see the discussion of Ben-Sasson, "Sabbath Violation Regulations," 191.
72. Ibid.
73. Ibid.; thus Ben-Sasson understood it ("Sabbath Violation Regulations," 191).

agreed with the highest halakhic authorities of Poland and Lithuania, of whom he was one. Furthermore, the reasoning provided for his ruling does not appear to be halakhically significant in connection with Sabbath observance. The landlord's loss is surely not a reason to rule permissively, and the formal designation of the ownership as being that of the landlord does not render the Jewish lessee any less the operator of the farm and the one who derives benefit from the work of Gentiles.[74] It is thus unlikely that R. Joel Sirkes based his opinion of the continued activity of the farm on the Sabbath upon his ruling in the matter of paying customs duties—which is what he was actually asked. Rather, he ignored the problem of permitting the work from the standpoint of the Jewish lessee.[75] We have no way of knowing how he would have answered this question had it been asked, just as we have no knowledge of the kind of "arrangements" the rabbinic court elders were asked to make by the Council of Lithuanian Communities in connection with the lessees of estates.

We do not know to what extent the actual behavior of the public corresponded to the demands of the institutions that supervised its religious behavior. Those who issued the regulations relied upon appointed officials who had the power to impose fines upon transgressors.[76] True, in matters universally accepted as forbidden, things that no Jew would consider doing, the public itself probably exercised its own informal kind of supervision. Learned men, who identified with

74. Support for our explanation comes from R. Joel Sirkes's wording: "Reuben is right and exempt from paying tax . . . since the land itself is the squire's, the Jew enjoying only the fruit, so the Gentile is in the middle. . . . Thus all the newborn are not considered firstborn, for the squire owns the animals, and the Gentiles plow and sow on Sabbath and festivals lest the squire lose." As far as the exemption for the rules of the firstborn is concerned, his halakhic proof is based on the fact that wherever a Gentile intervenes, the rules of the firstborn are invalidated. Had he thought similarly concerning the Sabbath, he should have continued by saying, "for this reason the work of Gentiles is permitted, etc."

75. The writers of responsa occasionally ignore minor but relevant problems, saying "I was not asked about that."

76. *Records*, 483. See Ben-Sasson, "Sabbath Violation Regulations," 185–186, about the supervision of the enforcement of the regulations. The author of *Korban Shabbat* (see n. 81 below) tells of the heads of the Slutsk community "who used to go around on Friday from house to house with their officials, two hours or more before nightfall, to inspect all the rooms [to see if work had stopped, and if not] they would break the vessels . . . so also in the homes of all the craftsmen and in all the shops and would close them down immediately" (p. 123).

the tendency of the authorities responsible for the regulations to comply
with the halakhic requirements, in all likelihood conducted themselves
according to the regulations. However, as we have already seen, this
field had always been wide open as far as the general public was concerned. The reproof coming from a contemporary of R. Meshullam Phoebus, to the effect that "people are not careful in telling a Gentile, even
on the Sabbath day itself . . . and they send Gentiles outside the *eruv*
[a Sabbath limit outside of which no Jew may carry any object] to bring
them supplies when they have the urge for wine or beer"[77]—such reproof, though aimed as a protest against "contemporary" developments,[78] sounds in fact like an echo of a warning sounded many generations earlier. The infraction was not new, although it undoubtedly
grew more common as a result of the conditions under which Polish-
Lithuanian Jewry subsisted economically in this period. Once the employment of Gentiles in various jobs came to be treated permissively
by contemporary Jewry,[79] it is doubtful that any public supervision
could reduce the phenomenon to the dimensions permitted by halakhic
precision.

The preacher R. Berechiah Berakh, the author of *Zera Berakh*, who,
of course, identified with the strict demands of halakhah when he undertook to rationalize the persecutions and massacres of 1648–1649,
termed the violation of halakhah in the field of the Sabbath Gentile one

77. The opinion of R. Jehiel Michael Morawceik, *Seder Berakhot* (Cracow, 1600),
8a, is adduced by Ben-Sasson, "Sabbath Violation Regulations," 183.
78. Ben-Sasson ("Sabbath Violation Regulations," 183) ascribes significance to
this concerning the special situation in Poland as reflected in the regulations.
79. R. Judah Leib Pohovitzer reproves his contemporaries again and again about
Sabbath desecration of the kinds mentioned here (the sources are adduced by Ben-
Sasson, "Sabbath Violation Regulations," n. 3), but he sometimes inserts a realistic
description of the situation: "The pious have to be familiar with Sabbath regulations
so as not to slip up on any of them. . . . We ourselves see that many have acted
mistakenly in a number of customs and laws and have treated a number of prohibitions as if they were permitted, like the manufacturers of brandy and the renters
of millstones and tax-collecting rights and selling liquor to Gentiles, some by renting
villages and towns from the lords of the estates and others by taking all the profits
for themselves. Their livelihoods depend on this, so it is impossible to tell them to
stay away from these occupations in order to refrain from violations" (*Kevod Hakhamim* [Venice, 1700], 19a). At any rate, he demands, at very least, that the restrictions included in the regulations be observed (he himself published the third set),
and if the Jew finds it impossible to do so, "he should give up that occupation even
if that means resorting to begging" (ibid., 26a).

of the most serious transgressions of the generation.[80] Another eyewitness of the same ilk, R. Bezalel ben Solomon Darshan, the author of *Korban Shabbat*, attributes the entire catastrophe to Sabbath desecration. His words comprise a mixture of description and evaluation of the current situation, as follows:

> We have to accept the decision of heaven; God is righteous, and we are wicked because of our many transgressions in desecrating the Sabbath and festivals. My object is not to besmirch the general public . . . but individually, most village dwellers in possession of *arenda* [leased villages], though there are good men amongst them, kindhearted men who deal charitably with the Gentiles as well as with Torah scholars whom they provide with a livelihood, yet most of them do not observe the Sabbath because their entire livelihood is linked to the villagers. . . . Not only are they remiss in not extending the sanctity of the Sabbath, they actually profane the sanctity of the Sabbath itself. . . . They buy and sell on the Sabbath in a deceitful manner through the agency of the villagers. They make themselves out to be as righteous as Phinehas and are extremely careful not to touch a coin on the Sabbath. It is as if they save the branch of the tree but pull up the roots. They order their Gentile servants to do such and such work, and they sit and teach them how to repair whatever has spoiled in the job. They are not careful about letting their animals rest on the Sabbath. Woe is me that I was witness to such things a number of times and had no way of offering a protest.[81]

80. *Zera Berakh*, pt. 2 (Hamburg, 1687), introduction. See Ben-Sasson, "Sabbath Violation Regulations," 189–190. R. Judah Leib Pohovitzer (*Kevod Hakhamim* 26a) cites this opinion approvingly.

81. Bezalel ben Solomon Darshan, *Korban Shabbat* (Warsaw, 1873), 121. The most significant Sabbath violation seems to have stemmed from leasing the estates. In both Moravia and Bohemia, where there was no such leasing, there is no trace of a similar phenomenon and certainly not to the extent of what happened in Poland. The Mähren regulations (n. 15 above) which include instructions concerning the supervision of the preparation of wine and so on (see indexes), do not relate to the problem of the Sabbath. The Noda bi-Yehudah says in one of his sermons: "I hear that the villagers do not finish early on Fridays and delay until nightfall, and even on the Sabbath itself their animals work in the fields, thus violating the Torah prohibition of 'so that [your animal] may rest, etc.' Those, too, who have their own fields may not cultivate them on the Sabbath, even by means of non-Jews—plowing, sowing, and harvesting, all this is public labor—neither by means of contracting nor especially working by the day." These are phenomena that did not originate in his day, and so he does not expect them to disappear. Ezekiel Landau, *Derushei ha-Tselah* (Warsaw, 1897), 25b.

This is a description of a farm working on the Sabbath, with the Jewish lessee supervising the work as on weekdays. Business with the local people continued by means of Gentile mediation, the only limitation being that the lessee refrained from touching money with his own hands. The halakhic authorities, rabbis and preachers, witnessed all this but could do nothing about it—either because of the widespread nature of the phenomenon, rendering it impossible to rectify, or because their own livelihood depended upon the economic prosperity of the lessee sector of the population. Together with his condemnation of the lessees for their desecration of the Sabbath, he does praise them for their charitable behavior, including their support of Torah scholars: "providing them with a livelihood."

7

Initial Industrialization
Problems in Italy

The Sabbath Gentile, one assisting the Jew to observe his Sabbath properly, became a permanent phenomenon as time passed, a sure indication
that not only individuals but also community institutions required his
services. R. Abraham Gombiner realized that in his own community of
Kalisch "they allow themselves to hire a Gentile under contract to remove the garbage from the streets, and the Gentile does the work on
the Sabbath."[1] R. Abraham, the author of *Magen Avraham*, assumed as
self-evident that this had been permitted in the past by a scholarly ruling
(". . . and we must conclude that a great rabbi handed down this ruling"),
and he guessed that this permissive ruling was based on the fact that
"because of the community ['s involvement] there is no ground for suspicion."[2] The ban on contracting is imposed on account of appearances,
but an entire community is not suspect.

1. *Magen Avraham* 244:8.
2. Ibid. According to this explanation, "it would appear permissible to build a
synagogue on the Sabbath by contracting; at any rate, I have seen that great scholars
did not want to permit this." The reason, in his opinion, was that since the Christians
do not allow work to be done publicly on their festivals, it would seem profane if
the Jews treated their own Sabbath more lightly.

An accepted custom in many synagogues was for a Gentile to extinguish the candles after the worshipers had left on the night of Sabbaths and festivals. When a scholar from afar visited one of these communities, apparently in the south of Germany, and questioned the custom, the reply was that "this has been customary since early times without anyone casting any doubt upon it; it is also well known that the community of Amsterdam conducts itself similarly."[3] R. Jacob Katz, the author of Shav Yaakov, a scholar of Frankfurt before whom this matter was brought, added that this was accepted behavior "in the great synagogue of Altona community; here, too, in our community it is customary for the Gentile to come, on his own initiative, and put out the candles."[4] This halakhic authority thus feels obliged to come to the defense of the custom. He explains the permissive ruling as stemming mainly from the fear of fire breaking out, which was liable to cause a far more serious desecration of the Sabbath. He is, however, also aware of the lenient ruling common in connection with matters not justifiable by this reasoning. It was customary in the synagogues to extinguish the Hanukkah candles after evening services and to light them again the following morning, during the morning service. On the Sabbath these acts were performed by a Gentile.[5]

From a question submitted to the author of the Noda bi-Yehudah, Rabbi Ezekiel Landau of Prague, we learn of a custom accepted "in many places, where a Gentile lights candles on the Day of Atonement at the hour of the closing prayer."[6] In his reply, he confirms that he found that the Prague community and Yampol in Vohlin, where he had previously been the incumbent halakhic authority, acted in just this fashion—showing that this custom was not a particularly German one. In an attempt to reestablish halakhic supremacy in all its detail, R. Ezekiel Landau overruled this custom—[at most, he permitted the carrying of an already lit candle]—just as the author of Shav Yaakov scolded those who allowed the relighting of the Hanukkah candles on Sabbath mornings. What is apparent here is a disparity between the lay concept of Sabbath observance and that of the halakhic authorities. The lay ap-

3. R. Jacob Katz, Responsa Shav Yaakov (Frankfurt-am-Main, 1742), sec. 15.
4. Ibid.
5. Ibid. He rules this custom out.
6. R. Ezekiel Landau, Responsa ha-Noda bi-Yehudah (Prague, 1776), Orah Hayyim 33.

proach preferred the symbolic religious ceremonies—lighted Hanukkah candles, reciting prayers of forgiveness at the closing prayer service of the Day of Atonement—to halakhic limitations on the use of a Sabbath Gentile even for purposes of fulfilling a religious obligation. The Noda bi-Yehudah himself says: "Who wants the congregation to recite the prayers [of forgiveness]? It were better that they not recite them and merely listen to the prayer leader recite them, rather than act in a way most authorities condemn."[7] The public, however, viewed their active participation in the emotive closing service as outweighing the ban on "telling a Gentile," which had at any rate become irreparably lax. The Hatam Sofer has supplied us with a description of the existing situation: "In our day, as a result of the Jews being scattered throughout the cold lands of the north, they must have their stoves lit on the Sabbath by Gentiles during their cold winters, and this has led to a proliferation of cases in which the Gentiles do many different jobs on the Sabbath for the Jews. The Gentiles in our lands have thus come to believe that such is Sabbath observance, the Jews themselves refraining from an act but telling Gentiles and having them perform it."[8]

Nevertheless, what was characteristic of the period when ghetto life was coming to an end was not so much the proliferation of cases of Jews using Gentiles on the Sabbath in personal matters and the like but rather the Jews themselves being engaged in various new jobs that had just become available to them. Jewish ownership of the means of production was common in earlier periods as well, when it raised questions about the employment of Gentiles on the Sabbath, as we have already seen. In this later period, the frequency of the phenomenon was multiplied, and halakhic authorities were more often consulted in this regard. Gur Aryeh ha-Levi, rabbi of Mantua, wrote to R. Samuel Aboab of Venice[9] about "*filatoio*, that is, the joining of attachments and wheels with which the craftsmen interlace silk." It was not only in Mantua that the Jews were involved in this industry. Rabbi Ishmael ha-Kohen of Modena writes of "the local custom of very early origin where the Jewish owner

7. Ibid. For the disagreement on the question of the limits of the ruling permitting the disregard of the law about "telling a Gentile—*shevut*" when fulfilling a religious precept is involved, see chap. 4, nn. 76ff.

8. *Responsa Hatam Sofer, Orah Hayyim* 59. For the halakhic context in which this was ruled, see chap. 11, nn. 28ff.

9. Samuel Aboab, *Responsa Devar Shemuel* (Venice, 1702), sec. 132.

of the *filatoio*" has a contract with the chief craftsman, who in turn employs secondary craftsmen.[10] This same responsum refers to an interesting ruling concerning something that took place in Gorizia,[11] another town in which Jews participated in this same industry. From an exchange of letters between R. Raphael Meldola and R. Joseph Irgas,[12] we learn about leather processing in a workshop belonging to a Jew; the workshop operated in Pisa, the hometown of the former.[13] During the days of R. Isaiah Bassan, that is, in the first half of the eighteenth century, there were two tannery owners, Reuben and Simeon, according to the description in existing sources, who lived in a village near Reggio. Originally there was "a tax on leather processing. Reuben acquired the rights from the landowner and set up house in the tannery."[14] The meaning of this was, apparently, that only a person who rented a workshop from the landowner was allowed to engage in his profession. Conditions changed, however, and over a period of time Jews set up other tanneries in town.[15] One of these Jews was Simeon, who rented his premises "from a Gentile in the village market, far from the Jewish neighborhood."[16] A description of this workshop follows below.

The situation described in all cases is that the Jews never desisted from their own Sabbath observance. None of the scholars who refer to the questions involved expresses any suspicion whatever that the Jewish owners of the workshops would actually take part in the operation of

10. R. Ishmael ha-Kohen, *Responsa Zera Emet* (Livorno, 1786), *Orah Hayyim* 32.

11. Ibid., in the heading of the responsum.

12. R. Raphael Meldola, *Responsa Mayim Rabbim* (Amsterdam, 1737), secs. 14–15; and see also R. Joseph Irgas, *Responsa Divrei Yosef* (Livorno, 1742), sec. 9.

13. R. Raphael Meldola's responsum (previous note) was concluded in Pisa. As for his dwelling place, see Nifi-Gerondi, *Toledot Gedolei Yisrael* (Trieste, 1853), 311 (y).

14. R. Isaiah Bassan, *Responsa Lahmei Todah*, the second part of *Todat Shelamin* (Venice, 1741), sec. 3 (56a). The case is described also in the responsum of R. Abraham Basilea, appearing in *Pahad Yitshak*, letter *sh* (76a), there being no doubt of the identity of the two descriptions. Details can also be deduced from an anonymous responsum adduced by Bassan word-for-word (ibid. 56a–b) and disputed by him.

15. Bassan only mentions Reuben and Simeon, but the anonymous sage he quotes says that after they were warned, "all the rest of the Jews, including those selling shoes, closed down their shops on the Sabbath" (ibid. 56b). R. Abraham Basilea opens by describing the custom of the other shopkeepers, and only then does he mention Reuben and Simeon. See n. 20 below.

16. Bassan, *Todat Shelamim*, sec. 3 (56a).

their plants on the Sabbath. But as regards their Gentile workers, the owners let them do their work on the Sabbath according to the stipulations agreed to, without paying attention to the question of whether these stipulations sufficed to remove the workshop owners from the halakhically defined boundaries of Sabbath desecration. The workers at the machines manufacturing silk in Mantua, whose conditions were submitted to the scrutiny of R. Samuel Aboab, were hired by the day.[17] This was also true of the workshop laborers for whose situation R. Raphael Meldola tried to find some remedy.[18] R. Isaiah Bassan writes that workers at the aforementioned Reuben workshop, too, were hired by the day, and he adds apologetically that since Reuben's workshop was hired from the landowner, "he was unable to do anything about having them stop work on the Sabbath."[19] Reuben, however, was not unique, and according to R. Abraham Basilea, "all the craftsmen engage in their crafts on the Sabbath in shops belonging to Jews, even when they are open to the public thoroughfare just as on weekdays."[20] Finally, a scholar arrived and warned them of the prohibition involved, as we shall see below. R. Ishmael ha-Kohen, too, complains of the "custom that has spread far and wide in this area, whereby the rich build various devices for stretching the silk (*filatura*, in their tongue) on their own property, the workers being hired by the day" and only the "chief craftsman" working by contract and even then not in every case.[21]

The division of labor between the Jewish owner of the workshop and his Gentile workers is clearly depicted by R. Isaiah Bassan in connection with the aforementioned Simeon. His rented shop "has two rooms, one an inner chamber and the other, an outer room open to the market. . . . Simeon put his merchandise in the inner room, where he sits every weekday and sells, whereas in the outer room he placed his cobblers and a Gentile in charge to cut the leather needed for the shoes. . . . On Fridays Simeon would hand over to the Gentile in charge the amount of leather needed for the Sabbath, for him to distribute among the cobblers. Before the onset of the Sabbath, he would close off

17. N. 9 above.
18. N. 12 above.
19. Bassan, *Todat Shelamim*, sec. 3 (56a).
20. Basilea, *Pahad Yitshak*, letter *sh* (76a). The status of the other shopkeepers is not sufficiently clear.
21. Ishmael ha-Kohen, *Zera Emet* sec. 32 (40b).

the inner chamber and take the key home with him, while the key to the outer room was always in possession of that Gentile who would open and shut the room on all weekdays as well."[22]

In Italy, as in other regions, as we have seen, the halakhic scholars viewed their role as one of supervision, to the best of their ability, of the conduct of the laymen. They would warn them of the prohibitions they were violating and would advise how to avoid them yet maintain the plants that were the source of their income. However, there was no unanimity concerning the proposed methods of circumvention. R. Gur Aryeh ha-Levi of Mantua seems to have tried to find a solution for the silk manufacturing plant in his town by having its workers, who had been hired by the day, become hired by the year,[23] in which case, following the view of Maimonides, their situation might be equivalent to those working under contract.[24] Moreover, since even working under contract was permitted only outside the premises of the Jew, he stipulated in addition that the workshop be rented out to a Gentile.[25] But R. Samuel Aboab had many reservations about this lenient ruling. Maimonides' permissive opinion was not entirely clear;[26] nor was it generally accepted. R. Abraham ben David disagreed with it.[27] The plant was still known by the name of its Jewish owner despite its being rented out, "and its workers labor for Jewish ends on Sabbaths and on festivals."[28] The fictitious basis of the permissive ruling would become painfully obvious "as soon as the Jews would stop working on Gentile hol-

22. N. 14 above.
23. We do not have R. Gur Aryeh ha-Levi's opinion and learn it only from the response of R. Samuel Aboab to it (n. 9 above).
24. Maimonides, *Hilkhot Shabbat* 6:12.
25. This, too, was one of the conditions of R. Gur Aryeh's permissive ruling, as learned from R. Samuel Aboab: "And so even if the two leniencies are joined together to make the house ready for renting to a Gentile, as you have written."
26. The doubt regarding Maimonides' opinion is whether he permitted it only if the non-Jewish laborer is free to do his job "whenever he wants," as he put it (*Hilkhot Shabbat* 6:12), or even if he is obliged to work continuously. R. Samuel Aboab merely hints at this uncertainty, but it is discussed fully in the debate between R. Raphael Meldola and R. Joseph Irgas; see n. 12 above.
27. R. Abraham ben David's opinion in his notes to Maimonides, *Hilkhot Shabbat* 6:12.
28. Aboab, *Devar Shemuel*, sec. 132.

idays but have the work continue in public, just like on regular weekdays, on divinely sanctified Sabbaths and festivals."[29]

R. Samuel himself suggested an alternative way of avoiding the prohibition, whereby the plant would be rented out to a Gentile throughout the year, in return for which the Gentile would process the Jew's silk in the amount the Jew would have processed without operating the workshop on Sabbaths or on festivals. The plant would be run on Sabbaths and festivals as well but not with the silk of the Jew. At the same time, there was no objection that in determining the amount of silk to be processed by the Gentile for the Jew, due account would be given to the fact that on the Jewish days of rest the workshop would be at the disposal of the Gentile for his own interests exclusively.[30] R. Samuel went so far as to restrict this lenient ruling by stipulating "that the building concerned not be known in the town under the name of its Jewish owner" and that it "not be of the kind that local people do not generally hire out."[31] Without acceptance of these preconditions, R. Samuel Aboab would not confirm the permissive ruling. In actual practice, this legal device fell short of what the workshop owner really wanted: He was not interested in renting out his plant to a Gentile; rather, he wanted to operate it himself. Not without cause did R. Ishmael ha-Kohen criticize R. Samuel Aboab's ruling as not permissive enough, saying that "this would not permit one to maintain a livelihood."[32]

Raphael Meldola and R. Joseph Irgas could not agree concerning the conditions of the desired lenient ruling. The former followed in the footsteps of R. Gur Aryeh ha-Levi and permitted the work on condition that workers be engaged by the year, whereas the latter required the processing of leather to be done under contract, that is, that the wages paid would depend on the output.[33] This contracting, however, was also banned if the work was performed on the premises of the Jew, but R. Joseph tended to be lenient on this point. Since the workshop was separate from the living quarters of the Jew, work in it was allowed "on condition that work on the Sabbath be done quietly, with the door

29. Ibid.
30. Ibid., at the end of the responsum.
31. Ibid.
32. Ishmael ha-Kohen, *Zera Emet* 32 (41a).
33. N. 12 above.

closed, so that passersby in the market do not realize that Gentiles are working there."[34] R. Raphael, however, could not accept this lenient ruling.[35]

A case that occurred in the province of Reggio resulted in extreme positions being adopted and led to a clash between the interested parties and to disagreement between halakhic scholars of the day. Here too the tanneries had engaged their workers on a daily basis,[36] with the tacit consent of the local rabbi, until a certain scholar warned the owners that, from a halakhic standpoint, they were desecrating the Sabbath.[37] He demanded that they cease work on Sabbaths and festivals and shut down their shops on those days. This anonymous scholar made no attempt to find—or perhaps he tried without success—room for a permissive ruling and therefore tried to establish the supremacy of religious law. Reuben, who had the franchise from the landowner, together with his associates,[38] actually accepted this ruling. They gave up the income of the day's work and had to compromise with their non-Jewish workers, who were not prepared to lose their wages for a full day's work.[39]

Simeon, however, who considered himself no less "God-fearing" than the other local residents,[40] conducted himself differently. One of the halakhic authorities who considered the problem called him a young scholar.[41] He claimed that he was unable to act like everyone else because of the pressure of his Gentile laborers. According to him, stopping

34. Ibid.

35. It is not clear to me what R. Raphael actually thought, whether he ruled permissively or prohibitively.

36. See n. 19 above. At this point R. Abraham Basilea's description differs from that of R. Isaiah Bassan, according to which the work itself was by contracting from the beginning, the flaw being that it was done "in the shop and with the tools of a Jew" (Pahad Yitshak, letter sh [76a]).

37. According to Bassan (n. 16 above): "The time came when Reuben decided . . . to stop work done in his house on the Sabbath by workers hired on a daily basis," meaning that Reuben decided this of his own accord. However, according to Basilea (n. 20 above): "And then someone came and forbade it," which is more likely.

38. Ibid., according to both sources, to which a third is added, Bassan's disputant, whose opinion is quoted precisely (Todat Shelamim 56a–b): "All the other Jews, including the sellers of shoes, closed down their shops on the Sabbath, for the awe of the Sabbath was upon them."

39. "And he succeeded in compromising with them," Bassan, Todat Shelamim 56a–b.

40. Ibid., as put by Bassan.

41. As worded by Bassan's disputant (n. 38 above).

the work of Reuben's workers on the Sabbath had already stirred up unrest in the area, and when his laborers heard that he was planning to do the same to them, "they complained vociferously to the local priest, the result being that the local uproar got the priest to threaten that if Simeon did the same, he would forbid all the Gentiles of the village to do any service for Jews on the Sabbath."[42]

Strict Sabbath observance on the part of Jews also hurt Gentile interests. We can thus understand R. Ishmael ha-Kohen's statement that "if the laborers do no work on the Sabbath, there will be a loud outcry against the [workshop] owners, which will certainly reach the land-owner."[43] It is, of course, possible that the non-Jewish workers' refusal to accept their enforced Sabbath idleness was merely a convenient excuse for Simeon not to have to accept the strict halakhic decision to close down his workshop. At any rate, "he turned to a scholar to see how he could avoid the problem of a possible Sabbath prohibition, and this charitable teacher [that is, a second-rate halakhic authority] . . . told him that from that day on the Gentile in charge should not sell any goods in the shop on the Sabbath day; in addition, he ruled that the Gentile in charge should rent the shop from its Gentile owner and prepare the contract in non-Jewish courts."[44] The assumption was that the work would be carried out under contract. The scholar added the stipulation that the shop be rented by the Gentile in charge, this being registered in court, so as to avoid the ban applying even to contracting when it is carried out in the home of the Jew.

By means of the ruling of this halakhic scholar, Simeon proposed to ensure himself of the halakhic backing required to counteract the ruling of the anonymous authority who had demanded the complete closing down of shops on the Sabbath. In addition, he ensured himself of a tangible economic advantage over the shopowners who had shut down their plants. At any rate, such differences of practice in so small a community were undoubedly considered intolerable. No wonder that the affair attracted attention and that the difference of opinion between the two anonymous scholars was brought before halakhic authorities of recognized standing. These, too, however, could not resolve their dif-

42. Bassan, *Todat Shelamim* 56a.
43. Ishmael ha-Kohen, *Zera Emet* 31 (40b).
44. Bassan, *Todat Shelamim*, sec. 3 (56a).

ferences. An unknown halakhic authority,[45] together with R. Abraham Basilea,[46] supported the scholar who had ruled stringently and banned the opening of the shops. R. Abraham's brother, Aviad Sar-Shalom Basilea, presented the problem to "the scholars of our [Mantua's] academy who said: 'Correct! Correct!'"[47] R. Isaac Lampronti, the author of *Pahad Yitshak*,[48] joined those ruling stringently, whereas R. Isaiah Bassan wrote a long and complicated responsum in support of the permissive ruling.[49]

The halakhic question at the center of the disagreement was whether the restriction stipulating that the work not be performed in the home of the Jew was applicable here. In the opinion of Bassan's disputant, a fictitious renting of the premises to a craftsman was of no avail, "since the finished product belongs to the Jew, who comes and goes all the time during the week in that shop to supervise the work, and so everyone says that the shop belongs to such and such a Jew."[50] Another reason for the strict prohibitive ruling was "because of the Gentiles," that is, because of the desecration of God's Name. It was for this reason that, according to the author of the *Magen Avraham*, contemporary halakhic masters had forbidden even the building of synagogues under contract: "What will they say of our law? That it is merely a matter of convenience!"[51] And "in addition, I would say that it involves a violation of the ban on contradictory behavior, for all the other Jewish shoemakers closed their shops on the Sabbath out of reverence for the Sabbath, and this would make it look as though some could rule leniently like Beit Hillel and others strictly like Beit Shammai—something that is not to be tolerated."[52] It is clear that the matter of con-

45. N. 38 above.
46. Adduced in Basilea, *Pahad Yitshak* 75a–77b.
47. Ibid., 77b. He himself refrained "from speaking of this matter, though I feel it is clear." The responsum (77b–79a) is apparently that of one of the rabbis of the academy, if not of R. Isaac Lampronti.
48. Ibid., 79a, but see previous note.
49. N. 14 above; the responsum stretches from 56a to 63a, to which a kind of appendix is added: 63a–66a.
50. Ibid., 56b. The scholar adds: "He himself knew that the rent paid by the workman to the landlord results from the addition the Jew added to his work above and beyond what had already been agreed upon." Simeon added to the workman's wages the amount he paid him in rent.
51. *Magen Avraham*; see n. 2 above.
52. Ibid.

tradictory praxis was not felt by this scholar to have halakhic validity. At the same time, it may have been decisive in the reasoning leading to a prohibitive ruling. R. Abraham Basilea repeated this halakhic authority's argument in great detail and says clearly: "I accept the authority of this individual so that even if this were the only reason, I would forbid it."[53] Still another scholar[54] repeatedly emphasized the informal reasons: "For this involves violating the ban on contradictory praxis as well as being a desecration of God's Name in the eyes of the Gentiles . . . in that they would see that Simeon's shop is open to his workmen, while those of other Jews are sealed, and they might think, God forbid, that Jews have two authorities, two Laws."[55]

R. Isaiah Bassan seems to have been the only scholar to support the permissive authority,[56] which, according to Bassan, had been attacked by the opponents for no reason at all. In considering the halakhic question itself, R. Isaiah claimed that only in connection with "attached" property such as fields, homes, bathhouses, and so on can the property be said to be known by the name of a Jew, in which case work on this property would be banned even if the Gentile is under contract. But when dealing with "movable" property such as tanning and shoemaking, no such limitation exists once the work is performed under contract, and it does not have to be performed in private. In addition to the evidence adduced from halakhic sources,[57] he also based his statements on the customs accepted by well-known communities such as Modena and Reggio, "where the butcher is Jewish and he has a Gentile selling on the Sabbath in the courtyard of the Jews, in the shop belonging to a Jew. . . . This is how they conducted themselves before renowned sages of the Torah who did not protest."[58]

From these and similar cases, analogies can be drawn concerning leather processing done by an expert craftsman. Although the work be performed in a room that is part of a shop belonging to a Jew, once it is rented out to a Gentile it is not considered to be known by the name

53. Basilea, *Pahad Yitshak* 77a.
54. See nn. 47–48.
55. Basilea, *Pahad Yitshak* 78b.
56. *Lahmei Todah* 56a–63a (see n. 14 above).
57. Ibid., all through the responsum.
58. ibid., 64a, and see also 60b, pointing out the accepted custom of giving the Gentiles laundry to wash, with their work being done openly on the Sabbath.

of the Jew.[59] As to the argument of "contradictory praxis," if it is at all relevant,[60] it can be directed against the opposing party, "for the local rabbi ruled permissively, whereupon someone else suddenly appeared on the scene to upset him and disagree with him, gaining obedient adherents. But this does not authorize him to compel the first rabbi to conform . . . for what the Torah really wants is that it should not appear as if there were two Torahs . . . and for this reason . . . he should only have prohibited it with the agreement of the first rabbi."[61]

We do not know what it was that moved R. Isaiah Bassan to rule permissively beyond what his colleagues were prepared to accept. This ruling was extraordinary, as R. Ishmael ha-Kohen put it, "in that he exaggerated . . . overly much in permitting work to be done with 'moveable' property, even publicly, as long as it does not take place in the home of the Jew."[62] R. Ishmael himself attempted to find a permissive solution to the problem of the silk manufacturers, one that was within halakhic boundaries as generally accepted but one that would also be feasible. As we have seen, he did not accept R. Samuel Aboab's cumbersome stipulations.[63] But he rejected out of hand R. Isaiah's permissive ruling and even referred to him "as a court that became habitually permissive, and therefore it is no wonder that the scholars of the day disagree with his decision."[64]

R. Ishmael ha-Kohen lived to an old age and was one of the scholars replying to the questions put by Napoleon Bonaparte to the Paris Sanhedrin in 1808. He searched for the middle road between the demands of the times and faithfulness to halakhic rules.[65] His responsa referring to Sabbath observance, however, were written at a stage when the main-

59. Ibid., further on.
60. Ibid., 62a, he compares the closing down of the shops of some of the Jews on the Sabbath with the statement in Yevamot 13b, discussing different customs on the eve of Passover: "The observer says he does not work, for he has none," which is, of course, a purely formal argument.
61. Ibid., 62b.
62. Ishmael ha-Kohen, Zera Emet 31 (40b).
63. Ibid., 32 (41a).
64. Ibid., 31 (40b).
65. Yehudah Rosenthal, "The Responsa of R. Ishmael ben R. Abraham Isaac ha-Kohen, Rabbi of Modena, to the Twelve Questions Put by the Emperor Napoleon" (in Hebrew), Mehqarim 2 (1966): 513–532; and see also on this, Meir Benayahu, Sefer ha-Hiyda (Jerusalem, 1959), 36–38.

stays of Jewish tradition seemed to be immutable.[66] In retrospect, a historian might discern in the multitude of issues that developed with increased Jewish involvement in the economics of their environment a sign of the impending change in the political and social status of Judaism. R. Ishmael's contemporaries, however, were not alert to the prospective significance of this phenomenon. It took time until halakhic authorities began to take into account the changing circumstances in making their halakhic decisions, circumstances that eventually led to mutually contradictory reactions on their part, to the devising of completely new permissive rulings or the development of hesitancy and retreat even from those leniencies that had already become accepted.[67] The give-and-take of the Torah scholars of eighteenth-century Italy, which we have just described, took place in an atmosphere of "business as usual," and a similar atmosphere pervades the give-and-take of most halakhic authorities in central Europe during the same period.

66. His book, *Zera Emet*, appeared in 1786.
67. To be discussed in the following chapters.

8

New Forms of Employment in Central Europe

Germany and Austria, along with Italy, were among the first regions to show signs of the new type of Jewish economic involvement—which then generated inquiries of halakhic authorities in connection with Sabbath Gentiles. Formal and informal supervision of the steps taken by community members seems to have been stricter here than in Italy and perhaps even stricter than it had been in Poland in previous centuries. There is no indication here of permissive conduct evolving inadvertently. Employing Gentiles on the Sabbath, not clearly precedented in local custom, was brought before halakhic authorities, whose guidance was sought in determining what should be done.

When the Austrian authorities decided in 1736 to grant the rights to manufacture and sell tobacco by lease,[1] a new source of livelihood was opened up to Austrian Jewry. When exactly the Jews managed to

---

1. See Ruth Kestenberg-Gladstein, *Neuere Geschichte der Juden in den böhmischen Ländern*, pt. 1, *Das Zeitalter der Aufklärung 1780–1830* (Tübingen, 1969), 104–105.

take their place in this industry is unknown.[2] We do have a legal document from the Jewish community of Prague, dated the thirteenth of Tevet 5525 (1765) and certified by the signatures of R. Ezekiel Landau and five members of his *beit din* in Prague. It has hitherto been ignored by historical research, even though it sheds light on the circumstances of such integration.[3] This document is a responsum to the question posed by "the illustrious Torah sage R. Wolf, son of the late S. Fränkel, concerning the tobacco he and his colleagues have leased: how to act both in selling it and in processing it."[4] We also know from other sources that the Fränkel family participated in the leasing of tobacco.[5] This source of ours reveals that the Jewish lessees undertook "to organize the industry properly and, after four years, to ensure the share of the empress in the profits."[6] The Jews, however, had rivals, "a group of merchants, non-Jewish, who also wanted to lease the tobacco franchise."[7] These competitors would now likely inform the authorities that their Jewish rivals, by preventing the manufacture and sale of tobacco products on Sabbaths and other festival days, would cause the empress a loss of part of her expected income. This fear was presented to underline the importance of the Jewish appeal for a halakhic ruling permitting continued processing and selling of tobacco on the Sabbath. An additional reason was "it provides a livelihood for a few hundred households in this area." This indicates that the tobacco franchise furnished a living for an entire stratum of Bohemian Jewry. The appeal, however, was

2. Professor Kestenberg says (ibid., 104) without adducing the source that a Jewish consortium held the franchise as early as 1741, and she assumes that already then the Fränkel family was involved. The franchise had to be renewed every so often, of course, and the source adduced below, which Kestenberg did not have before her, testifies to the determining of the conditions of the new franchise.

3. This court order was printed by R. Jacob Koppel ha-Levi at the end of his responsum (which we shall study in the next chapter) in *Shomer Tsiyyon ha-Neeman* 75 [(Iyyar 26, 1849)]: 150b.

4. Ibid. This family appears under a number of different names: Fränkel, Hoenig, Hoenigsberg, and Kaf, i.e., Kuttenplan, its first place of origin. See Kestenberg, n. 1 above, and according to the list of names, p. 409.

5. Kestenberg, n. 1 above.

6. A court order (n. 3 above); Kestenberg, *Neuere Geschichte*, 105 n. 48, indicates a tradition whereby the head of the family invented a new process of tobacco manufacture and proposed a new organization of the sales. Perhaps the contract mentioned here is connected with this proposal.

7. All the quotations in this section and the next are from *Shomer Tsiyyon ha-Neeman* (n. 3 above).

prompted also by the fear of direct economic loss, a fear that played a role in the ruling of Italian sages as well. For despite the cessation of work on the Sabbath, "they will have to pay the workers and will therefore lose thousands." This reasoning led the judges of the rabbinic court to declare "that there is no greater 'temporary necessity' than this," meaning that there was justification for making an effort to find a solution that exhausted the limits of permissiveness. The legal document, however, contains only the conditions upon which the permissive ruling was based but not their logical basis. We shall thus have to guess how the scholars of Prague reasoned their instructions within their closed forum.

The first condition was for the owners of the franchise to cancel the contract they had already signed with "the craftsmen," for its original wording made no provision for the problem of the Sabbath. The new contract would be based on "an estimate of how much the craftsmen could finish in a year, were they not to work on the Sabbath or on festivals." The chief craftsman would undertake to supply the estimated number of bales of tobacco in return for "a fixed annual sum to be negotiated with him." This was also the advice given by R. Samuel Aboab to the silk manufacturers,[8] and this example may be assumed to have influenced the scholars of Prague. Through such a legal device, the employment of the foreman and his workers became a matter of contracting. In fact, they of course had no intention of turning the main craftsman into a contractor who would invest his own money in the plant and take responsibility for manufacture of the goods. Giving him the work as if by contracting is obviously a fiction, for "any expenditure he [the master craftsman] incurs in connection with his workers must be fully repaid by the owners." Although the workers work on a daily basis, "this need not bother them [the owners], for whatever he [the craftsman] does, he does of his own accord," and he is being engaged under a contracting engagement. The obligation to pay for labor done by the workers is part of the recompense given the foreman for the contracting he has undertaken. This seems to be the interpretation of the halakhic basis for a permissive ruling. Although the contract was signed on the basis of an estimate of the number of bales to be processed, excluding Sabbaths and festivals, actually a larger number is taken into account, the stip-

8. See chap. 7, n. 30.

ulation being that "they give him a fixed portion of each surplus bale, whether few or many, as it is agreed between the parties"—that is, a kind of second contracting agreement.[9] From here on, "if he works on the Sabbath, he does so of his own accord." It is, however, forbidden for work, even on a contracting basis, to be done on Jewish premises. The solution to this problem was that "the building in which the work is done is to be rented out to the chief craftsman for a small sum per annum," the assumption being that the tobacco processing plant did not basically belong to its Jewish owner but rather was rented by him. That being the case, it was not publicly known as Jewish premises and could thus be rented out to a Gentile.[10] Such contracting was permitted on the basis of the supposition that the Gentile may well not engage in this work on the Sabbath at all because he is capable of completing it on weekdays. From here on, if the Jew sees the Gentile working at this job on the Sabbath, he is obliged to protest.[11] For this reason the halakhic authorities added that "none of the partners to this agreement are to reside in that building on the Sabbath or on festivals."[12] This restriction does not apply to the Jewish servants of the partners. Because they are under no obligation to protest, they may be present in the workshop. Such permission is, however, based on the further condition that the servant must be present "when the agreement is reached with the chief craftsman." Since working on Jewish premises is forbidden because an observer may suspect the Jewish owner of employing workers on a daily basis in his plant, the servant's presence when the agreement is signed

9. This one agreement seems to have been sufficient to pay the craftsman for each bale, but actually there was no intention to employ him as a contractor. He receives his basic wages as they evaluate what he has earned for the bales made during the week. The contracting fees paid for each bale can be "either high or low" (in the responsum of the Noda bi-Yehudah, n. 18 below, concerning the sale of tobacco, it says "a fixed amount, even a single penny") and appear merely to render the whole deal halakhically proper.

10. The permissive ruling was given by R. Moses Isserles, *Orah Hayyim* 243:2, according to *Or Zarua*, in the name of the geonim.

11. Ibid.: "For the Jew who has a portion [therein] and can protest, if he sees the Gentile working on the Sabbath, should protest." The obligation to protest is mentioned in *Shulhan Arukh, Orah Hayyim* 252:2 and is discussed by the *Magen Avraham* 9.

12. A court order (n. 3 above).

serves to rule out this fear.[13] But that is not all. The work of a beast of burden was required by the workshop, and this scholarly document explains how this may be permitted on the Sabbath.[14] Yet after all the permits were given, it was recommended that the work not be done "in that part of the building adjoining the street but rather in the inner rooms opening onto the courtyard."

Up until now we have discussed the ruling permitting the manufacture of tobacco. Its sale requires a similar permit. The Gentile salesmen rent the franchise for a year for a fixed amount, and in addition "they are to receive a fixed portion, even a small percentage, of every bale sold." "They will not state explicitly that he will sell on the Sabbath, merely that he is to be employed on a monthly or yearly basis," according to a contracting arrangement. "And then the non-Jew acts for his own benefit . . . and works of his own accord to gain that fixed portion; the Jew does not oblige him to do his work on the Sabbath." The legal document concludes, saying that "we have permitted this in the aforementioned ways for temporary needs," and it is signed, as already noted, by R. Ezekiel Landau, author of *Noda bi-Yehuda*, together with the five members of his illustrious rabbinic court.[15]

The wording of the ruling, its style, the detailed stipulations of its permissive contents, together with the ability to support every point of view that takes into consideration the economic requirements of the community—all these are characteristic of Rabbi Landau. This ruling is undoubtedly his own work; the others merely affixed their signatures to a completed document.

These characteristic traits of Noda bi-Yehuda's halakhic rulings are apparent in his responsum to a question posed by the same family seventeen years later. Two brothers, R. Israel and R. Moses K. P. (Kutten-

---

13. This is a significant innovation, for the problem is not limited to close acquaintances, and R. Moses Isserles, *Orah Hayyim* 244:1, ruled that even if one lives among Gentiles, one must take guests into consideration. See *Noda bi-Yehudah*, 1st ed., (Prague, 1776) 12, where he limits this misgiving from another point of view.

14. The court order gives advice of two kinds: The animal must belong to the workman whom they pay for his services, or they give their animal to the workman as a gift.

15. The signatories are Meir Bumsla, Judah Leib Kaswin, Asher Anshel Ozersch, Solomon Zalman Emrich, Moses Ginzburg Shapira.

plan) moved to the imperial capital, Vienna. R. Ezekiel Landau confers on them a rabbinic title and negotiates with them as though they were well versed. His reply clearly indicates that the brothers not only proposed their question but also suggested a basis upon which the required permit might stand: "Concerning your opinion that I shall undoubtedly find a way to rule permissively in this matter of commercial transactions, the ban on which is solely rabbinical [not biblical], this is an important statement."[16] On the basis of permission concerning the processing of tobacco that entailed real work, the brothers could logically assume that it would be the same with regard to their opening a sales and loan business, which, in halakhic terms, involved only a rabbinic ban. They were referring to "this shop in the house in which they live, with the shop opening onto the street and Gentiles not having to pass through their rooms, but merely directly from the street into the shop."[17] No mention is made of the type of merchandise sold in this shop, but it is clear that it was tobacco, "which franchise they obtained by the kindness of his Excellency the Emperor, on condition that they sell at a lower price than the Gentiles."[18] The franchise does not seem to have been conditional upon the sales continuing on the Sabbath, but, at any rate, "if the entrance to the shop is closed on the Sabbath the emperor may not be pleased, in which case our rights may be canceled and much be lost."[19] The involvement of royal interests was mentioned here, of course, to emphasize the urgency of the permissive ruling.

This involvement became even more significant when the brothers were granted another franchise, the right to open a "loan bank," when they apparently sought to combine the two types of business under a common roof in the shop that itself was part of their living quarters. The bank had to be open at all times, "for one cannot shut the door in the face of a borrower."[20] Engaging in the sale of tobacco is not new for them, but up until now "the shop opened onto a Gentile thoroughfare, with a Gentile sitting in it." This Gentile received "a fixed wage, such

16. *Responsa Noda bi-Yehudah*, 2nd ed., *Orah Hayyim* 29. The responsum is dated Elul 1782.
17. Ibid.
18. Ibid. At the end of the responsum he writes that they should pay "one penny per bale." The "bale" is the unit mentioned in the court order as well.
19. Ibid.
20. Ibid.

and such per week or such and such per annum."[21] The brothers thought that in this way they were satisfying halakhic requirements. From now on they needed an authoritative permit, since the shop was being moved to their own home, and their ownership of it was now being openly demonstrated.

In his responsum the rabbi first criticized what the brothers had been accustomed to doing up until now: paying the non-Jew for a month or a year at a time is insufficient for a permissive ruling to be given, for if the Gentile draws his salary whether "a buyer comes in or not," it turns out that whatever "the Gentile sells on the Sabbath he does only for the benefit of the Jew." The way for permission to be granted is that which was laid down in the court document for the year 5525 (1765), where the wages for the entire period of service, be it a month or a year, must be supplemented by "a fixed amount per thousand bales sold, or per hundred bales, as they decide, or even per single bale," even if this additional amount is "just a single penny."[22] In this way the employee is engaged on a contracting basis, the Gentile works for his own benefit, and the Jew's profits accrue incidentally, as it were.

The problem in the question posed by the brothers was the moving of the business to their house. As we have already noted, this difficulty plagued many halakhic authorities in previous generations and would yet trouble future generations as well. Formally, the reason for the ban was that passersby would suspect the owner of engaging his non-Jewish workers on a daily basis. Noda bi-Yehudah considered making an innovation. Accordingly, if the work the Gentile was to engage in was merely one banned by rabbinic sources to ensure a complete Sabbath standstill, then, since if the Jew was suspected of having told the non-Jew to perform this work, "he would merely be suspected of transgressing a secondary injunction of this kind—and perhaps there is no need to rule strictly in such a case."[23] But in the end he only raised this possibility "in theory but not in practice,"[24] whereas he based the per-

21. Ibid. The brothers thus simplified the permissive process ever since the court order.
22. Ibid.
23. Ibid., 12b, beginning, "from now on."
24. Ibid. The passage begins with the words "This seems to me to be theoretically so but not to be practiced," but this reservation refers to what was said in the previous passage.

missive ruling he eventually handed down, for "fear of losing the franchises," on another innovation: "They are to rent out the shop in which the non-Jew will be sitting . . . to the non-Jew, for when the non-Jew brings in the goods he will be bringing them into his own premises, for renting out for a day is considered a transaction." This permissive ruling was made conditional upon "the Gentile sitting in the shop by himself; and even during the week no Jew is to sit with him and help him sell."[25] At any rate, the work would be done before the eyes of the Jewish landlord, and according to the court document of 5555 (1795) he was forbidden to stay there lest he be obliged to prevent the work being done even though it was being done under a contracting arrangement. Noda bi-Yehudah undoubtedly gave in considerably in granting this ruling in order to compromise with the demands made by "the lay leaders," who were important members of his community and whom he considered observant Jews attempting to strengthen their economic standing within the limits prescribed by halakhah.[26]

The extent to which these circles tried to have the best of both worlds—to participate in the surrounding economic activity yet to observe formal halakhic restrictions—may be deduced from the question requested by one of the above-mentioned brothers, R. Israel, as to whether it would be permissible for him to prepare "a seal . . . in his handwriting so that every Sabbath day, while he sits with the great lords in the office, he can have a Gentile affix the impression of the seal to documents he is supposed to sign."[27] At this point, however, even the Noda bi-Yehudah's innovative capacity was exhausted. He mentions the ruling by the author of Or Zarua, whereby writing in "their," that is, Gentile, script was merely a rabbinic prohibition. However, he continues, this was a minority opinion. "Even if we say that it is reliable in emergencies, even then telling a Gentile to do something banned rabbinically to ensure complete Sabbath rest is not so small a matter."[28]

---

25. Ibid.

26. The strangeness of this responsum is that he rejects at the end the very basis for a permissive ruling that he himself had laid down at the beginning; while the basis on which it actually relies is not discussed at all—renting out—and appears as a kind of deus ex machina. This is not at all simple, and the Hatam Sofer is very unhappy with it, Orah Hayyim 58.

27. Responsa Noda bi-Yehudah, 2d ed., 33. The question was put orally.

28. Ibid.

Even so, the refusal to give the requested permission was phrased weakly: "It is thus difficult to produce a ruling permitting such for the gentleman."[29] It is more surprising that the rabbi refrains from scolding the questioner about the circumstances leading him to make his request for a permissive ruling, for sitting in the office on the Sabbath is the same as turning it into a workday even if one is careful not to do any creative labor. The rabbi of Prague seems to have been aware of the limits of his authority concerning this stratum of his community, illustrious by virtue of its wealth and good relations with the authorities, although formally they admitted a subordinate position regarding halakhic authority and its representatives.

The ruling of Noda bi-Yehudah, responding to the challenge presented by econmic conditions by exercising his "vantage of leniency," must not, it seems, be considered merely an individual tendency. Of course, not many could rely on their familiarity with halakhic literature and their inventiveness to the degree that he could. But the opening up of new livelihoods to Jews was likely to persuade others as well to exhaust permissive avenues or, at least, to refrain from turning away people in need of halakhic assistance.

Tobacco processing was only one of the industrial developments in which Jews took part. R. Mordecai, president of the rabbinic court of the Leipen community and one of Noda bi-Yehudah's most outstanding disciples, was asked about a textile plant that belonged to a Jew but did not shut down on the Sabbath.[30] The external circumstances of the case facilitated a lenient approach: The workshop was not located in a Jewish residential area, and its owner did not live on the premises. "The workers are not hired daily but, rather, are given the work by contracting."[31] It is unclear whether these were the accepted employment conditions or whether the rabbi had instructed the owner of the factory to arrange things this way in order to circumvent halakhic problems of Sabbath desecration. At the same time, it was not an easy matter to decide whether the continuation of the work on the Sabbath did not contradict the term "contracting," for this term embodied the idea that the employee work whenever he sees fit and not, by necessity, on the Sabbath.

29. Ibid.
30. *Noda bi-Yehudah*, 2d ed., 38. The responsum is dated Adar 1789.
31. Ibid.

It could also be claimed that, despite its distance, the workshop was known to belong to a Jew; even though local residents knew this work was being done by contracting, visitors passing by might suspect that daily workers were performing the Jew's work.[32] We do not know how R. Mordecai overcame these problems, as his decision has not survived, and our knowledge stems only from the writings of his master, the Noda bi-Yehudah, who questioned several of his disciple's claims while confirming his permissive ruling. "Since it is well known that this factory always works by contracting, and since it is located on a street of Gentiles and there is no fear of visitors, you did well to rule permissively, especially since closing down the plant would involve a considerable loss, for the workmen would not want to cease working, and the Jew would have to pay their salaries for nothing."[33] Once again we find a full admission that economic requirements pressured halakhic authorities to make special efforts to find a basis for the requested permissive decision.

Not all halakhic authorities, however, were willing to make this effort, as we will determine from the testimony of R. Jacob Emden, who maintained a contrary position. It all began in the days of the rabbi of Hamburg, R. Ezekiel Katzenellenbogen, who in 1742 was asked about handing textiles over to dyers to "draw nice pictures on them with various hues and colors, very artistically."[34] The stipulations of the agreement between Jew and Gentile are not sufficiently clear.[35] At any rate, R. Ezekiel viewed it as a simple matter as it falls under the lenient rulings handed down in connection with businesses shared with Gentiles and ended up saying: "So there is no doubt whatever; this is fully allowed, there being no grounds whatever to forbid it. I wish you good fortune and prosperity."[36] Rabbi Jacob Emden considered Rabbi Katzenellenbogen's decision carefully, though his wording is concise and

32. The discussions in the reply of the rabbi concern these questions.
33. Ibid., at the end of the responsum. Emphasis on the size of the loss appears here without distinguishing between a loss and the prevention of profit.
34. R. Jacob Emden, *Sheilot Yaabets* 2:60.
35. In the description of the question a partnership is discussed, but from the rest of the text it seems that the work was handed over by contract.
36. Emden, *Sheilot Yaabets* 2:60. The responsum contains no detailing of the conditions for the permissive ruling, and it merely mentions that "the Gentile works in his home." The details may have been handed down orally, the document testifying only that the rabbi approved of the deal.

somewhat obscure. At any rate, he, too, confirmed the ruling but stipulated three conditions: that the workman be paid "for every piece he decorates," that the work be conducted on the non-Jew's premises, and that the Jew not tell him to work specifically on the Sabbath "and certainly not supervise the pace of his work on Sabbaths and festivals."[37]

According to Rabbi Emden's version, the original circumstances did not last long. The Jewish employer enlarged his business and instead of handing over processing of the textiles to the craftsman, he set up "a large industrial plant on his own premises where the workmen perform various types of work such as dyeing the calico apparel . . . beating the material, bleaching it, and dyeing it . . . and ironing it, and all kinds of repairs"[38]—a typical shift from delivering work to the workmen on their own premises to using the capital to set up factories on the premises of the capitalist. As far as the work to be performed on the Sabbath, the conditions, of course, changed completely: The work is no longer done by contracting on the Gentile's premises. The plant belonged to the Jew, who would "pay his workers their wages daily."[39] Nonetheless the Jew wanted to rely on Rabbi Katzenellenbogen's permissive ruling and, according to Emden's allusions, his ruling was confirmed by Rabbi Katzenellenbogen's successor, Rabbi Jonathan Eybeschuetz.[40] The latter's successor, Rabbi Isaac ha-Levy Horowitz, also "allowed him to engage in his work on Sabbaths and festivals, made no protest, and did nothing to stop him."[41] Rabbi Jacob Emden, however, from whom the plant owner wanted to get an explicit permit for his factory, rejected the request decisively.[42]

All the arguments for granting permission—valid when the work was handed over to a Gentile—were now invalidated by setting up the factory. Rabbi Emden, however, added "that even if all the new circumstances supported granting the requested permission," it should be rejected because this case involves "a great desecration among the Gen-

<hr/>

37. Ibid.
38. Ibid.
39. Ibid.
40. Here too Emden uses this opportunity to besmirch his rival who had already passed away: "The idolator . . . by whom permits and prohibitions are purchased for money."
41. Ibid.
42. Ibid., and further on, in sec. 61.

tiles who see how the Jews do not observe their Sabbaths, and things are being performed publicly and with much to-do."[43] We have already noted the role played by the motif of desecration in the ruling of other scholars.[44] And it would yet play a decisive role in the reservations expressed by certain halakhic authorities concerning work permits granted by their contemporaries who attempted to compromise with generally felt pressures of the economic conditions of the nineteenth century.[45] In R. Jacob Emden's day, such a perspective was untypical. We have already seen the halakhic experts of the same period in Italy and Germany attempting to maintain customary permits and even to expand their validity. Emden's particular attitude may be attributed, of course, to his extraordinary personality—on the one hand, his zealotry and, on the other, his sensitivity to signs of laxity in the observance of the tradition.[46]

Yet it seems that an additional explanation is required by virtue of his special public status, to which he himself points in a responsum we have considered here. Rabbi Emden played no rabbinic role, for he was not responsible for the conduct of any specific community. His rulings obligated whoever accepted them and no one else. He was thus able to demarcate limits of ideal conduct that he was clearly incapable of enforcing. He was willing "to mark the boundaries of Jewish conduct and not to broaden the already existing gaps that result from our sinful lives, . . . and if I could, I would certainly close them as strongly as I was able."[47] In fact, he was actually divesting himself of any responsibility for present custom, as he himself said: "And as for me, I recite a daily blessing, 'Blessed is He who has not created me a servant of the community, so that I do not have the power to protest to transgressors.' "[48] Scholars who had such power had to be careful not to hand down rulings that their power was insufficient to enforce.

43. Ibid., 61.
44. See chap. 7, n. 2.
45. See chap. 10, n. 31; chap. 11, n. 53.
46. It is easy to make out Emden's nature from his own autobiography: *Megillat Sefer* (Warsaw, 1897).
47. Emden, *Sheilot Yaabets* 2:60.
48. Emden was accustomed to employ this saying—a play on the abbreviation a-b-d (head of the *beit din*) and *eved*, "slave." See Hayyim Joseph David Azulai, *Shem ha-Gedolim* (Vilna, 1853), 48b.

9

Sabbath Observers as a Minority

Jewish involvement in the manufacturing processes characteristic of postfeudal economies began, as we have seen, as early as the period of the ancien régime. Their economic involvement became more intense with the collapse of the ancien régime, which led to a change in the political status of the Jews. Even where Jews were not granted full and equal rights—outside of France and Holland Jews reached this stage during the last third of the nineteenth century, and in eastern Europe only in the twentieth[1]—their range of economic opportunity improved vastly. The kinds of personal occupations and investment channels open to them increased and became more varied;[2] and questions relating to Sabbath observance now multiplied accordingly, to be dealt with by contemporary halakhic authorities.

The varied subject matter, however, was not the only sign of changing times. The very status of the Sabbath among the Jews was changing, as the entire Jewish religious tradition found itself in a state of flux.

1. For details, see Jacob Katz, *Out of the Ghetto* (Cambridge, Mass., 1973), 161–175.
2. Ibid., 176–190.

Unlike earlier generations, when halakhic Sabbath observance was ax-
iomatic in Jewish society, the breakdown of traditional society, coming
as it did together with the collapse of the ancien régime, was accompanied by Jews throwing off the yoke of the Sabbath or at least being
more lax in observing its regulations. At the same time, and linked with
the change in political status of the Jews, community leaders and rabbis
lost their authority and ability to enforce Sabbath observance as well
as observance of religious precepts in general.[3]

There still was, of course, a broad sector of the Jewish public, in
certain regions encompassing the majority of the community, that was
careful to observe the Sabbath. The businesses of these observant Jews,
as they encountered Sabbath problems, provided the reason for discussion of Sabbath Gentile matters in contemporary halakhic literature.
The number of responsa concerning this topic dating from the nineteenth and twentieth centuries is actually greater than the number of
questions and answers posed by earlier generations.[4] From the standpoint of principles involved, there is no difference between the halakhic
rulings handed down by contemporary authorities and those given in
earlier times. As always, they reflect the acceptance of the obligatory
character of talmudic rulings, with all their variegated exegetical di-
versity. Contemporary halakhic authorities, however, were aware of the
fact that no longer did the entire Jewish community recognize the binding authority of halakhah. This awareness had its influence upon their
considerations and even found expression in their conclusions, be they
strict or lenient, as we shall yet see.

At this time, however, not all regions were alike. We may distinguish three situations in which halakhic authorities found themselves
that were characteristic of the three subdivisions of Europe in the nineteenth and twentieth centuries. In western Europe, especially in Germany, over a period of a generation or two the social, unifying basis for
the acceptance of halakhic authority deteriorated. A rabbi, even if he
served as the leader of a pious community, knew that his rulings obligated only those who had remained faithful to the ancestral tradition
or who had determined, after hesitation, to accept the yoke of the halakhah.

3. Ibid., 142–160.
4. This can easily be seen from the *Otsar ha-Sheelot u-Teshuvot*, vol. 4, ed.
Menachem Kahana Shapiro (Jerusalem, 1981), secs. 243–247.

In eastern Europe as well, halakhic authorities knew that the unity based on halakhah that had in the past characterized the nation no longer existed. They knew of Jews in western lands who denied the validity of halakhah and refused to obey it, and they sensed that in the east, their own position was not as assured as it had been in earlier times. As secular authority in the region passed from the Poles to the Russians and Austrians,[5] community leaders found taken from them the power they had enjoyed to enforce religious observance by means of either excommunication or physical duress, power that had previously been granted them by the state. Religious authority, represented by halakhic scholars, now depended upon the community's spontaneous acceptance of it and was still strong enough to prevent open breaches of traditional behavior but not strong enough to prevent critical consideration of its details as expressed by those Maskilim who absorbed the sounds of rebellion in the west and echoed them in the east, although using different tone and style. The danger of violation of religious discipline was thus present, albeit latent, at least at the margins of society, leaving the halakhic authorities no choice but to take this into consideration.

Nevertheless, the main factor that motivated halakhic scholars to seek out new solutions to Sabbath problems was not socially marginal but rather central, stemming from that sector of the community that considered itself unquestionably subject to halakhah but that confronted its limitations in respect of the new forms of employment that came along. The increase in appeals made to halakhic experts by lessees, factory and workshop owners, and so on seeking ways to maintain the sources of their livelihood placed the halakhic authorities in a new situation to which they had to and did react—though not uniformly, as we shall see below.

A unique situation, being a mixture of eastern and western conditions, developed in Hungary.[6] Most of the large Jewish communities in Hungary formed or achieved stability only as a result of the contemporary economic development of the country, which characterized the period of Magyar national rebirth. Part of the Jewish population com-

5. See Raphael Mahler, *History of the Jewish People in Modern Times* (in Hebrew) (Merhavia, 1955), 3:34–38, 160–169.

6. See Nathanel Katzburg, "The History of Hungarian Jewry" (in Hebrew), in *Pinkas ha-Kehilot: Hungary* (Jerusalem, 1976), 19–39.

prised immigrants or children of immigrants from neighboring lands—
Bohemia, Moravia, and Galicia—who integrated themselves into the
country's new economic conditions and ignored the bounds of tradition,
which had ceased to have decisive influence on their decisions in other
walks of life as well. In opposition to them were the Jews who had
remained faithful to old-style Judaism, and a bitter battle was waged
between the representatives of these two camps until, in the last third
of the nineteenth century, most of the Jewish communities split into
separate communal entities, the Orthodox and the Neologists. However,
long before the organizational split, halakhic authorities realized that
the entire Jewish public did not accept their rulings. They were faced
with a dilemma: Should they aim their decisions at the undecided, making it easier for them to bear the burden of religion under the new conditions? Or should they rule strictly, lest the defection reach those Jews
who still remained halakhically observant even at the expense of economic advantage? Although it is generally thought that most Hungarian
halakhic scholars chose the second way, they nevertheless had no uniform or even unambiguously directed system, as we shall yet see.

As we have already noted, most of the problems concerning Sabbath
observance that arose in the modern era arose as a result of the broadening potential of Jewish livelihood. In Germany, the first two generations of integration were characterized by attempts to channel Jewish
youth into agriculture and handicrafts.[7] Secular authorities of numerous
states, Baden, Württemberg, and others, encouraged this tendency, and
Jewish public opinion viewed it as an important means of diverting the
Jewish community from the one-sided adherence to matters of finance
and trade. This aspiration is clearly echoed in the halakhic question
raised by Rabbi Koppel Loewenstein, the rabbi of the community of
Galingen, in the periodical Shomer Tsiyyon ha-Neeman in 1849, concerning a youngster who had studied a craft and wanted to open a workshop employing non-Jewish assistants.[8] Emphasizing the necessity of a
permissive ruling, the rabbi adds: "Crafts are important, for they provide
the craftsman with a livelihood. Jews have repeatedly been told not to

7. See Katz, Out of the Ghetto, 181–183, and the sources cited there.
8. Shomer Tsiyyon ha-Neeman 67 (1849): 134a–b. For Rabbi Loewenstein, see
Franz Hundsnurscher and Gerhard Taddey, Die jüdischen Gemeinden in Baden
(Stuttgart, 1968), 106.

SABBATH OBSERVERS AS A MINORITY 137

engage any longer in trade, but rather in crafts."[9] As to the question itself, Rabbi Abraham Wechsler, a disciple of R. Wolf Hamburg of Fürth, the rabbi of the community of Schwabach,[10] had anticipated him. The master dealt with a similar question on another occasion[11]—a signal of the public effort to redirect people to choose handicrafts.

Jews also turned to agriculture, not as farmers working land with their own hands but at least as the owners of lands cultivated by others. Halakhic literature preserves certain traces of the halakhic problems arising from this situation. R. Jacob Koppel ha-Levi, rabbi of the community of Worms, mentioned in 1849 that it was customary in the district of Alsace for every landowner "who was not agriculturally proficient to hire a knowledgeable supervisor; this is the general custom . . . in this region for landowning Jews, and has been very common for more than fifty years, ever since the Jews of this country have enjoyed the freedoms of citizenship."[12] Of course, German Jewry did not enjoy similar privileges. Nevertheless, from Württemberg, which preceded most other German states in granting Jews additional privileges, two problems placed before halakhic authorities have reached us: One concerns a partnership with a Gentile in land belonging to a Jew, and the other concerns the Jew's servant working in the fields [on Sabbath] without the Jew explicitly instructing him to do so. The first question was put to R. Wolf Hamburg by R. Gabriel Adler, the rabbi of Mühringen.[13] R. Joseph Schneitach, rabbi of Freudenthal,[14] dealt with the second problem. The first question was resolved permissively in accordance with the opinion of the questioner,[15] whereas the second, a more serious affair, was summed up by the rabbi as follows: "Despite all the lenient

9. See *Shomer Tsiyyon ha-Neeman* 67, leaf a.
10. Abraham Benjamin Wolf Hamburg, *Simlat Binyamin* (Fürth, 1840), 25b (the responsa are unnumbered). The rabbi calls the disciple who has put the question to him "R. Abraham Schwabach" and terms him *dayyan*. At the same time, there is no doubt of his being identified as Rabbi Wechsler, here named after the town in which he served. He served as rabbi of Schwabach from 1814; see *Pinkas ha-Kehilot: Germany-Bavaria* (Jerusalem, 1973), 364.
11. Ibid., 84a–85a.
12. *Shomer Tsiyyon ha-Neeman* 74 (1849): 148b.
13. Hamburg, *Simlat Binyamin* 17a.
14. R. Joseph Schneitach, *Responsa of Rivam* (Drohobycz, 1890); *Orah Hayyim* 19; for the author, see Leopold Loewenstein, "Zur Geschichte der Juden in Fürth," *Jahrbuch der jüdische-literarischen Gesellschaft* 8 (1911):114.
15. Hamburg, *Simlat Binyamin* 17a, and further on.

opinions, we have no authority to rule permissively against the opinion of the greatest halakhic authorities, who forbid this when there is no question of great loss and damage."[16] The landowner was allowed to elucidate how great a loss and damage he would really incur. Rabbi Schneituch added that questions of this ilk were not overly common. He tended to ignore the fear of appearances because "at this time it is uncommon for a Jew to own many fields";[17] anyone witnessing the workers toiling in the fields would not imagine that all this belonged to a Jew.

The expectation of those who granted emancipation to the Jews and the hope of Jews who accepted was that as the Jews integrated into their surroundings they would participate proportionately to their number in all fields of endeavor, including agriculture. But this expectation proved illusory.[18] We of course know of wealthy men such as Israel Jacobson,[19] the Rothschilds,[20] and others who acquired estates. But in these cases, such a step was less a matter of seeking out a new source of livelihood or even of a worthwhile capital investment than it was an attempt to integrate into aristocratic society—and these individuals did not seek halakhic rulings concerning Sabbath observance on their estates. Regarding the main body of Jewish citizens, the middle class, agriculture was not very attractive even if religious problems were ignored. This was certainly true concerning observant Jews who, in maintaining a farm, were liable to confront difficulties over and above the problems that deterred other Jews from seeking their fortunes in this type of work.[21]

Jewish involvement in crafts also turned out to be a passing phenomenon, although when Jewish integration was just getting under way

16. *Responsa of Rivam* 9b.
17. Ibid., 8b.
18. For that expectation, see my article, Jacob Katz, "German-Jewish Utopia of Social Emancipation," in *Studies of the Leo Baeck Institute*, ed. Max Kreutzberger (New York, 1967), 65–72; and for the disappointment, in my book *Out of the Ghetto*, 176–190.
19. See Heinrich Schnee, *Die Hoffinanz und der moderne Staat* (Berlin, 1954), 2:144–149.
20. Jean Bouvier, *Les Rothschilds* (Paris, 1960), 233–239.
21. Among all the questions concerning Sabbath observance put to Rabbi Bamberger, only one pertains to agriculture; Isaac Dov Bamberger, *Netia shel Simhah* (Deba, 1928), *Orah Hayyim* 4.

during the early decades of the nineteenth century, even Orthodox circles harbored prospects in this direction, as may be deduced from the
correspondence between R. Wolf Hamburg in Fürth and his disciple,
Rabbi Abraham Wechsler, religious authority of the Schwabach community.[22]

In 1821, a master shoemaker employed assistants in his workshop,
"in the special workroom in the house inhabited by the craftsman."[23]
The workers were employed under a contractual arrangement, as was
customary among all the craftsmen of the area, with no connection to
problems of Sabbath observance.[24] The rabbi of Schwabach, turning to
his mentor, tended to rule permissively on the basis of the example of
customs duty collection, by which the contracting arrangement enabled
the halakhic sources to permit work to be carried on in the Jew's own
home "lest he lose heavily, and the present case would result in a greater
loss."[25] R. Wolf Hamburg approved of this ruling but not for the reason
advocated by his disciple. He ruled on the basis of two precedents,
which, in their time, were also quite bold: the permissive ruling handed
down by R. Isaiah Bassan concerning shoe manufacture[26] and that given
by the Noda bi-Yehudah concerning the establishment of a bank in the
home of the owners in Vienna, based on the renting out of the room in
question to the Gentile overseer of the business.[27] In this particular case,
R. Wolf Hamburg added another element to his ruling—an unprecedented halakhic innovation—that it be announced in the synagogue that
the basis for the matter was contracting, so as to alleviate the fear of
"appearance."[28] Regarding his motive for this permission, R. Wolf mentioned two decisive considerations. His disciple had compared the loss
incurred by the shoemaker with that incurred by the tax collector, and
he added: "This is a better case as it does not involve only the loss of

22. See n. 10 above.
23. Hamburg, *Simlat Binyamin*. The date of the question is mentioned there,
28b.
24. Ibid., 29a.
25. Ibid., 28b.
26. See chap. 7, nn. 56ff. The source is Hamburg, *Simlat Binyamin* 26b–27a.
27. See chap. 8, nn. 20ff. The source is Hamburg, *Simlat Binyamin* 27a–b.
28. Hamburg, *Simlat Binyamin* 28a. The writer defends this derivation of the
permissive ruling in light of the protest received from a scholar, the old rabbi Moses
Harris of Ansbach, of which the questioner tells his teacher (ibid., 28b–30a).

profit, for without it he cannot make a living."[29] The second consideration: "There is also the fear that other Jews will be unable to gain the permit to go into this business . . . the precept of being fruitful and multiplying also being involved."[30] Master craftsmen were allowed to marry and settle in the area, in addition to the regular local population.[31] Permitting the craftsmen to engage in their occupation thus opened the way to the establishment of additional families in the area.

This permissive ruling was, however, conditional upon the workshop being separated from the craftsman's home. "We do, however, have to warn [members of the household] not to come into the [work]room on the Sabbath and certainly not to keep the workers company at all. The door should be shut in such a way that passersby in the street not sense that the Gentiles are working on the Sabbath—in such a way it is permitted."[32] These were conditions difficult to live up to because of the overcrowded living quarters. This is underscored in the continuation of the story. That same craftsman moved to another house, lived there in "a large hall" that "was divided by boards. . . . In the outer part he works throughout the week, and it is impossible to reach the inner section except via this outer room."[33] In this way, the Gentile laborers did their work on the Sabbath in full view of the craftsman and his family. The craftsman's "pious" wife[34] was afraid at this point that her home was not free of Sabbath desecration and attributed the calamity that befell her—the death of her two sons—to this transgression. R. Wolf Hamburg agreed with her[35]—an indication of the similarity between popular conceptions and the thinking of the halakhically trained mind.

Either because of this affair or for other reasons, R. Wolf Hamburg retracted his permissive ruling, even when the workshop was completely separate from an individual's living quarters. In the 1840s, R.

29. Ibid., 27a.
30. Ibid.
31. See Jacob Gotthelf, *Historisch-dogmatische Darstellung der rechtlichen Stellung der Juden in Bayern* (Munich, 1851), 111.
32. See Hamburg, *Simlat Binyamin* 28a.
33. Ibid., 29a.
34. Ibid., 176a.
35. Ibid., 29a, 30b: "And the woman did well to attribute to this sin the death of her sons."

Wolf Hamburg was once again asked about a tailor who wanted to employ craftsmen "but was not allowed to do so outside his home because of the law of the land and rules of the craftsmen's guild."[36] This time he banned the arrangement, explaining this change in his ruling by the changed circumstances. The first case had taken place "in a small town," in which there was no fear of the workmen coming to disregard Sabbath restrictions as a result of his ruling. The new case (in the thirties and forties) was different, "with many unobservant craftsmen," especially "in a large, heavily populated town."[37] He also attributed the first, permissive ruling to the special circumstances of the family: The shoemaker was not observant of halakhic detail, and it was his wife who sought the lenient ruling.[38] In this way, the rabbi tried to portray his earlier decision as a temporary measure. Nevertheless, a study of the first ruling shows that its composer viewed it as a solution applicable to the entire stratum of religiously observant craftsmen and that he changed his mind because of his inability to enforce religious observance, that is, to ensure that the entire Jewish community would continue to obey halakhic injunctions. In 1821,[39] this end could be achieved in small, outlying towns, but by the 1840s throughout the country, it no longer could.

R. Wolf Hamburg personally witnessed the collapse of the order of traditional society.[40] He served as a religious authority in the community of Fürth, maintained a large yeshiva, and expected to be appointed rabbi of the community. However, toward the end of the twenties, with the rise to power of the would-be innovators in the community who enjoyed the support of the Bavarian secular authorities, the academy was closed. His students were exiled from the town, and his own position was limited to the rabbinate of the study hall of the pious faction. He was considered a relic of the older generation—born in 1770—unwilling to compromise. His strict ruling in the case of the tailor was more typical of his overall leanings than his lenient decision in the case of the shoemaker. The tailor's assistants also worked under a contracting

---

36. See n. 11 above.
37. In a footnote at the end of his book, 176a.
38. Ibid., 176a.
39. For the date, see n. 23 above.
40. For his life story, see Leopold Lowenstein, "Zur Geschichte der Juden in Fürth," *Jahrbuch der jüdisch-literarischen Gesellschaft* 6 (1909):209–214.

arrangement, and his doubts stemmed from a fear of outward appearances, which were ignored by many halakhic authorities because of the considerable financial loss entailed. The composer of the question himself had relied on this consideration, claiming that "there can be no greater loss than this where one's livelihood depends on it."[41] Rabbi Hamburg, however, refused to accept this claim, defining the damage to be incurred by the tailor as a "prevention of profit"[42] and scolding him for abandoning the custom of "many Jewish craftsmen in this country who, just the same, cease working on the Sabbath."[43] The rabbi's objection seems to have been to the tailor's seeking his livelihood by this unacceptable way of engaging non-Jewish helpers in his workshop.

Rabbi Hamburg was not alone in this position. R. Menahem Mendel Kargau,[44] a contemporary and resident of the same town, when asked about a Jew interested in acquiring a stagecoach agency (fahrende Post),[45] who, of course, would have to send his messengers with their vehicles on the Sabbath as well, refused even to review the specific case: "Even if this were a clear case that could be permitted, I refuse to rule in such a case, where the matter will be made public and as a result others will come to rule leniently in other matters as well."[46] He was aware that, in this way, he was preventing a Jew from engaging in a certain type of livelihood, but the religious interests of the public, as he interpreted them, were decisive, as opposed to the interests of the individual. In his opinion, this particular person, whom he considered to be "one who hearkens to the voice of rabbinic authority—otherwise, why should he ask?"[47]—had to give preference to public interests. The rabbi thus addressed the halakhic scholar who was mediating between the two, saying: "Thus, my friend, persuade him not to touch something problematic, so that he may be rewarded for restraining himself."[48]

These two relics of the older generation in Fürth were considered extremely authoritative by halakhic scholars of the following generation

41. Hamburg, Simlat Binyamin 85a.
42. Ibid.
43. Ibid.
44. On him, see n. 40 above, Lowenstein, pp. 118–119.
45. Adduced by Rabbi Isaac Dov Bamberger, Netia shel Simhah, pp. 5–7 n. 2.
46. Ibid., 6.
47. Ibid., 6–7.
48. Ibid., 7.

in Germany, many of whom were their disciples. However, regarding the avoidance of new kinds of occupations, the latter did not maintain the strict rulings laid down by their mentors, as demonstrated by the case of the craftsman discussed in the pages of *Shomer Tsiyyon ha-Neeman*. The circumstances of this case were identical with those of the two craftsmen concerning which R. Wolf Hamburg finally changed his permissive decision. The proponent of the lenient view, Rabbi Loewenstein,[49] and also Rabbi Jacob Koppel ha-Levi of Worms,[50] ignored Rabbi Hamburg's ruling. They were, however, undoubtedly aware of it, for they added to the other grounds for their permissive ruling the requirement that an announcement should be made in the synagogue,[51] a basis that was Rabbi Hamburg's own innovation. These two halakhic scholars do not conceal the motivations for their permissive ruling. We have already adduced Rabbi Loewenstein's statement encouraging the study of crafts;[52] Rabbi ha-Levi, in referring to new employment opportunities open to Jews, speaks of "emergencies when one's livelihood sometimes depends on this."[53]

Considerations of this kind had originally been taken into account by Rabbi Hamburg, but he abandoned them because of the increase in the number of the nonobservant[54] and adopted an ultrastrict attitude. This later attitude of his turned out, however, to be in conflict with the current reality and seems to have lost all its supporters among German halakhic authorities. The fact that the editor of *Shomer Tsiyyon ha-Neeman*, R. Jacob Ettlinger, published these permissive rulings without any comment of his own must be interpreted as a lack of reservation on his part. The advocates of a lenient approach were also unexpectedly

49. See n. 8 above.
50. His statements there in *Shomer Tsiyyon ha-Neeman* (1849) 74–75, 148a–b, 157a–b; for Rabbi Levy, see S. Rothschild, *Beamte der wormser jüdischen Gemeinde* (Frankfurt am Main, 1920), 15–20.
51. See *Shomer Tsiyyon ha-Neeman*, 134b, 150b. Even without evidence it is impossible to assume that they were not familiar with the book of a rabbi considered to have been the leading halakhic authority of their country in the previous generation.
52. See n. 9 above.
53. See *Shomer Tsiyyon ha-Neeman*, 150b.
54. His phrasing in a note at the end of his book to explain his changed opinion (n. 37 above).

supported by R. Moses Schick, at the time still the spiritual leader of the small Hungarian community of Jergen[55] and not yet the influential authority he was destined to become. His statements are self-explanatory.[56] From the standpoint of one far from the scene of events, Rabbi Schick considered the question as a theoretical one "not for implementation."[57] His conclusion was permissive: "If no way is found to allow him to do so, he will unwillingly abandon his craft during the week as well; and in cases of so great a loss, the question of external appearances is minor."[58] This consideration, rejected by Rabbi Hamburg, was thus relegitimized by an independent and unexpected source. R. Moses Schick was certainly unaware of R. Wolf Hamburg's decisions, for otherwise he would not have refrained from mentioning them.

The heirs to the halakhic authority of the two Fürth scholars were their disciples, R. Isaac Dov ha-Levi Bamberger,[59] the rabbi of Würzburg, and R. Jacob Ettlinger, chief halakhic expert of Altona-Hamburg.[60] The former studied under both of them;[61] the latter studied for a while in the academy headed by R. Wolf Hamburg[62] but was undoubtedly known to Rabbi Kargau as well. It seems that the later generations were no less learned than their predecessors and certainly no less determined to maintain halakhic requirements in all their minutiae. It was historical development during their period of religious leadership that altered the circumstances that halakhic authorities had to consider. The two earlier rabbinic giants died during the fifth decade of the nineteenth century, Kargau in 1840 and Hamburg in 1850. Until then, most German Jews

55. Concerning him, see chap. 11.

56. The opinion of Rabbi M. Schick was printed in *Shomer Tsiyyon ha-Neeman* 86 (172a), 87 (174a–b), and was included in his *Responsa* (Munkács, 1880), 95, and will be quoted accordingly.

57. In the last section of the responsum.

58. Ibid.

59. On him, see Shlomoh Schmidt, "The Rabbi of Würtzburg: His Image and Work" (in Hebrew), in the *Bamberger Family Volume* (Jerusalem, 1979), 8–14.

60. For him, see Yehezkel Dukes, *Ivva le-Moshav* (Cracow, 1903), 114–124; A. Posner and E. Freiman, "Rabbi Jacob Ettlinger," in *Guardians of Our Heritage*, ed. Leo Jung (New York, 1958), 231–243.

61. Schmidt "Rabbi of Würzburg," p. 9.

62. So according to Posner-Freiman, "Rabbi Jacob Ettlinger," 233, though without citing the source.

still lived traditional lives.[63] The struggle between the Jews adhering to tradition and those trying to break away from it seemed to relate to the character of the entire community in the future. From midcentury on, the trend toward throwing off the shackles of tradition grew ever stronger, as a result of demographic changes, urbanization, and other secularizing agents,[64] leaving the traditionalists unmistakably in the status of a minority.

This does not mean that the majority divested itself completely of all traditional characteristics. Consistent assimilationists and members of the Reform camp were themselves still a minority. The majority camp sandwiched between the two minorities still maintained links with traditional forms. Its community institutions, synagogues and schools, were unmistakably Jewish, and the major religious symbols—Sabbaths and Jewish festivals—still determined the rhythm of family life. This camp was distinguishable from the Orthodox minority by the nonchalant fashion with which it treated the remains of these religious symbols. If conflicts arose between religious observance and economic interests or personal comfort, these would be likely to prevail. Most of the adherents of this group dissociated themselves from the supervision of halakhic authority. Halakhic rulings from now on would be aimed at the Orthodox minority, which continued to entrench itself, if not in actual separate communities, at least in self-integrating circles. Nevertheless, the borderline between the minority subordinating itself to halakhic authority and those Jews adhering loosely to traditional forms was not always clear.

An ideological and educational fight for the souls of the undecided was waged by the Orthodox camp. The question was no longer one of enforcing halakhic authority throughout the Jewish community but rather one of attracting individuals and persuading them to accept this

---

63. This was the conclusion of the two scholars who checked the commonly accepted version, as if the modernization process came to an end soon after it began at the close of the eighteenth century. Jacob Toury, "Deutsche Juden in Vormärz," *Bulletin des Leo Baeck Instituts* 8 (1965): 65–82; Steven M. Lowenstein, "Pace of Modernization of German Jewry," *Leo Baeck Institute Year Book* 21 (1976): 41–56; idem, "The 1840s and the Creation of the German-Jewish Religious Reform Movement," in *Revolution and Evolution: 1848 in German-Jewish History*, ed. W. E. Mosse, A. Pauker, R. Ruerup (Tübingen, 1981), 255–297.

64. For a description of the process, see Lowenstein, *Pace of Modernization*.

yoke. Signs of this struggle are occasionally discernible in halakhic give-and-take, with the scholars considering the question of whether a certain halakhic ruling to be handed down would drive Jews away instead of attracting them.

There is an example of just such hesitation in a case involving the two aforementioned rabbinic authorities, the rabbis of Würzburg and Altona. The matter under consideration was halakhically similar to the question unambiguously turned down by Rabbi Menahem Mendel Kargau[65] and was brought before Rabbi Bamberger by his son, Moses Aryeh, district rabbi in Bad Kissingen.[66] A local Jew made his living by owning horses and carriages that served the visitors to the famed health resort. This Jew had undertaken "to have ready for one of the summer guests, a prince, a carriage and horses every day together with one of the Jew's servants, who would be at his disposal;[67]—Sabbaths, of course, included.

This was a very problematic decision to make. At first glance, a permissive ruling was possible on two conditions: that the owner of the carriage sell the horses to his Gentile carriage driver "from Sabbath eve in a complete and valid sale and that he have no benefit whatever from the profits made by the taker [the carriage driver], a non-Jew, on the Sabbath."[68] The rabbi ruled in detail how the horses were to be sold, in complete accord with halakhic requirements for concluding a transaction[69]—and yet he was still unsure if all the doubts concerning the deal had been resolved. The horses remained in the domain of the Jew, and "it is forbidden to remove any object from the home of a Jew on the Sabbath."[70] He concluded that a third condition had to be added: to rent "the stall and the place for the carriage" to the carriage driver. In addition, the horses' feed had to be sold to the carriage driver before the Sabbath. One doubt still remained: The carriage driver was, after all, the Jew's "servant," his steady worker, a fact that increased the fear

65. See n. 45 above. Rabbi Kargau's responsum was printed by Rabbi Bamberger's son, who edited his responsa and noted the similarity between the two cases.
66. Bamberger, *Netia shel Simhah*, 5–7 n. 2; *Orah Hayyim* 6.
67. Bamberger, *Netia shel Simhah*, 3.
68. Ibid.
69. Ibid., 3–4.
70. Ibid., 4.

of outward appearances, for both the driver and the horses were known to belong to the Jew.[71]

The factor encouraging the quest for a way to permit the deal was the "financial loss," a factor always considered sufficient for a permissive ruling whenever the prohibition was based on a fear of appearances. But Rabbi Bamberger's desire to take into account all the rulings that tended to ban the deal was the very factor that weakened this consideration, for from a purely formal point of view, this was none other than a case of "loss of profit. And Providence, having commanded us to observe the Sabbath, can be depended upon to reward the observant."[72] This sentence, uttered with some anguish, expressed the principle that the rabbi wanted the person who had requested the permissive ruling to accept—but he was not sure if the latter was willing to do so. He concluded: "At any rate, in the way described above [that is, by fulfilling all the conditions] there may be no reason to rule strictly."[73] But Rabbi Bamberger still did not want to make such a decision by himself. He permitted the Jew to act accordingly to the rules of his decision for a single Sabbath[74] and in the meantime requested that his son put the same question before his father-in-law, R. Jacob Ettlinger of Altona.

Rabbi Ettlinger's response reveals that the gentleman involved was not just any prince, but the German kaiser himself,[75] who was accustomed to vacation with his family in Kissingen.[76] And the carriage owners of the town, including the Jew, were hired to be at the disposal of the royal party at all times. It is understandable that even if the Jewish carriage owner had been pious, it would not have been easy for him to give up the honor and fame that would have accrued to him by serving the kaiser's family. This, then, was the source of Rabbi Bamberger's inner struggle and, to a large extent, that of Rabbi Ettlinger as well. From a halakhic point of view, however, the opinion of the latter was the more definitive. He described all the innovations as "devices" used

71. All of this—ibid.
72. Ibid.
73. Ibid.
74. Thus according to young rabbi Bamberger, ibid., 5 (the middle of the responsum).
75. The responsum of Rabbi Ettlinger, ibid., 4–5.
76. Ernst Günther Krenig, *Bad Kissingen, Bilder aus seiner Geschichte* (Würzburg, 1964), 34–71.

to "conspire to transgress against a Torah ban." There were no exten-
uating circumstances. The deed would be done when everyone "knows
that the building, the carriage, and the horses belong to the Jew." He
also defined the loss incurred as a mere "loss of profit." Neither is there
in this case a way to claim "lack of choice." The rabbi's assessment was
that "if he says that he has no desire to be one of the carriage owners
rented for the royal party . . . no one will protest his decision or compel
him to carry out what he undertook."[77] He did not doubt that the ruling
to be made would be prohibitive in nature; he did, however, doubt if
the person involved would accept it. If he indeed refused to do so, the
question as to the obligation of the local rabbi and his advisers, the
halakhic authorities, would arise: Would they be obliged to make a public protest against this refusal to accept their authority, or could they
keep silent?[78] In this way, the question concerning the behavior desired
of the questioner became one concerning the desirable response of those
asked.

Rabbi Ettlinger found a compromise solution. The younger Rabbi
Bamberger was to tell the person concerned that he, his father, and his
father-in-law had struggled to find a way to permit the deal and forestall
financial loss, but "after all our attempts we found no way to do so, and
so he should trust in Providence to compensate him fully and announce
that he does not wish to be included in the carriage owners hiring themselves out to the kaiser's family. But if he refuses to do so, then, in order
to minimize the transgression by means of the sale, he should act in
every respect as he had on the previous Sabbath. . . . And in that case
we can take comfort in having not given him permission." This advice
was given to the young rabbi by his father-in-law "to free you of all ill-
feeling toward you."[79] The rabbi of Würzburg accepted his in-law's injunction happily and instructed his son to tell the Jew who had made
the original request that "if he does not accept the prohibitions, he
should at least act in such a way as to minimize the sin." He then
repeated to his son: "Make it very clear to him that neither you nor we
are granting him permission, even if he behaves in this fashion, and that
we are only telling him this to reduce the dimensions of his transgres-

77. For all of this—n. 75 above.
78. Ibid., 4.
79. Ibid., 5.

sion." One last piece of advice: "Do not take it to heart if they speak harshly to you, and certainly do not answer them; let us give thanks to God that He found us a place among those who study His law and observe His precepts, etc."[80]

This seems to be a clear expression of the change in the status of the halakhic authorities. They no longer have the power to enforce their rulings physically, and they even lack the public support needed to have the questioner accept their ruling. Ignoring a halakhic ruling would likely cause the rabbi no little embarrassment, which explains the delicate phrasing and words of advice used by the rabbis in replying to the question put to them.

In this particular case the problem was solved to the satisfaction of both sides. Rabbi Jacob Ettlinger added a practical suggestion to his halakhic ruling, that the Jewish carriage owner reach an agreement with one of his Gentile colleagues that should he be requested to serve the royal family on the Sabbath, the non-Jew would provide his carriage in place of the Jew's. The younger Rabbi Bamberger, the final editor of the responsum, could happily inform the reader that "the Jew concerned accepted the ruling of the scholars" and accepted the rabbi's advice.[81] The solution was thus found thanks to the cleverness of the halakhic scholar and not to his authority.

The desire to take into account all the strict rulings, on the one hand, and the fear lest his contemporaries be unable to accept them, on the other, guided the reasoning of the Würzburg rabbi in a number of other responsa as well. It was customary in Würzburg for Jewish butchers to sell their merchandise, kosher meat, together with Gentile butchers in the market designated for the purpose. The Jewish butchers would sell nonkosher meat to non-Jews, and these sales were carried out on Sabbaths as well, by means of a Gentile employee.[82] As soon as he arrived in Würzburg in 1839, Rabbi Bamberger expressed doubt whether this concept was halakhically valid; but his own mentor, Rabbi Mendel Kargau, assured him that when the Gentile works "under a contractual arrangement . . . , because of the loss entailed . . . it is best to ignore

---

80. All of this—ibid.
81. Ibid.
82. The situation is described in his question put to Rabbi Ettlinger in the sixties (see n. 85 below), in R. Isaac Dov ha-Levi Bamberger, *Responsa Yad ha-Levi*, ed. Shlomo Adler (Jerusalem, 1965), *Orah Hayyim* 42.

the matter and not react strongly."[83] The supervision of the conduct of the butchers was always difficult for those in charge, and R. Kargau's advice not to clash with them was intended to solve a problem liable to occur in every traditional community.[84]

Nevertheless, the changing circumstances raised new problems in this field, too. At a later stage, no later than the sixties,[85] the secular authorities allowed the butchers to open butcheries in town. A number of Jewish butchers did so while continuing their custom of putting a non-Jew in their stead on Sabbaths in order to sell to non-Jewish clients. The rabbi, however, doubted that the old permit would still be valid in the new circumstances in which the butchery belongs to the Jew and is known by his name. He thus turned to his in-law, Rabbi Ettlinger, and described the dilemma, for the butchers "shout that if they are not permitted . . . they may very easily lose their entire trade. And if you and I know that such a claim would not be made by those who trust in God, it is still very difficult to convince such ignorant people to accept the tradition of the covenant."[86] In this case, too, Rabbi Ettlinger made it clear that the butchers' behavior was forbidden. In his opinion, these new circumstances, where the butchery belonged to the individual Jew and was known by his name, rendered invalid the "permissive ruling handed down by the late R. Kargau."[87] He would also not concede that there was any great loss in this case, "for the butcher can see to it that no meat remains on Sabbath eve, and if there is any left over he can sell it to a Gentile at only a slight loss" or keep it on ice. "Furthermore, if we permit this because of a capital loss strictly on account of the heat, what reason is there to permit it in the cold winter? It is apparent that

83. Ibid.
84. See chap. 7, n. 58, concerning the permissive ruling accepted in the Jewish congregations of Italy. R. Joseph Teomim, the author of *Peri Megadim*, was asked about this by a Jew of Lvov and relates that "some say that it was customary to permit it," adding that "if a great scholar permitted them to do so, my opinion is of no value." His opinion was that if the case was well known, then there was no way to permit it. *Peri Megadim, Orah Hayyim* 244.
85. Rabbi Bamberger's appeal to Rabbi Ettlinger is undated, but he calls him "my in-law." Rabbi Ettlinger's daughter, who married Rabbi Bamberger's son, was born in 1842 (see the *Bamberger Family Volume*, 14). Thus, the responsum could not have been composed prior to 1860.
86. Ibid.
87. Ibid., 31.

the butcher will not make a distinction between summer and winter."[88] In short, Rabbi Ettlinger wanted the butchers to accept all the halakhic reservations, and he relates that "here in our community there are fourteen Jewish butchers who make most of their living from the Gentiles, yet none of them thinks to ask me to allow him to sell meat on the Sabbath by means of a Gentile, from his own house." He concluded his reasoned opinion with the following sentence: "In my humble opinion, especially in this undisciplined generation in which the nonobservant who sell on the Sabbath are unfortunately numerous, we must rule especially strictly so as not to invite adverse criticism."[89]

The butchers were, of course, under the supervision of the rabbi, upon whom the decision depended whether they could sell meat to the Jewish public. The rabbi could be strict with them, but this is not true of other storekeepers who were not under his control.[90] The strong-handed approach with the butchers thus served as a kind of counterweight to the weakness of the rabbis shown toward the Jewish community in general. Whether the rabbi of Würzburg, too, was able to enforce his authority over his butchers is not known. We have no expression of his showing a desire to rule strictly with observant Jews as a reaction to the indifference toward religious authority demonstrated by others. What was characteristic of his approach and, fundamentally, of that of Rabbi Ettlinger as well was a sense of obligation to live up to the requirements of the halakhah, as they emerged under the new circumstances, without making allowances for accepted customs or tradition. This approach is what prompts him to examine the conduct of the butchers as he found it when he arrived in Würzburg[91] and to reexamine it when conditions change, lest new circumstances have invalidated existing permissive rulings already in force. Rabbi Bamberger's conduct was no accident, as may be seen from his ruling about the Sabbath Gentile in reply to another question.

88. Ibid.
89. All of this—ibid.
90. About eighty years earlier the rabbi of Hamburg, Rabbi Raphael Cohen, was prevented from chastising a Jew for having desecrated the Sabbath in public; see my book *Out of the Ghetto*, 148.
91. Rabbi Bamberger seems not to have been satisfied by Rabbi Kargau's first responsum, and he brought a further doubt before him, as may be deduced from Kargau's second reply to him (Bamberger, *Responsa Yad ha-Levi*, 31).

This question originated in Fürth. Its wording was lost, but its content was preserved by the responder. The case concerned an agent selling lottery tickets, a typically Jewish occupation at this time, who, "now that things have changed . . . , wants to engage a non-Jew to work . . . on our holy Sabbath as well."[92] Rabbi Bamberger adds: "I will not repeat the superfluous details," that is, he would relate only those details he considered relevant from a halakhic point of view. From our standpoint, however, one detail was important, and this may be reconstructed from the content of the reply: This question did not originate with an individual but, rather, with many people,[93] that is, all the agents whose livelihood depended upon this matter. And it is clear that the "things that had changed" were that the authorities issuing the lottery tickets made their sale by the agents conditional upon their being sold on the Sabbath as well[94] It is clear that the rabbi purposely ignored that circumstance and strove to consider the question abstractly, on the basis of principle. This was how he acted in omitting the involvement of the royal court in the question of the carriage owner, wording the problem as if it involved "a certain prince."

The study of the rabbi's response also reveals that in Fürth itself there was a dispute between two halakhic scholars, Rabbi Joel Getz and Rabbi Tebli,[95] as to whether or not the affair could be permitted by letting the Gentile employee keep the profits of the Sabbath and renting to him the shop for Sabbaths.[96] The rabbi accepted the opinion of the

92. Ibid., 41.
93. The matter is rendered explicit in the question put by the scholar who wanted to permit it, inter alia, relying on the Magen Avraham (see chap. 7, n. 2): "For in a matter of the public there is no suspicion, and so in the matter before us where those asking are themselves more than one, it should also be permitted" (ibid., 29a).
94. Lotteries were an important source of livelihood in the country. See Wolfgang Zorn, Kleine Wirtschafts und Sozialgeschichte Bayerns 1806–1932 (Munich-Passing, 1962), 31.
95. The responsum was written to Joel Getz, and Rabbi Tebli (once misspelled as Tamli) is mentioned in the debate from the viewpoint of one objecting to the permissive ruling.
96. That renting out the room was a condition of the proposed permissive ruling can be seen from the reservations expressed by the responder concerning this ruling, whereas he included the following condition in the permissive ruling he himself proposed: "The entire proceedings of the Sabbath shall belong only to the person engaged in this matter, the Jew not benefiting from it at all" (Yad ha-Levi, 30). This, without discussing the matter, is an indication that it was agreed to by the scholar ruling permissively as well.

opponent of the proposed arrangement and would only give his permission if the matter were arranged so as to satisfy the requirements of all the rulings: "The Jew should set aside a separate room for the person working on the Sabbath,"[97] that is, a kind of Sabbath shop alongside the weekday shop—a completely impracticable proposal. He overcame the problem of loss of livelihood incidentally, as it were, by defining the case as one of "loss of profit" and not "loss of principle."[98] Even if the stipulation of a separate room for Sabbath sales were kept, there would still be another condition, "that you know the person asking the question to be a pious Jew, who will keep those conditions. . . . In such a case, perhaps after the deliberation it will be possible to rule permissively."[99]

Even though the rabbis of Altona and Würzburg differed from one another as regards decisiveness and hesitation, basically their approach was the same. Each is willing to accept responsibility for any permissive ruling only if he has not in any way risked overlooking any opinion in halakhic tradition, and it is unnecessary to note that they refrain from any attempt at devising innovative and unprecedented permissive rulings. This extreme caution, lest the agreed boundaries of halakhic flexibility be violated, is obvious in their strict interpretation of the concept of "loss." Fear of loss is, of course, what prompted the questioners to bring their problems before the halakhic authorities, and taking such loss into account plays a certain role in determining the boundaries of the prohibition on "telling a Gentile," as we have seen. The later authorities, however, made a distinction between loss of principal and prevention of profit, thus limiting their flexibility to cases of loss of principal only. In actual practice, this depended upon the evaluation made by the halakhic authority of the case before him—whether the loss entailed was to be considered of the one sort or of the other. In the case of the butchers, Rabbi Bamberger seems to have accepted their claim that by not selling meat on the Sabbath their very livelihood was endangered.[100] His colleague, Rabbi Ettlinger, overruled this claim completely, however.[101] In the case of the carriage owner of Kissingen, too,

97. Ibid.
98. Ibid., 29.
99. Ibid., 30.
100. See n. 85 above.
101. Nn. 87–88 above.

Rabbi Ettlinger ruled "that this is only a loss of profit";[102] and Rabbi Bamberger went even further in the case of the lottery agents, when an entire group of family men considered their livelihood to be endangered. He nevertheless defined their loss as only one of profit.[103] The desire to consider concrete cases as if they were merely theoretical is revealed in Rabbi Bamberger's custom of omitting the actual details of the case in his wording of the question,[104] unlike the practice of previous generations of halakhic authorities, who went into great detail in describing the situation that gave rise to the problem and even admitted that these conditions were what encouraged them to extricate the questioners from the predicament in which they found themselves.

This seems to be an expression of the change in the function of the halakhah following the contraction of its actual social basis. As long as traditional Sabbath observance was characteristic of the entire Jewish community, the role played by the halakhic authorities entailed only supervising the prevention of violations of established Sabbath practice, the principles underlying it being detailed explicitly in halakhic literature. Halakhic rulings certainly depended upon written halakhah for their validity, but their role was not one of expressing their underlying principles so as to create a new reality. Their only function was to regulate existing reality. The halakhic give-and-take preceding the actual ruling itself was intended to draw two Sabbath patterns closer together: the one reflected in halakhic literature and the one placed before the halakhic authorities reflecting social reality. The obligatory ruling was influenced by both focuses of the give-and-take, as our historical discussion has shown throughout.

Now that most of the Jewish community had ceased to observe the Sabbath according to traditional patterns, as occurred in western Europe as early as the second half of the nineteenth century, the halakhic authority lost one of his two bases, the one anchored in religious social life. From this time on, questions reaching him in connection with the Sabbath came from the minority desirous of observing the Sabbath as decreed by halakhah. In his responsum the scholar could no longer take into account accepted community norms, for these had lost their le-

102. N. 77 above.
103. N. 98 above.
104. Nn. 75, 93 above.

gitimacy as the continuation of established tradition. The anguish voiced repeatedly by halakhic authorities, to the effect that many Jews are no longer observant and that contemporary life was that of a non-observant generation, and so on, seems aimed at explaining the necessity of not ruling leniently, lest the masses hear of such a permissive ruling and use it to justify further nonobservance. From the point of view of phenomenologists, these complaints reflect the recognition of the halakhic authorities that they no longer have a behavior pattern enjoying relative but well-defined authority. The halakhic scholar, *in his own responsa*, was now left solely with the literary source from which to abstract the obligatory norms, but the questioner had to decide for himself if he was willing and able to live accordingly, his decision being final.

Rabbi Isaac Dov Bamberger seems to represent this new type of halakhic authority in its purest form. He sees no reason to excuse himself for his tendency to rule strictly. He really does not desire to rule strictly; on the contrary, his doubts and hesitations show that he would have preferred to reach a permissive conclusion had he been able to base such a conclusion upon the authority of the sources in their entirety, which he felt obliged to take into consideration.[105] His halakhic rulings—conditioned on this single principle—deliberately overlooked the ability or inability of the questioner to live by them. In the final analysis, each and every individual in the Jewish community had to make his own decision as to whether he wanted to be considered halakhically Sabbath observant: The role of the halakhic authorities was not to make this decision for him but merely to teach him the precise meaning of Sabbath observance. This principle also guided his colleague, Rabbi Jacob Ettlinger, and we shall encounter this approach with halakhic authorities in later generations outside Germany as well.

---

105. Rabbi Bamberger's desire to meet the demands of all rulings is clearly emphasized in his instructions to the owner of the carriage concerning how he was to make the horses and wagon the property of the Gentile. He insisted on the wagon because the Bah had written (246) that "a pious man must be strict in connection with the resting of his implements," taking into account the opinion of the Rokeah, a single opinion ignored by halakhic authorities ruling in matters of the Sabbath. The acquisition is carried out by means of *meshikhah*, as ruled by most of the authorities. Nevertheless, he stipulates receiving money from the Gentile so as to meet the requirements set by the minority; *Netia shel Simhah*, 3–4.

The system of giving halakhic rulings that ignored reality was not, of course, the only way halakhic authorities could react to the situation in which those accepting their rulings had become a minority. Rabbi Azriel Hildesheimer, the outstanding disciple of R. Jacob Ettlinger, conducted himself differently in response to the request of one of his students to agree to a permissive ruling already confirmed by an illustrious scholar, R. Meir Bergel of Rawitsch. It allowed the construction of a synagogue to proceed on the Sabbath by means of a contractual arrangement—"where all great authorities of the previous generation retreat from applying the power of leniency." Hildesheimer added: "It is true that at the present time we unfortunately have to choose a minimal evil or even search out ways to permit something lest if we rule strictly our ruling will not be accepted, and the deed will be done though it be prohibited."[106] He viewed his generation as "spiritually impoverished, tested day after day by those who openly violate the sanctity of the Sabbath."[107] And so "it is proper and even religiously required to rule permissively wherever possible."[108] His willingness to rule leniently had its limits, of course. When a Jew requested permission to build his own home, by contracting, on the Sabbath because "of a great loss of three or four hundred reichstalers a year," his negative ruling was unambiguous: "Concerning this loss, the Almighty will surely compensate you in other ways and on one day can make up for any possible loss."[109] At any rate, Rabbi Hildesheimer attempted to take into account the concrete conditions in which his questioner found himself: a merchant, the partner of a Gentile in a mercantile firm, whose company could not be known by a name other than his own;[110] a banker, whose Gentile agent was obliged by the rules of banking to be able to purchase bonds and securities on the Sabbath in an emergency;[111] the factory owner whose buildings had burned down and whose Gentile partners were urging the contractors to hurry and continue building even on the Sab-

---

106. *Responsa* of Rabbi Azriel Hildesheimer (Tel Aviv, 1969), *Orah Hayyim* 32.
107. Ibid., 34 (p. 36).
108. Ibid., 36–37.
109. Ibid., 33. For the synagogue building, because it is on behalf of the public, there was a way to rule permissively that would not apply to a private building; see ibid., 32.
110. Ibid., 36 (sec. e) 37, 38.
111. Ibid., 40.

bath.[112] In this last case, the rabbi based his permissive ruling, *inter alia,* upon the fears of the questioner that a delay in the reestablishment of the factory might lead his clients to transfer their business permanently to a rival firm. Accordingly, he defined the feared damage in halakhic terms as "loss of principal" and not mere "prevention of profit."[113]

Although Rabbi Hildesheimer took into account those whose adherence to halakhah was lax—those who might be led by prohibitive decisions to act in violation of halakhah[114]—most of his responsa appear to have been aimed at the pious, whose subordination to Orthodox life patterns was absolute. This seems to be characteristic of the period. Hildesheimer returned to Germany from Eisenstadt, Hungary, in 1869. At this stage, neo-Orthodox communities were being established, the most outstanding being that of R. Samson Raphael Hirsch in Frankfurt, but also others, which copied its example. Jews belonging to these congregations maintained Orthodox lives not merely as a result of conservative leanings. They had been educated to view precise observance as an ideal endowed with spiritual significance, and their loyalty to it was above reproach.[115] The halakhic questions that these Jews brought to the rabbi were not accompanied by an ultimate demand for a permissive ruling. The request was rather for guidance that would allow the individual to live with a clear halakhic conscience.

From the wording of Rabbi Hildesheimer's responsa it is clear that this was the kind of Jew with whom he had to deal. If he was able to propose two alternative solutions, one better grounded halakhically than the other, he would advise his questioner to choose that one; if this was impractical, he suggested relying upon the second. If it was possible to enter a real partnership with an independent Gentile so that the business could bear the latter's name only—this would be better. If this was

112. Ibid., 35.
113. Ibid.
114. N. 106. In building a synagogue, the matter depends, of course, on the opinion of a majority of the congregation, and there he may have feared that those who scorn halakhah may be triumphant.
115. Max Wiener described the German Orthodox Jews correctly as being clearly aware of the detailed observance of the commandments, more than the awareness common in periods when the tradition appeared to be in automatic control; Max Wiener, *Jüdische Religion im Zeitalter der Emanzipation* (Berlin, 1933), 77–81.

THE "SHABBES GOY" 158

impossible, one could settle for a formal partnership with an official of the business, with the name of the Jewish owner remaining the one displayed.[116] Concerning the problem of the bankers, it would be preferable for the agent to purchase the debentures for himself on the Sabbath and then resell them to the bankers after the Sabbath was over. When he was told "that according to the rules of the trade this method was extremely difficult," he permitted the transaction to be carried out in the name of the banker himself.[117] Rabbi Hildesheimer was familiar with the saying of the sages, "Do not call 'evil' that which can be good." And he used it in the sense attributed to it in Tractate *Berakhot* of the Talmud:[118] If you are capable of observing a commandment in a better fashion, do not settle for observing it in a worse way.[119] This principle appears to have been applicable and, at any rate, to have been applied in public only where the rabbi was more a religious counselor than an enforcer of halakhah by virtue of his authority.

116. *Responsa* of Rabbi Azriel Hildesheimer, *Orah Hayyim* 36 (sec. a), 37.

117. Ibid., 40.

118. *Berakhot* 30a; the example here is of prayer to be recited when standing still rather than while walking around, as explained by Rashi: "Since I can pray standing up, for my group is standing, I will not be called bad for praying while walking around even though it is permitted." In *Bava Kamma* 81b the statement is adduced to condemn someone "whose fruits are no longer in the fields, yet he forbids others to enter his field"—this seems to be the simple meaning.

119. The saying appears in his *Responsa, Orah Hayyim* 32, 34 (p. 37), 35. I found this use of the saying in one of R. Solomon Kluger's responsa, *Ha-Elef Lekha Shelomoh* (Bilgora, 1931–1932), pt. 1, 127; *Ketav Sofer, Orah Hayyim* 44.

10

Galicia: The Use of a Bill of Sale

The drastic change that occurred in Jewish history during the modern era is clearly reflected in the different rates of development experienced by western European and eastern European Jewry. From a broad historical perspective, one may distinguish similar internal and external factors nibbling away at the foundations of traditional society in both regions. The weakening of institutions of feudal government and the absorption of rationalist ideas accompanying this development eventually reached eastern European lands as well, with the consequential fundamental change in Jewish society. But the fact that eastern Europe lagged behind the western part of the Continent led to the emergence of a gap between the two Jewish groups, which, until the beginning of the modern era, in the second half of the eighteenth century, might very well have been considered two wings of one and the same society, that of Ashkenazic Jewry.

The difference in the rate of change does not negate the similarity in the substance of the development, as demonstrated by the fact that the same problems facing the Jews of western Europe eventually came to trouble their eastern brethren as well. And matters of Sabbath observance, of the kind we are considering, can serve as an example of this parallelism.

The division of Poland that occurred at the beginning of the modern era led to the result that different sectors of eastern European society did not develop simultaneously. Galicia, which was annexed by the Austrian Empire, abandoned the forms of a semifeudal economy before the Russian provinces did. This process directly affected its Jewish population. The policy adopted by the authorities, especially during the reign of Kaiser Joseph II (1780–1790), was aimed at eliminating the status of the Jews as economic middlemen between the landowners and farmers and directing them toward independent economic activity in agriculture, crafts, industry, and other fields required by Austria's developing market economy.[1] This goal was perceived to be utopian at the time, and as far as agriculture was concerned remained so for the future. At any rate, signs of a new economic order began to appear, as reflected in the establishment of factories. The problem of Sabbath observance in these industrial plants arose here as it had earlier in western countries.

The halakhic factors delimiting the problems were apparently identical with the factors upon which halakhic precedents had been based in the west. But social conditions here had for a very long period of time made it necessary for broad strata of the population to engage in economic activity involving both Jews and Gentiles, so that the various details of Sabbath observance had already come up against very basic difficulties. From our discussion of what transpired in sixteenth- and seventeenth-century Poland-Lithuania we recall how difficult it was for communal or higher authorities to supervise proper Sabbath observance, especially with regard to leasings, small and large, outside areas of Jewish settlement. The types of livelihood prevalent at that time were maintained by the Jewish community until the expulsions from the villages that took place in the period of Kaiser Joseph II (and to no small extent, afterward as well); and the halakhic authorities continued to acquiesce in the popular permission given to the sale of drinks in Jewish houses, the employment of servants on leased estates, and so on. Just as in the seventeenth century Jewish preachers attributed the adversities of 1648–1649 to the numerous cases of Sabbath desecration, so Rabbi Solomon Kluger ascribed the decrees of Joseph II to the same transgression. In 1851 he wrote: "In the past, Jews who rented the villages and estates used to desecrate the Sabbath, and so did the bartenders, as has been

1. See n. 21 below.

explained in the books; for this reason the Satan provoked the decree that Jews may no longer live in the villages, and much bartending has ceased because of this sin."[2]

R. Solomon Kluger was aware that violations committed in the past were not curbed; some even achieved permanence in public life. In his debate with the scholar who disagreed with his permissive ruling concerning a "Sabbath Gentile," his opponent claimed that R. Solomon ignored the fact that in the relevant case there was also a matter of Sabbath wages. This was R. Solomon's reply: "I made no mention of the prohibition of Sabbath wages because in any case, at the present time, this has become as if entirely permissible."[3] By "at the present time" he seems to have been referring to recent generations and not specifically to his own day. In the same context he added: "The reason for this seems to me to be that for performing a *mitsvah* one is permitted to accept Sabbath wages, as we find in chapter 306 [of *Shulhan Arukh*], and so we rely on the opinion propounded by R. Moses Isserles, chapter 246 [this should read 248], that at present even traveling to business is considered a matter of *mitsvah*, for it is hard to make a living, and so one is permitted to accept Sabbath wages."[4] The halakhah referred to in paragraph 306 concerns the hiring of a cantor, mentioning that some permit this "because it is for the purposes of *mitsvah*"; R. Moses Isserles' ruling in paragraph 248 follows that of Rabbenu Tam in the matter of setting sail in a boat, where he rules permissively because setting out in order to make a living is to be considered a *mitsvah*.[5] It is certain that no one originally imagined combining these two permissive rulings and applying them to a third matter, Sabbath wages, thus overruling their prohibition.[6] However, once the taking of Sabbath wages came to

2. Solomon Kluger, *U-Vaharta ba-Hayyim* (Budapest, 1934), 64 (43a). Concerning this responsum and its date, see nn. 30ff. below.

3. *U-Vaharta ba-Hayyim* 65 (44b).

4. Ibid.

5. Concerning the cantor, see *Magen Avraham, Orah Hayyim* 306:8; Rabbenu Tam's ruling was discussed in chap. 3, nn. 33–34.

6. I found no signs that halakhic authorities used Rabbenu Tam's ruling in other fields. R. Joseph Saul Nathanson, however (*Shoel u-Meshiv*, 1st ed., 2:66 [Lvov, 1869] [30a]), overruled R. Solomon's reasoning "as, according to him, one cancels out all matters of Sabbath income dealt with in *Shulhan Arukh* 244, 245 and the other sections."

be accepted, any ex post facto justification was preferable to declaring the public erring and sinful.

However, such an ex post facto justification as suggested en passant by R. Solomon Kluger in the course of a debate does not mean whole-hearted agreement. In other responsa, R. Solomon takes the prohibition of Sabbath wages into account,[7] thus demonstrating the degree of confusion to which a scholar of his ilk was subject. Sometimes his desire to justify the permissive rulings—created by virtue of the pressure exerted by difficulties in making a living—was predominant; at other times he preferred to try to restore halakhah to its pristine status. Such indecision on his part is especially apparent in connection with the most daring permissive custom of his day: the use of a bill of sale to circumvent the prohibition of "telling a Gentile," with all its relevant implications.

It is not known who invented this type of permissive ruling and who first authorized it. As early as 1854, R. Abraham Teomim of Buczacz, the author of Responsa Hesed le-Avraham, wrote: "We know of no halakhic authority who mentions permitting the building of one's house on the Sabbath by the legal fiction of selling it to a Gentile, as was permitted in the case of leaven [on Passover]."[8] R. Abraham ignored the discussion of his contemporary R. Solomon Kluger, who had dealt with this question from a practical point of view thirty years before in his book Sefer ha-Hayyim, printed in 1825,[9] in which he stated that in contrast to "the age of the Talmud and early halakhic authorities . . . nowadays . . . it has become customary in a number of places to act permissively in matters of Sabbath observance, to allow it by selling to a Gentile."[10] It is likely that this practice began before the 1820s. Even if halakhic authorities refrained from considering this matter, this does not mean that in popular circles, especially in connection with leasing outside the Jewish settlements, this way was not utilized to assuage guilty consciences, perhaps under the tutelage of unknown halakhic authorities. The selling of hamets (leaven), common throughout the Jewish Diaspora, could very well have served as an example to be em-

7. Ibid., 66, 71, and especially Solomon Kluger, Ha-Elef Lecha Shelomoh (Lvov, 1910), 103, 106, 125.
8. Abraham Teomim, Hesed le-Avraham (Lvov, 1857), 1:20.
9. Solomon Kluger, Sefer ha-Hayyim (Zholkva, 1825).
10. Ibid., 244:6 (31a).

ulated, as mentioned by R. Abraham Teomim[11] and by other halakhic authorities considering that same matter, as we shall yet see.[12] At any rate, this custom was first documented in writing in the 1820s by R. Solomon Kluger, in connection with a textile plant in the town of Rawena, nearby Brody, where R. Solomon lived.[13]

The matter involved "a factory owned by merchants operating in a building known to belong to a Jew, in which the non-Jews do their work on the Sabbath, as they have been doing for several years. Lately some people have protested against this desecration of the Sabbath, especially since some of the work performed by the Gentiles is of a type that is biblically prohibited.[14] The owners of the factory replied that the work was performed under a contractual arrangement and "also that they sell the building and the wool to a certain Gentile and he sells to other Gentiles."[15] This apparently meant that the sale was made to one of the workers, who employed the others on Sabbaths.

The plant owners clearly did not act upon their own initiative. We find that "they used to write out bills of sale in the presence of local rabbbis."[16] Permission to operate the plant by means of this sale was thus granted by the local rabbinic court. The scholar who put forth the question, apparently a member of the court, did place the matter before R. Solomon Kluger together with the reasoning behind the permissive ruling. The basis for the latter was that the work was done under contract. Since this was not allowed, in the case where the plant was known by the name of a Jew, the scholar who ruled permissively proposed three reasons for the removal of that stigma. First, closing the plant on Sabbaths and festivals would lead to its liquidation, in which case the loss involved was of "equipment worth several thousand gold coins." Second, the plant was sold to a Gentile, and if this was to be considered a fiction, "such a fiction was permitted in respect of rabbinical prohibi-

11. N. 8 above.
12. Nn. 24, 37 below.
13. Concerning the nature of the factory involved, see below. The location of the case is not mentioned in the responsum, but R. Solomon mentions it in *Ha-Elef Lecha Shelomoh* 127. The term "town" refers to Rawa Ruska. See *Pinkas ha-Kehilot: Poland* (Jerusalem, 1980), 2:498–499.
14. *Sefer ha-Hayyim* 30b.
15. Ibid.
16. Ibid., 31a.

tions." Third, contracting is forbidden in connection with the house of a Jew because of the suspicions that might arise; but in the case "of many individuals there are no suspicions"; since the factories were owned in partnership, the prohibition was invalidated.[17]

The scholar who defended the permissive ruling in the town of Rawena considered the sale to the Gentile secondary to the two other factors. R. Solomon disagreed. He was not satisfied with the two permissive considerations raised by his questioner, although he nevertheless considered the sale justifiable, but paradoxically so. Since the matter involved the fear that it would be misinterpreted, it all depended on whether the passerby had any reason to suspect that the Jew was employing the non-Jew in an illegitimate way. In an earlier time, when it was not customary to permit such an arrangement by means of the sale, the Jew would have been suspected of having employed the Gentiles on a daily basis. Now, with the bill of sale common, everyone knew that there was a permissible method and no one would think that the Jew had acted contrary to the rule: "Rather than enjoy it in a prohibited fashion, one would achieve it in a permitted way."[18] The very enactment of the permissive ruling thus created the basis for the ruling itself, reasoning that could be accepted only by someone who failed to aspire to restoring religious life according to the pattern that could be reconstructed on the basis of the ancient sources. He obviously considered the communal conditions under which he lived a sufficient guarantee of Sabbath observance.

R. Solomon Kluger's reliance upon the community guarantee of Sabbath observance was expressed in yet another halakhic argument. In their fears of misinterpretation of appearances, halakhic authorities had taken into consideration visitors as well.[19] These guests, unaware of the local permissive customs, might suspect the owner of the factory of employing Gentiles on a daily basis. R. Solomon invalidates this fear:

17. Ibid., 30b.
18. Ibid., 31a. The expression, "rather than enjoy it while it is prohibited, etc.," is not to be found in R. Solomon's writings, but R. Abraham Teomim (n. 8 above) uses it.
19. The matter is adduced in the Beit Yosef 244 as an Ashkenazic responsum, its source actually being in the writings of R. Meir of Rothenburg (Pesakim, ed. Kahana, 193), and the Noda bi-Yehudah discusses the subject (Orah Hayyim 12, 1st ed.). See chap. 8, n. 13.

"For the visitor certainly knows that if this were a case of Sabbath dese-
cretion, the townsmen would surely have discerned it. Thus even if the
owner is suspected of desecrating the Sabbath, all the other people of
the town are certainly not suspected of it."[20] As there is communal
supervision of Sabbath observance, it may be assumed that anything
done in public is done with permission.

The establishment of factories is one of the signs of the change that
took place in the economic life of the Jews of Galicia after the Austrian
annexation. It involved a shift in the center of gravity from the coun-
tryside to the towns.[21] The extra publicity accompanying urban activity
was perhaps the reason it became impossible to ignore deviations from
halakhah: Problems of Sabbath observance were thus brought before the
recognized halakhic authorities. And so either the unofficial permissive
ruling concerning the bill of sale was approved in this way or it was
created under pressure of circumstances. At any rate, once the permissive ruling was confirmed, it was applied as well to leasing activities
and similar enterprises, and R. Solomon Kluger writes that if "there was
a person owning a distillery or the like and I could see that it was necessary for his livelihood . . . I would allow him to write out a bill of sale
in ways valid according to the insight vouchsafed to me by the Almighty."[22] He was not the only notable halakhic authority to approve
of this permissive ruling. He showed his reply to the people of Rawena
to R. Ephraim Zalman Margolioth and Rabbi Meir Apta, who approved
of it.[23] There is certainly no doubt that the permissive ruling regarding
a bill of sale was already common before the revolutionary year of 1848
and that it was already known in Hungary. The Hatam Sofer replied in
1835 to the rabbi of the community of Egerszeg in connection with "the
regulations concerning a Jew selling to a Gentile to avoid the prohibitions of leaven and of work on the Sabbath"; and whereas concerning
the leaven he confirmed the permissive ruling, he rejected with both
emphasis and pathos the "fictitious sale" in respect of both shops and

20. *Sefer ha-Hayyim* 31a.
21. For the changes in the lives of Galician Jewry following the area's annexation
to Austria, see Filip Friedmann, *Die galizischen Juden im Kampfe um ihre Gleich-
berechtigung (1848–1868)* (Frankfurt am Main, 1929); A. J. Brawer, *Galicia and Its
Jews* (in Hebrew) (Jerusalem, 1965), pts. 1, 2.
22. *U-Vaharta ba-Hayyim* 42b–43a.
23. *Ha-Elef Lecha Shelomoh* 127.

fields in connection with the Sabbath, concluding with the statement that "anyone approving of it gave his approval erroneously"[24]—which means that the subject under discussion was an actual case and that a certain halakhic authority had made use of the permissive bill-of-sale ruling.

In Galicia itself, R. Solomon Drimer, the rabbi of Skole, writes toward the end of the 1830s that the landlords of his community wanted to write a bill of sale for a distillery of brandy.[25] According to his narrative, he was inclined to give in to their demand because of the "new decrees concerning the excise," a raising of taxes by the government that made it difficult for the distillers to stop working on the Sabbath. It seems likely that the landlords of Skole, having heard that some rabbis relied on the convenience of a bill of sale, asked that their own rabbi join them. As we have intimated, he tended to rule permissively but felt it necessary to consult his former master, R. Abraham David Wahrmann (the compiler of *Daat Kedoshim*), the rabbi of Buczacz. This great halakhic authority and hasidic master replied "that he preferred not to rule on this matter, neither permissively nor strictly"; and this was what his disciple did finally, as well. He replied to those who had appealed to him that he did not want to deal with the matter but that "if they approach another rabbi who writes out for them the formula of a bill of sale, I will not protest; this is what they did, traveling to a rabbi living nearby who wrote for them the formula of a bill of sale." This attitude of "do nothing" but not protesting either was maintained by R. Drimer ten years after the death of his master, the author of *Daat Kedoshim*, who passed away in the fall of 1840, when the change in the status of the Jews following the revolution of 1848–1849 placed the question of work permits on the Sabbath squarely on the agenda of the greatest halakhic experts of the day.

The shock waves generated by the revolution overturned many of the foundations of the ancien régime and also uprooted the set of decrees

24. *Hatam Sofer, Orah Hayyim* 113. The *Hatam Sofer* does not mention a bill of sale explicitly, but the comparison with the sale of leaven indicates that this was the case.

25. The story is included in a responsum composed by R. Solomon Drimer in *Responsa Beit Shelomoh* (Lvov, 1855), 36 (24a). The responsum is dated Tevet 5611 (January 1851). On it and on R. Abraham David Wahrmann, see *Entsiklopedia Ligedolei Galicia*, ed. M. Wunder (Jerusalem, 1982).

that had delimited the areas of Jewish activity. The emancipation that had been promised during the upheaval was abrogated when the revolution was suppressed. Nevertheless, most of the limitations affecting the integration of the Jews into the economy disappeared. This change was felt especially in connection with the leasing of land. Until then Jews had access to leasing only by circumventing the laws of the land; from then on this became legitimate and common.[26]

Echoes of the change that took place can be heard in contemporary halakhic rulings. R. Abraham Teomin relates in 1856: "When the law was promulgated by the Kaiser permitting Jews to acquire villages, and the number who purchased villages for themselves increased, I was asked by the landlord, Simeon Bische of Brody, and by many others . . . what they should do on Sabbaths and festivals."[27] The opening remarks of R. Hayyim of Zanz to his study of the subject is similar: "Not long ago, when the Jews were allowed to live wherever they wanted, the renters and buyers of estates became numerous."[28] This situation eventually convinced the writer to approve of the bill of sale, as we shall yet see.

R. Solomon Kluger distinguishes between the prerevolutionary period, when the people who sought permissive rulings were "a very small minority," and the postrevolutionary period, when many people engaged in leasing, even "those who had no need of it," that is, whose livelihood was secure without it.[29] He mentions three requests made of him during the first two years after the revolution, one of them from the community of Zolkiew, another from Czortkow, and the third, to which he was replying, from "Rabbi Shalom ben Israel of Ruzhyn."[30] Although he was

---

26. See Friedmann, *Die galizischen Juden*, p. 8. Purchasing land was not permitted (ibid., pp. 79–84), but the empirical rules vacillated as did their interpretation, and there were also ways of circumventing them. At any rate, in the internal sources we shall deal with below leasing and purchasing are mentioned together.

27. *Hesed le-Avraham* 21. A similarly worded question was also put to R. Aaron Moshe Taubes, the author of *Toafot Reem* (Zholkva, 1850): "Concerning the question you sent me in the name of the householders of the state of the kaiser . . . of what they should do in the villages they purchased under their name, in accordance with the emperor's permission"—he ruled permissively without a bill of sale.

28. Hayyim Zanz (Halberstam), *Divrei Hayyim* (Lvov, 1875), 1:7. For the date and content of the responsum, see nn. 57ff. below.

29. *U-Vaharta ba-Hayyim* (n. 2 above).

30. Ibid.

accustomed to permissive rulings of this kind, he rejected the first two, as well as the request made by Rabbi Shalom Joseph (his full name). In his responsum to the latter, he explained his change of mind, even rebuking him and his father for even asking.

R. Solomon did nothing to hide the fact that his rejection was not related to the pure halakhic aspects of the case. The numerous cases of people making their living in this new way, which for other halakhic authorities was considered good reason to pursue a permissive ruling, as we shall see below, persuaded R. Solomon to rule strictly, for "Sabbath desecration has, due to our many sins, become commonplace to such a degree as to make the Sabbath indistinguishable from weekdays. . . . Moreover, how terrible it will be if work ceases on their day of rest, Sunday, and God's holy day, the Sabbath, is desecrated and treated as a weekday."[31] His objection stemmed mainly from his reservations concerning the political factor, the equal rights granted the Jews, which was responsible for the situation that had developed. The emancipation was a curse, an act of Satan, a call "for the Jews to be like the Gentiles" contrary to their destiny, "for the Jews have to be separate . . . and not be counted together with the Gentiles, so that a single law applies to both."[32] A person who exploits the law of emancipation for his own benefit by purchasing an estate in a land not his own is like a person agreeing to the idea that the same emancipation invalidates the uniqueness of the Jews. Purchasing a home outside the Land of Israel was permitted only because of necessity. "But buying additional villages and fields and vineyards and thereby violating the injunctions of the sages has never been countenanced," anyone acting in such a way being almost as if he had despaired of redemption. R. Israel of Ruzhyn, a very influential authority with his hasidic followers, was the right person to protest: "And now, not only have you not protested; on the contrary, you have assisted many . . . to take part in that evil decree."[33]

When R. Solomon rejected the permissive bill-of-sale ruling for reasons that may be termed historical or religio-national, he rediscovered its halakhic faults. Formerly, in his responsum to the community of Rawena, he claimed that "there was in this sale no fear of fictitious-

31. Ibid., 43a.
32. Ibid.
33. Ibid., 43b.

ness,"[34] whereas now he accepted the opinion of those who ruled strictly, "that in matters of biblical prohibitions a bill of sale is of no help because it is fictitious."[35] Previously he discounted the fear of the act being misinterpreted on the grounds that everyone was aware of the existence of a way to obtain a permissive ruling by means of a sale.[36] Now, thirty years later, after this permissive ruling had undoubtedly spread far and wide, he says, "On the Sabbath such a custom is unknown (in contrast to the sale of leaven on Passover). . . . And so ruling permissively here must not become customary, for it is an affront to the Sabbath."[37] He writes impassionedly to the son of the hasidic leader who had asked him: "Please believe me, after all the strained permissive rulings handed down in this matter, it is better to eat meat of doubtful fitness . . . than to hold by these permissive rulings."[38] He ends his responsum saying: "Let the matter be forgotten and not even spoken of."[39]

R. Solomon's wish, however, was not fulfilled. The permissive ruling at issue was not forgotten. If he cast suspicion on it, others held by it, and it seems likely that his own opposition was not long lasting. This opposition had developed at the very end of the revolution,[40] out of fear of the threat it posed to traditional values. Once everything had settled down and the world had returned to its earlier habits, his fears settled, too, and once again he ruled permissively as he had done in earlier days. He lived for twenty years after the revolution. The conditions that held following the revolution undoubtedly necessitated such permissive rul-

34. *Sefer ha-Hayyim* 31a.
35. *U-Vaharta ba-Hayyim* 43a. R. Solomon rules in a number of his responsa according to this opinion. *Ha-Elef Lecha Shelomoh* 99, 100, 102, 104, 105; *U-Vaharta ba-Hayyim* 69, 72. By contrast, he rules permissively in ibid., 65, 75, 76. The responsa are undated, but it is likely that the contradictions are a function of time. See below in the text.
36. See n. 18 above.
37. *U-Vaharta ba-Hayyim* 4a. He knows that this ruling contradicts his first one and writes: "Though in *Sefer ha-Hayyim* we ruled to make a distinction in this; at any rate this must not be relied on where the problem is acute and the Sabbath is regarded lightly."
38. Ibid., 43a.
39. Ibid., 44a. According to R. Solomon he was not the only one to condemn what the Ruzhyn family did, "but they do not dare speak out" (ibid., 44b).
40. His responsum to the Ruzhyn family is undated but was given in R. Israel's lifetime: He died in Heshvan 1851; thus the responsum was written before that year.

ings: Not only had the number of people seeking such a ruling multiplied, but also the number of authoritative halakhic experts confirming it grew, like R. Abraham Teomim, who replied to the question posed by the landlord of Brody, as we have already seen.

We do not know why the landowner of Brody took his request for a permissive ruling to R. Abraham of Buczacz rather than to R. Solomon Kluger of his own town. At any rate, R. Abraham did not refrain from answering him; neither did he refer him to the famed local halakhic authority (although R. Solomon was not the chief rabbi of the place, his appointment being to the position of "preacher"). He also ignored the discussion of this subject to be found in R. Solomon's *Sefer ha-Hayyim*, even though the basis of his permissive ruling was not very different from that of his predecessor. R. Abraham's point of departure was that "the landowners who have acquired the estates . . . should they cease work and not cultivate their fields on Sabbaths and festivals even by means of Gentiles, they will suffer great loss."[41] His permissive ruling is complex: Fields are to be hired out and the animals to be sold. It is clear that both the hiring out and the sale are mere formalities, thus matching the opinion of authorities who ruled that such fictions are permissible even with such biblical prohibitions as having one's animal cease work on the Sabbath.[42] R. Abraham solves the problem of suspicion and appearances by means of fine distinctions rooted in the new situation that has developed: "Now that the Jews have been permitted to buy villages, they will have to rent them out to Gentiles because of the loss involved in preventing work from being done on the Sabbath. This renting out will be a very common thing and so it will become a matter of public knowledge that the work is being performed in a permitted fashion."[43] R. Solomon Kluger claimed in his responsum in *Sefer ha-Hayyim* that since the permissive bill-of-sale ruling had become common in recent generations, prevalent conditions had changed from what they had been in the days of the Talmud and early halakhic authorities, and the fear of misinterpretation by an observer was reduced. R. Abraham Teomim relied upon conditions yet to come about to supply the grounds for his permissive ruling: "Especially after this permissive

41. *Hesed le-Avraham* 21 (19a).
42. Ibid., at the end of the responsum.
43. Ibid., 19a.

ruling becomes known by virtue of all the purchasers of villages who will act accordingly, it will become well known amongst the Jews that this matter was done in a permitted fashion."[44]

The approval of any respected halakhic authority would further spread this ruling, which involved a vital economic interest. However, it could achieve a secure position for itself only through the authority of a central figure. And this occurred when R. Hayyim of Zanz, who bore the title *Admor* (hasidic leader) and was a prominent halakhic authority, gave his approval—though not without hesitation. He describes this hesitation in his "responsum concerning the leasing or purchasing of estates by a Gentile on the Sabbath in order to do work on them,"[45] at the beginning of which he testifies: "You, my friend, must realize that I have never even considered ruling permissively against the *Shulhan Arukh* and the Talmud, which forbid [certain things] because of the possibility of misinterpretation."[46] If early authorities ruled permissively in connection with tax collecting, farming, and minting money, "they are allowed to rule permissively . . . not we small figures . . . and so I have never ruled permissively for anyone to make use of a bill of sale."[47] This proves that requests had reached him at an early stage, that is, before the wholesale purchase of estates following the revolution that led him to change his mind. He describes the flow of events, something he repeats in yet another responsum.[48] He realized that he remained isolated in his opposition: "I have heard that in the province of Lvov the great scholars of the generation permitted it. And this is the way people act in all our communities."[49]

The permissive ruling was based on a bill of sale. And although he had seen such a document prepared by two scholars, R. Mordecai Zeev

44. Ibid.
45. *Divrei Hayyim* 1:7.
46. Ibid.
47. Ibid.
48. *Divrei Hayyim* 2, *Orah Hayyim* 22. This responsum is dated winter 1861. For the date of the first one, see below. The descriptions in the two responsa are mutually supplementary.
49. *Divrei Hayyim* 1. It is unclear who "the great scholars of the generation" are. When the responsum was written (see below) there was no chief rabbi in Lvov. Halakhic rulings were entrusted to R. Simhah Nathan Ellinberg, who was a *moreh tsedek* (an assistant rabbi). R. Joseph Saul Nathanson was appointed head of the rabbinic court only in 1859; see Solomon Buber, *Anshei Shem* (Cracow, 1895), 98.

Ettinger and R. Joseph Saul ha-Levi Nathanson,[50] he had doubts about the formulation of the document. The public impression was that the prohibition had been overridden, thus giving rise to many cases of "public Sabbath desecration, some of which occurred because the bill of sale was written improperly by unqualified people."[51] This means that some people permitted themselves to carry on even without a bill of sale, whereas others relied upon documents that could not withstand critical review. In light of this situation, he too ruled permissively on the basis of the examples provided by early authorities' rulings in connection with taxes and coinage, on condition that the bill of sale be worded in such a way as to remove all doubts regarding its validity. He composed such a document and gave it to the person who had appealed to him for a permissive ruling.[52]

In joining those who ruled permissively, he wrote, "I decided to clarify the matter according to the Talmud and early authorities."[53] He thus admitted that at first the permissive ruling seemed to him merely an emergency measure, and that only ex post facto did he make it a halakhic ruling grounded in the sources—an admission almost unprecedented in the writings of halakhic authorities. His justification for this was itself original. R. Hayyim remained firm in his initial belief that there was a prohibition based on the likelihood of misinterpretation in connection with a sale, just as there was in connection with renting or contracting. Yet this prohibition is to be ignored according to the rule (adduced in *Shabbat* 4a) that it is better for a person to commit a trivial transgression if this saves him from committing a more serious one.[54] A second support is found in the rule, "Similarly he is compelled to release his maidservant to prevent her from being treated disgracefully"[55] (*Gittin* 31b), "for where violations are common, it is permitted to commit a trivial transgression so as not to commit a serious

50. "I learned of a permissive ruling from *Mefarshei Yam*" (see *Divrei Hayyim*), i.e., from the compilers of the work of that name, the commentary on the treatise *Yam ha-Talmud*, compiled by R. Joshua Heschel Orenstein (Lvov, 1825). R. Joseph Saul Nathanson did approve (in 1856) of the permissive ruling based on a bill of sale (*Shoel u-Meshiv* 2:31).
51. *Divrei Hayyim* 2, *Orah Hayyim* 22.
52. The wording of the document is given at the end of the responsum (1:7).
53. Ibid.
54. Ibid., and 2:22.
55. Ibid., 2, and in a similar wording already in pt. 1.

one."[56] In other words, in this case too it is permitted to ignore the prohibition prompted by fear of misinterpretation rather than become involved in actual Sabbath desecration.

The first responsum, which contains this important testimony regarding the development of his permissive ruling and that of others, is undated. In yet another responsum, however, dated 1856, R. Hayyim already mentions the document he composed.[57] Hence, his change of mind took place around the time of the revolution of 1848–1849, a date fitting the description of the circumstances: Jews were permitted to settle anywhere and they took economic advantage of the new political situation. The second responsum, in which the rabbi repeats his description of the situation, is dated 1861, and it is obvious that in the meantime this permissive ruling had taken root in the Jewish community. From this time on, there really was no longer any fear of misinterpretation, "for now it is known to every Jew that this is permitted."[58] There was no longer any reason to suspect that the matter had been performed in violation of halakhah—reasoning already adduced by R. Solomon Kluger and R. Abraham Teomim.

Yet, R. Hayyim never denied his conviction that his permissive ruling and those given by others were nothing more than the result of compromise with the pressures exerted by prevalent conditions. He called his own permissive ruling "a permissive ruling clear to everyone,"[59] meaning that his bill of sale was acceptable according to all schools of opinion. But formal justification was one thing and a sense of moral embarrassment was another. He uttered words of condemnation of all the permissive rulings, including his own: "You, a learned rabbi, are to know that in my opinion all these permissive rulings are problematic, since they are mere verbal arguments. One feels that they are not right, for practically everyone will know and say that the Jew works on the Sabbath by the way of his representatives."[60] Despite the evidence he adduced from the sources, his permissive ruling was never

56. Ibid.
57. Ibid., 1:5.
58. Ibid., 2:22.
59. Ibid., 2:29. In the responsum (2:22), he calls it "a correct wording according to all authorities."
60. Ibid., 2:22. The context proves that the attributes refer to his permissive ruling as well.

any more than an emergency measure: "I relied on the verse, 'The time has come to act for God; it is time to violate Your Torah.'"[61] His ruling is therefore not a general decision upon which anyone can depend. "I ruled permissively for many people owning estates, but for a God-fearing person who may be assumed to be ready to accept whatever he is told I forbid work on the estate during the Sabbath by means of a bill of sale"[62]—a distinction that was certainly very difficult to maintain. The rabbi once visited the home of one of his followers, "the illustrious and learned R. Herzl Bernstein of famed descent,"[63] and heard how this landowner, acted "in his enterprises by selling to a Gentile on the Sabbath." The rabbi cast doubt upon this behavior and immediately upon arriving at his house told him that it would be better for him to follow the permissive ruling of the bill of sale he would give him.[64]

It really is difficult to imagine that the rabbi's permissive ruling was limited to "simple people" and that his own disciples were not allowed to rely on it. R. Hayyim's influence affected the community of his followers in the provinces of Hungary in close proximity to Galicia, and his bill of sale reached them. He was at first willing to give it to anyone requesting it of him,[65] but here its use was challenged, and this led him to react defensively in what amounted to a retreat. His responsa to Hungary were sent to two rabbis. One was Rabbi Hayyim Meir Zeev Hartmann[66] of the community of Samloya in Transylvania, and the other was anonymous.[67] In his earlier responsum, written in 1867, he repeats in brief the basis of his permissive ruling and the circumstances of its derivation in light of the complaints made by Rabbi Hartmann, who had expressed doubts. R. Hayyim concludes: "Of what use are your arguments? The ruling is clear and has been approved by a number of halakhic authorities of this land. However, if the rabbinic authorities

---

61. Ibid.
62. Ibid. Also 1:7. He concludes: "Wherever he is unlikely to violate a serious prohibition, we must not rule permissively, which is how I conduct myself here."
63. Ibid., 1:5.
64. Ibid.
65. Ibid., 2:30. He writes: "For a rabbi among my adherents asked me for a copy of the bill of sale, and I sent it to him."
66. Ibid., 2:29. The name of the rabbi is not mentioned, but he served in Samloya and died shortly after. See *Shem ha-Gedolim me-Erets Hagar* (Jerusalem, 1959), sec. 8, par. 28 (34a).
67. Ibid., 30.

of Hungary see reason to be cautious and fear a scandal, please warn the people of your region in my name not to rely on my ruling, because it is limited to its own place and time. . . . I have written in this spirit to another area in Hungary as well."[68] Hence this was not the first time he had heard of reservations expressed by halakhic authorities in Hungary. He wanted to put an end to argument and requested "that he refrain from troubling him with this matter again, for he should not hope for a reply"[69]—a dissonant phrase that does not testify to the writer's calm and detached attitude on the subject under discussion.

Now taught by experience, R. Hayyim hesitated to send the anonymous rabbi the bill of sale he had requested. The questioner himself had apparently expressed his fear that nonobservant Jews would mock the permissive bill-of-sale ruling and disparage it as legal fiction. R. Hayyim replies to this challenge incisively: "In this respect, we have learned 'do not be overly righteous'; we shall not rule more strictly than our predecessors who allowed such legal fictions . . . and did not worry about possible mockery on the part of contemporary nonbelievers [literally Sadducees], for why need we take into account the laughter of the wicked? They will perish and we shall act in accordance with the Torah."[70] The "wicked," that is, Maskilim, disparage the laws of the Talmud that permit the use of legal fictions. If contemporary scholars were to refrain from using such fictions because of the criticism voiced by the Maskilim, they would seem to be "cooperating with the wicked. . . . But we will not retreat from the customs of our forefathers."[71]

In the next chapter we shall describe the situation of Hungarian Jewry, typified in this period by the deep split between the Jews who had abandoned their traditional way of life and those who continued to adhere to it. The fact that some Jews challenged the validity and legitimacy of tradition deterred those faithful to the tradition from deviating from its patterns, even under formal halakhic auspices. The orthodox Jews of Galicia, too, were engaged in a struggle with the innovators in the circles of the Maskilim and the economic upper class. These in-

68. Ibid., 29.
69. Ibid., at the end of the responsum.
70. Ibid., 30.
71. Ibid. Nevertheless, at the end of the responsum he writes: "And if you want a copy of the bill of sale, let me know and I will have it copied."

novators wanted to attract the Jewish community to rational patterns of behavior and ways of thought, which were considered a precondition for saving the masses from idleness and ignorance. In their opinion, or at least according to their declared programs, their goal was not conditional upon abandoning the principles of Jewish religion. Community life in all its facets, including that of Maskilim and would-be reformers, carried on, at least in public, the observance of sanctified religious customs, especially the Sabbath and festival days.[72]

Warnings and complaints of Sabbath desecration in connection with matters of the Sabbath Gentile had been voiced even in the periods of absolute traditional predominance. The tension existing between the principled demands of halakhah and their actual practice was especially noticeable in this area. Now, with the introduction of the new forms of livelihood, these complaints became more frequent and echoed throughout the deliberations of the halakhic authorities considering the problem. The prevalence of Sabbath desecration according to halakhic definition led R. Hayyim to acquiesce in the permissive bill-of-sale ruling, and R. Solomon Kluger, who replied to a question concerning an ironing workshop and permitted its Sabbath operation by the same means, concluded his responsum with the following sentence: "The permissive ruling I have just written down is clear and beyond all doubt I wish seeing it as a permit by the purchasers of villages and towns or by their renters who desecrate the Sabbath in public in matters of biblical prohibition without anybody objecting."[73] This means he would approve of the landowners using this bill-of-sale ruling—in direct contrast to the stand he had taken in his reply to the household of the rabbi of Ruzhyn. This responsum is undated, but it seems to be late, written at the time that the leasing and buying of estates was commonplace. It is, at any rate, certain that R. Solomon began once again to rely on the bill of sale. This is demonstrated by his responsum to Rabbi Baruch Meir Frisch, the rabbi of Czortkow, who wrote him "about the lessors of villages who are forced to cultivate the land by means of Gentiles, with the animals and other requirements of the agriculture belonging to the Jews."[74] The questioner adds "that it is impossible to write out a bill

---

72. See Raphael Mahler, *Ha-Hasidut veha-Haskalah* (Merhavia, 1961), chap. 2, and esp. 57–69.
73. *U-Vaharta ba-Hayyim* 65 (45a).
74. Ibid., 76.

of sale for all of it because each time they sell the animals and buy others in their stead."[75] The bill of sale is thus considered a commonplace, an accepted permitted tool—a situation that prevailed only after the revolution. Not only does R. Solomon express no reservations concerning the use of the bill of sale, but he actually announces that the purchase of new animals need not hinder the transaction: "I formulated and wrote a number of bills of sale, and I did so in such a way that they would apply even to as yet nonexistent situations," that is, to animals yet to be purchased.[76]

This is not the only example of a lack of consistency in the stands adopted and the rulings handed down by R. Solomon. At one time, he condemns "those who brew beer in their breweries, which really implies a biblical prohibition, and it has scandalously become permitted on the Sabbath by means of a sale."[77] But from another responsum we learn that in his town there was "a large brewery, with a lot of work, and on each Sabbath they used to sell the brewery together with all the implements and all the grain to a Gentile by means of a bill of sale."[78] It so happened that on the festival of Rosh Hashanah they forgot to hand over the bill of sale and did not discover this fact until nightfall: "And to prevent the work means a great loss, and so I sought a way to permit this."[79] He sought and found a way, by means of a daring combination of various permissive rulings,[80] the weakness of which he was well aware. "Thus it seemed proper to look for a way to rule leniently where a great loss was involved. . . . This is why I allowed this, but no analogy should be drawn from this to other cases. And moreover I told them to undertake to give a certain sum to the poor"[81]—a way of punishing the

75. Ibid.
76. Ibid.
77. Ibid., 65 (44b).
78. Ibid., 66.
79. Ibid.
80. He relies on relinquishing his ownership of the plant, of all the work of the brewery. Brewing the beer is permitted by the Torah. And since "it is only a rabbinic ban, we can certainly say it is permitted by means of a Gentile." The Gentiles were hired to perform a certain job and so are considered working under contract according to one ruling (Maimonides), "and they work at their own initiative." As far as misinterpretation is concerned, "since they work every Sabbath and this is done by a bill of sale, anyone seeing them will assume it has been sold."
81. *U-Vaharta ba-Hayyim* 45b.

factory owner for forgetting to hand over the bill of sale, a device for which the rabbi had difficulty finding a halakhic reference[82]—and which actually serves as a kind of atonement, as shown by the end of his statement: "At any rate, it is fitting for him to undertake to give a certain amount to charity as punishment and atonement; perhaps this was not permissible, and may the good Lord grant atonement for me and save me from errors and show me wondrous aspects of his Torah."[83]

R. Solomon's inventive genius know almost no bounds, yet he refrained from exploiting it equally in every case.[84] It seems that the vacillations in his halakhic rulings are not to be attributed only to the characteristics of his nature and temperament.[85] The people who put their problems before him did not always expect a permissive ruling. Sometimes it was the rabbi of the town or local talmudic scholars who found fault with the behavior of the public in matters of Sabbath observance. They appealed to the great authority of the day for support in their struggle, and he provided it eagerly: "The question is about what the purchasers or renters of *paraffinatsia* [establishments for producing and selling liquor] should do on the Sabbath. Your excellency knows how correctly he protests both regarding the *goralnie* [distillation of spirits], which is a great source of public Sabbath desecration, and regarding agriculture, whatever work is being done . . . I hope he is obeyed."[86] In a similar vein he replies to Rabbi Schmelke of Sasov: "Concerning the religious zeal with which he battles the people of his town who all do business with the beams from which sawdust is made. . . . Your excellency did well to make an outcry so that all the people of his town, from the very greatest to the smallest, know that it is utterly forbidden."[87] He thus supported those who would rule strictly in mat-

---

82. He relies on R. Moses Isserles in *Orah Hayyim* 307:4, that when one hires a Gentile to transport one's goods, and the Gentile takes them from the owner's house, he deserves to be punished. R. Solomon makes this a precedent for anyone who has forgotten, and the halakhists ruled permissively because of a great loss. See ibid., 45b–46a.

83. Ibid.

84. For his inconsistency, see n. 35 above.

85. Saul Nathanson, in his debate with R. Solomon Kluger concerning the use of a machine for the baking of *matsot*, describes him as someone who hastens to collect opinions in support of his own and does so uncritically; see the pamphlet *Bittul Modaah* (Lvov, 1859).

86. *Ha-Elef Lecha Shelomoh* 128.

87. *U-Vaharta ba-Hayyim* 77.

ters in which he had ruled leniently when necessary. In the town of Pomorzani the local rabbi permitted the owner of a brandy distillery to continue work on festivals "by means of a bill of sale and by paying an inclusive price,"[88] but the owner of the plant broadened this permissive ruling with the rabbi's knowledge to include the Sabbath as well. Two talmudic scholars, however, questioned the validity of the ruling even as regards festivals, for their community knew of no such precedent. R. Solomon praises the questioners: "Let the matter subside so that no one will permit this from now on; the rabbi himself did not act correctly in permitting him to do so on festivals."[89]

Both the halakhic give-and-take and the comments made by R. Solomon Kluger and his colleagues reflect a situation typified by the lack of uniformity in community behavior in this area and the absence of a uniform response on the part of the halakhic authorities to what was transpiring. This lack of uniformity was not caused by dissident behavior of Jews rejecting halakhic discipline. The halakhic authorities quoted here did not justify their rulings by claiming fear of dissident conduct, as did the halakhic authorities of Germany and, as we shall yet see, those of Hungary. On the contrary, R. Hayyim of Zanz was seen to ignore intentionally the critical comments made by critics of the Maskilim.[90] The Sabbath, with its set patterns and central restrictions, was deeply rooted in the life and consciousness of the community, which leads us to believe that infractions of a marginal nature, such as the employment of Gentiles to serve Jews, could be repaired or even plastered over by virtue of halakhic inventiveness. The change in behavior resulted from the pressure of economic necessity; and its being cloaked in halakhic guise—selling the business in a manner derived from the example of the bill of sale for leaven—was neither proposed nor applied by rabbinic or other halakhic authorities. The innovative ruling was created in order to pacify the religious conscience of those who were forced into the change. The halakhic authorities fulfilled the function of ratifying the remedy by compelling it to accord with strict halakhic requirements.

This reaction of theirs was not the only possibility; they might also

88. Ibid., 69.
89. Ibid.
90. N. 71 above.

have overridden the innovation and uprooted it. The fact that they refrained from doing so testifies to the involvement of scholars in community life, which allowed for a fruitful mutual influence. Operative here was the ancient rule of "Go out and see what the people do" (*Berakhot* 45a), together with its rationalization, "If they are not prophets then they are at least the disciples of prophets" (*Pesahim* 66a). A condition of its functioning was that the community be considered a reliable partner in the shaping of halakhah. Such was the case perhaps for the last time in Jewish history before the widening of the gap that separated the behavior of a majority or even a minority of the community from halakhic requirements as formulated by its interpreters and champions.

11
Nineteenth-Century Russian and Hungarian Jewry

The advantage of the bill of sale over the other solutions to the problem of the Sabbath Gentile was its mobility, the ease with which it could be transferred from one place to another and from one matter to another. Instead of examining a case from different perspectives in order to arrive at a halakhic ruling based on the sources, a process that only genuine halakhic authorities were in general willing and able to do, here was a tool that could be wielded by any rabbi. He could now issue his ruling without taking personal responsibility but could instead rely on the formulator of the document (such as R. Hayyim Zanz, whose formula was circulated in his responsa, which were published in 1875)[1] or on accepted custom. Accordingly, the use of the bill of sale spread rapidly. R. Moses Teomim of Horodenka said about the time of the publication of R. Hayyim's book: "Go out and see what the people are doing—they write a bill of sale for every Sabbath enterprise carried out by Gentiles

---

1. See chap. 10, nn. 45ff. R. Hayyim Baruch, *Birkat Hayyim* (Lublin, 1896), 4; see "a bill of sale said to have been written by the rabbi of Ciechanow," i.e., R. Abraham ben Raphael Landau, who died in 1875. This case came up in his lifetime.

by means of a fictitious sale."² (He adds that this is the custom with mourning as well, when the mourner is not allowed to work. "When his relative is on his deathbed, he sells his factory to someone else, so that the ban on work will not apply to it.) While this testimony might be interpreted as referring solely to the provinces of Galicia, other sources reveal that this solution was accepted at an early date in Russian communities as well.

Russia lagged behind the western lands, including Austria, which controlled Galicia, not only in granting civil rights to Jews but also in broadening the basis of their economic existence. At any rate, it was impossible to keep the situation static over a long period. Even czarist Russia was propelled along the road to political reform by economic pressures and social change, such as the liberation of the peasants in 1861. Two years earlier, rich Jews had been permitted to settle beyond the Pale of Jewish settlement and to take part in the economic development and industrialization of the state.³ Jewish capitalists and investors were now engaged in enterprises beyond the limits of the economic activity for which there were religiously acceptable norms of conduct, such as for the observance of the Sabbath and Jewish holidays. It is true that some of the more enterprising Jews, especially among those who settled outside the Pale, belonged to those who sought new religious forms and ignored the restrictions imposed by Jewish tradition. At any rate, the new economic involvement affected all sectors of the Jewish community, most of whom considered themselves bound by Jewish religious law as interpreted by its traditional representatives. Thus, questions stemming from Jewish ownership of factories operating on the Sabbath were also brought before acknowledged halakhic authorities— the same sort of questions that had been considered by the rabbis of Galicia one generation earlier.

2. Moses Teomim, *Orian Telitai* (Lvov, 1880), 160 (at the end of the responsum). He means to emphasize, in contrast to the opinion of others, that wherever people rely on a fictitious sale, a handshake is insufficient but rather a bill of sale is required. In general, this means that using a bill of sale is a current custom. R. Joshua Horowitz, (author of *Ateret Yehoshua* [Cracow, 1931], 30) writes to someone who heard that he did not rely on a bill of sale: "It was not the law that forbade it, for the sages of recent generations have ruled to permit it, and who can contradict their ruling?"

3. See Bernhard D. Weinryb, *Neueste Wirtschaftsgeschichte der Juden in Russland und Polen*, 2d ed. (Hildesheim, 1972), 1–24.

If the purchase and leasing of estates became a common phenomenon in Galicia toward the end of the 1848 revolution, this phenomenon
repeated itself in Russia after the liberation of the peasants. At that time
many of the aristocracy could barely maintain their estates, and, consequently, Jewish capitalists were permitted to buy or rent them. The
description written by R. Aryeh Leibush Bolekhover, author of *Shem
Aryeh* and the rabbi of Zaslav since the 1860s, matches the situation
referred to by R. Solomon Kluger and R. Hayyim of Zanz perfectly:

> I have given serious consideration to matters of Sabbath observance
> that arise wherever the government has given the Jews permission
> to rent fields and gardens and to cultivate them by means of non-
> Jewish workers known as "possessions" and wherever permission
> has been given to purchase land and cultivate it. For many of our
> people have been hiring these "possessions" from their owners and
> plowing, sowing, harvesting, and sifting. These tasks are performed
> by non-Jews who refrain from work on Sundays. Not laboring on
> Sabbaths as well creates considerable hardship. . . . Therefore they
> request permission to allow this, in whatever way such a permissive
> ruling can be given according to the regulations of our holy
> Torah. . . . The truth is that some of them are God-fearing in their
> hearts and would avoid doing any work on the Sabbath, but many
> say that this is a decree they cannot accept under any circum-
> stances. . . . I have also been asked about this by certain rabbis, and
> this is my opinion in this matter.[4]

However, before the rabbi presents his solution he tells of what
others have done: "Several halakhic authorities write bills of sale for
an entire year or the entire period for these 'possessions' that they sell
to a non-Jew, and they rent him the entire business."[5] The writer condemns this procedure as "a very ugly thing and an outright lie, viewed
as a mockery by everyone . . . far worse than anything else prohibited
by the sages because of outward appearances."[6] The fact that such an
arrangement had won the approval of R. Hayyim of Zanz had not yet
become publicly known: His book *Divrei Hayyim* was to appear two
years after the printing of *Shem Aryeh*. But R. Abraham Teomim's book
Hesed le-Avraham was certainly known to R. Aryeh Leibush. It is also

---

4. Aryeh Leibush Bolekhover, *Shem Aryeh* (Vilna, 1873), 1:2.
5. Ibid., 2b.
6. Ibid.

possible that Teomim's perspective was the basis for those rabbis who made use of the bill of sale after him. At any rate, Rabbi Leibush challenged this ruling and completely dissociated himself from it.

He proposed an alternative method of ruling permissively, based essentially on making the non-Jew a partner in the purchased or hired estate and dividing the income between the two in such a way that the work done on the Sabbath would belong to the Gentile and that of another day of the week to the Jew exclusively. The problem was that such an arrangement was mentioned in halakhic sources as the basis for a permissive ruling only when the field was received by the already constituted partnership, with the balancing of the Sabbath by some other day being the basis for the partnership itself. In this case, however, the Jew first buys or hires the estate on his own and then wants to make the non-Jew his partner under the aforesaid condition, a step unprecedented in the halakhic sources. To circumvent this difficulty, R. Aryeh Leibush proposed that the buyer or renter sell the estate—a purely formal sale, of course—to another Jew and then buy it back from him, this time in partnership with the non-Jew, the partnership, like the sale, being purely formal and fictitious. "Such a thing is easy to do,"[7] as the rabbi put it. Such an arrangement was certainly not beyond the capability of a person desirous of meeting halakhic requirements while actually circumventing them. It is however difficult to understand why R. Aryeh Leibush viewed this arrangement as less offensive and less a mockery than the use of the bill of sale. At any rate, his protest against the bill of sale did not prevent its spread, so that at the end of the century R. Jehiel Michal Epstein, the compiler of Arukh ha-Shulhan, could grant the custom validity, testimony to its firm position in the community. The following is the ruling of Arukh ha-Shulhan in the section concluding the discussion of employing a non-Jew under a contractual arrangement and so on:

> Now in cases where the only possibility is to employ workers on a daily basis, like in the brandy and beer distilleries and where Jews run post offices for the government or employ horses . . . and especially those who have factories, the only solution is to sell the entire business to a non-Jew by means of a halakhically binding sale. . . . This is now the accepted custom in all countries: to write

---

7. Ibid., 3a.

out bills of sale for all land-leasing deals that cannot be done by contracting. . . . Everyone should make out such a bill of sale with the help of his community rabbi, who will tell him how to do it.[8]

This evidence of the spread of this custom is valid for those countries of eastern Europe familiar to Rabbi Epstein, who was one of the luminaries of Lithuanian Jewry, with the exception of Hungary, which in the nineteenth century had been separated to a large extent from the mainstream of Jewry, even within the rabbinic world. Of course, Hungarian Jewry did not escape the need to grapple with the new problems including those of Sabbath observance. However, its reaction to these problems was unique, as we have already seen in connection with the refusal of R. Hayyim Zanz's disciples to accept their rabbi's permissive ruling unconditionally.

We may observe parallels between halakhic problems that engaged rabbinic authorities of other countries and those of Hungary from the questions brought before the primary authority of Hungarian Jewry, R. Moses Sofer of Pressburg, known as the Hatam Sofer. He was asked about "a Jew who had leased from a landlord a number of villages together with their fields. The landlord also rented to him for his purposes a number of Gentile villagers to do the work of the Jew, both indoors and in the fields, whatever was required. Similarly, the landlord leased him beasts of burden to work the fields, with the Jew taking responsibility for the animals. . . . What is to be done on the Sabbath?"[9] The prevailing conditions were semifeudal. The landlord leased the fields to the Jew, together with the vassals and animals to cultivate them. From the continuation of the responsum it seems that the Jewish renter wanted to hand the fields over to a Gentile, whether in actuality or formally is unclear, so as to circumvent the ban on doing work on the Sabbath. Similarly, a question arose concerning one "who had rented a distillery from the landlord and had a Gentile worker hired out to him for a year."[10] This, too, reflects the continuation of the premodern economic order. Broad sectors of Hungarian Jewry were still at this time

8. Jehiel Michal Epstein, *Arukh ha-Shulhan* to *Orah Hayyim* (Pietrokov, 1903–1907), *Hilkhot Shabbat* 244:24.
9. Moses Sofer, *Hatam Sofer, Orah Hayyim* (Pressburg, 1855), 57. The responsum is not dated.
10. Ibid., 59.

making their living from the economic activity carried out under the auspices of the magnates on whose land they lived. The Hatam Sofer stated what he "used to say to sellers of brandy," who were obligated to sell their product on the Sabbath. His advice was the same as that of the authorities who enacted the regulations in Poland: "They are to sell everything on Friday to their Gentile foremen to such and such an extent . . . and whatever is left over is to be returned to the Jew who will buy it back from the Gentile after the Sabbath."[11]

The Hatam Sofer, however, also dealt with problems resulting from the acceptance of franchises from the authorities, like the questions already dealt with by the Noda bi-Yehudah:[12] "tobacco salesmen" trying to find a halakhic way to sell their merchandise by means of a Gentile on the Sabbath[13] and "a Jew who bought the rights to the sale of salt, so that no one could sell salt without his involvement," the stipulation being that "the shop may not be closed at any time."[14] Another case concerned a Jew who "leased the sale of salt from the authorities for a period of three years"[15] and desired to have his Gentile partner permitted to do the selling on the Sabbath. The Jews who actually encountered these problems in practice sought to resolve them with the help of the local halakhic authorities. And the problems came before the Hatam Sofer by means of the intermediaries: either the local rabbinic authorities or the lay communal leaders who considered themselves subject to halakhic authority. During the last decade of his life, at least— he died in 1839—he was informed of attempts to violate traditional Sabbath limitations: shopkeepers selling their merchandise on the Sabbath, or arranging for Gentiles to take their place without getting permission from the authorized halakhic experts, and so on.[16]

The Hatam Sofer had no need of these indications in order to realize the threat to the integrity of traditional life in this period of revolution and change that had occurred in his own youth.[17] He was aware of the

11. Ibid., 58. For the advice of the compilers of the regulations in Poland, see chap. 6, n. 35.
12. See chap. 8, nn. 1ff.
13. Hatam Sofer 63.
14. Ibid., 113, toward the end of the responsum, beginning "in my opinion."
15. Ibid., 58.
16. See nn. 38ff. below.
17. See Jacob Katz, Halakhah and Kabbalah (Jerusalem, 1984), 353–386.

fate of western communities, including that of the city of his own birth, Frankfurt, where the previously unifying traditional halakhic framework had been shattered with the arrival of the Enlightenment, on the one hand, and the tremors of revolution and war, on the other. Against the background of these attempts he developed his famed system, mainly the attempt to halt the erosion of tradition by the sanctification of all its aspects and details: Instead of trying to lighten the burden, he strove to reinforce tradition by demanding strict halakhic observance. He expressed this opinion in connection with the matter under consideration here as well. Concerning the question of delegating the job of repairing buildings in the Jewish neighborhood to a Gentile contractor after the city was shelled during the Napoleonic war of 1809, he began his responsum as follows: "Since, unfortunately, the people of this generation are completely unruly, it is proper to place a fence around the Torah, not by ruling permissively but by ruling strictly."[18] In practice, the perspective he adopted in this case contradicted the principle he had previously enunciated. He combined the permissive reasoning developed in various rulings, that of Rabbenu Tam allowing a Gentile to work in a Jewish building under a contractual arrangement with that of the authorities who ruled that where many are involved, there is no fear of misinterpretation. "And in order to make sure we can publicize the details by means of an announcement in the synagogue,"[19] with chance visitors understanding "that no Jew would act perversely in public, so that it must have been permitted according to instructions of halakhic authorities."[20] This was clearly a matter of great urgency for the members of his community. In addition, he could rely upon his conscientious community not to interpret the emergency ruling as a general permission.

In fact, the Hatam Sofer was conscious of the economic pressures compelling individuals to come before halakhic authorities in search of permissive rulings, and he responded to the limits allowed by his understanding of the halakhah. Moreover, he was careful not to overrule other halakhic authorities who were more far-reaching in their permis-

18. *Hatam Sofer* 60.
19. Ibid., 21b, beginning "but."
20. Ibid., end of section beginning "however." This is a kind of argument used by R. Solomon Kluger; see chap. 10, n. 20.

siveness than he. He replied to the father of a favorite disciple of his, himself apparently a talmudic scholar, who had inquired of him in connection with the leasing of villages with all the necessary equipment, as follows: "I find it very difficult to give my opinion in this matter for a secret yet obvious reason, but it is even more difficult not to answer you, and so I shall tell you my opinion briefly, as a person acts when he has no choice."[21] No explanation is given of the "secret yet obvious reason." The Hatam Sofer may have agreed with those of earlier generations who viewed anxiously the danger of widespread violations in leasing affairs, or he may have been critical of a Jew making himself master of an estate with its accompanying vassals. At any rate, as long as he found no clear halakhic reason to oppose the leasing, he studied the matter on its own merits and ruled permissively. He allowed the Jew who had the franchise on the sale of salt to hand it over to a Gentile under conditions he recommended to the sellers of liquor, that is, that the Gentile buy on Friday from the owner of the franchise the salt he proposed to sell on the Sabbath.[22] As for the Jew who proposed to operate by means of his Gentile partner—if the Gentile was a real partner, he could be awarded the selling on the Sabbath under a contractual arrangement, which would be a halakhically unassailable arrangement, whereas if he "were in actual fact the Jew's servant and the partnership established merely to facilitate Sabbath sales, it is difficult to agree"[23] but apparently not impossible. However, such permission contained one restriction: that "the Jew not sit nearby and supervise."[24] It will be recalled that R. David ben Samuel ha-Levi, the Taz, had authorized such a procedure.[25] But the Hatam Sofer rejects it ("a careful Jew will keep away from it"), leaving the decision to the person involved: "As for the Jew sitting there in the shop on the Sabbath, anyone interested in accepting that ruling may permit himself to do so, but I decline to be a party to it." He concludes his statement with a wish that "the one who observes the Sabbath according to halakhah enjoy unlimited reward"[26]

21. N. 9 above.
22. N. 14 above.
23. N. 11 above.
24. Ibid.
25. See chap. 6, n. 49.
26. N. 11 above.

In this way he encourages the Jew to act strictly, but without wording his reply as a ruling that obliges its recipient to accept it. The Hatam Sofer's responsum regarding the *Breihaus*, the beer distillery, addressed to a Rabbi Lima[27] is especially enlightening. R. Lima "had bravely sought out a way to rule permissively . . . for his Excellency," but the identity of both his Excellency and Rabbi Lima is unclear.[28] At any rate, the Hatam Sofer sought to strengthen the rabbi's ruling, which was based on the employment of a Gentile under a contractual arrangement, "that he take some of the beer distilled for himself as well, thus benefiting from the work itself, so that he will resemble a tenant, and the arrangement will be permissible."[29] As far as the fear of misinterpretation was concerned, that it might appear that the Jew is employing the Gentile on a daily basis, R. Lima was of the opinion that "since the building was located in a completely Gentile village, with only one or two Jews living there, who will know of this tenantlike arrangement? . . . There is thus no fear of misinterpretation."[30] The Hatam Sofer challenged the first part of this ruling, for a tenant who receives a third or even a quarter of the produce of the field really works for this recompense, whereas in our case the owner of the distillery would have to pay his employee a daily or weekly wage, the portion given him of the fruits of his labor (one barrel per vat) serving merely to make the entire arrangement one of contracting so as to circumvent the prohibition—which is deceitful. The Hatam Sofer, however, found a solution to this problem. He fixed "the salary of the employee for every hundred distilling operations during the year or half a year"[31] without determining when precisely the Gentile would do the work.

The Hatam Sofer was also unhappy with R. Lima's treatment of the element of misinterpretation. The isolated locale of the place of work did not seem to him a sufficient reason to rule permissively. For his part, he sought other reasons to conclude permissively, either because

27. N. 10 above.
28. W. Bacher published in *Magyar Zsido Szemle*, 9–10 (Budapest, 1892–1893), the list of people who corresponded with the Hatam Sofer. To Lima's name he added a question mark (ibid., 9:707) because he was apparently uncertain whether a printing error had crept in or not.
29. *Hatam Sofer* 59.
30. Ibid.
31. Ibid.

of an expected heavy loss or because he discovered that Maimonides had not made the fear of misinterpretation dependent specifically upon Jewish suspicions,[32] "for Jews are not suspected of Sabbath desecration, so everyone will assume that the Jew is acting in a halakhic manner." What was meant by fear of misinterpretation was the besmirching by Gentiles who might say, "The Jews are not observing their Sabbaths."[33] But in modern times this fear no longer existed, for Jews and Gentiles alike had already become accustomed to the concept of Sabbath Gentiles, "the Gentiles in our countries believing that this is the way the Sabbath is observed: Jews refrain from doing certain things, but rather tell a Gentile [to do them], and he performs the work."[34] Nevertheless, despite the fact that the Hatam Sofer helped bolster Rabbi Lima's permissive ruling, he refused to associate himself with any responsibility for it:

> At any rate I shall not be involved in this permissive ruling. This is what we pray for—that we make our living in an allowed fashion and not by transgressing. This does not mean refraining from stealing or robbing, for this is not in the hands of Heaven. This refers to forbidden things we may have to permit to avoid a loss of livelihood—that Heaven save us from such phenomena![35]

In this case, as in the others considered above, the motif of the "unruly generation" plays no part. The factors deciding the halakhic ruling are economic need and the rules of halakhic tradition as interpreted by the halakhic authority. Some importance is to be attributed to the degree to which the halakhic authority himself was involved in the matter. A question posed by members of his own community prompts him to make special efforts to find a way to allow the matter. Similarly, one may sense a special obligation to deal with the question put by the son of the anonymous rabbi in connection with the leasing of the villages,[36] even though the nature of this obligation remains obscure. As a famed halakhic authority, the Hatam Sofer considers himself

32. Maimonides in his commentary on the Mishnah *Avodah Zarah*, end of chap. 1.
33. These are the Hatam Sofer's words (59), not those of Maimonides.
34. Ibid.
35. Ibid., at the end of the responsum.
36. Ibid., 57.

obliged to ponder every question in the main put before him by a rabbi requesting his decision. His rulings are of three kinds. If he finds a clear basis for a permissive ruling, he rules this way without hesitation. If he doubts the validity of a permissive ruling accepted by others, as in the two cases discussed above, he passes the responsibility for the decision back to the questioner. But if the matter involves what in his view is a mistaken ruling, such as the case of the preacher "whose permissiveness led him to allow tobacco sellers to engage in their trade by means of a Gentile on the Sabbath, by relinquishing their ownership of the tobacco on Friday,"[37] a ruling unprecedented in halakhic literature, he overrules the decision placed before him. At any rate, the discussion is carried out in each and every case on a purely halakhic basis.

The situation is different when widespread violations of tradition are insinuated into his considerations. In 1829 the leaders of the community of Wardein (present-day Oradea) came to him with the following: "What are the rules affecting the [Jewish] partner of a Gentile"[38]— the very question he had considered in the case of salt sales. This time his answer was different. If the Gentile is taken into partnership only for Sabbath business, the prohibition is absolute; if the two are active partners in the business throughout the week, "then on the Sabbath the Gentile alone takes part." Business profits on that day belong exclusively to the Gentile, "and no member of the family of the Jew is to be seen or to be present in the shop."[39] This ruling is strict on two points, which are actually three in comparison with the ruling in the case of salt selling. In that case the Gentile partner was allowed to work under a contractual arrangement whereby some of the profits earned on the Sabbath would belong to the Jew; and even making his servant a partner was not completely ruled out. Similarly, Jewish supervision was not permitted, but neither was it forbidden. In contrast, according to the last decision, the entire Sabbath income belonged to the Gentile, and the Jew was explicitly prohibited from entering his shop.

It is not difficult to guess what caused the Hatam Sofer to "veer to the right." The problem posed by leaders of the Wardein (Oradea) com-

---

37. Ibid., 63.
38. *Hatam Sofer, Hoshen Mishpat* 195. The date of this responsum is made clear by its link with the sermon mentioned in n. 46 below.
39. See *Hatam Sofer*, sec. c.

munity had four aspects: First, what is the punishment for a Sabbath desecrator? Second, "Is a person who opens his shop on the Sabbath and sells and buys to be considered a Sabbath desecrator, or should a distinction be made between one who opens his shop completely and one who does so only partly?" The third question concerned the partnership with the Gentile. The fourth was as follows: Are there in the Hatam Sofer's own community, that of Pressburg, "people who conduct themselves permissively in this kind of matter?"[40] It is thus evident that Wardein—a rapidly developing community that absorbed new residents, including migrants from the neighboring countries[41]—had violators of tradition who were looking for excuses to operate their businesses on the Sabbath. Faced with this situation, the leaders of the community requested assistance in their struggle from the highest-ranking halakhic authority in the country. They may have required the Hatam Sofer's ruling in order to convince the secular authorities to help them uphold the principles of Jewish faith. Such a situation is hinted at in the Hatam Sofer's responsum, in which he writes: "It is forbidden for anybody known to be Jewish to open his shop or engage in trade. . . . If he does not obey and it is impossible to coerce him to do so with the help of the state authorities, then he is to be expelled from the Jewish community; he is devoid of any religion and is no longer qualified to testify in court or to take an oath."[42] Such wording would likely impress the secular authorities.[43] Further along in the responsum he writes that in Pressburg, too, even though "there are no Jews who desecrate the Sabbath in public," the halakhic authorities are sometimes in need of assistance from the secular authorities to back up halakhic rulings.[44] In such circumstances the Hatam Sofer wanted to rule unambiguously on the question of partnership as well; he permitted it only on condition

40. Ibid., at the beginning of the responsum.
41. For the development of the community, see *Pinkas ha-Kehilot: Rumania* (Jerusalem, 1980), 2:61–65.
42. See *Hatam Sofer*, end of sec. b.
43. The simplistic wording of the entire responsum, too, indicates his desire to placate those who were not versed in the halakhic depth of the questions.
44. According to the Hatam Sofer sec. d, it happened that a Jew "opened his shop on his day of mourning, and Mr. Fischgal, sent to close it, threatened to punish him if he opened it before he got permission from halakhic authorities." The authorities were certainly not versed in the rules of mourning, and the leaders of the community requested their intervention and got their desire.

that the Jew not benefit from any profits made by running the business on the Sabbath and that he not have any reason to take an interest in whatever transpired in his shop on that day.

Six years later the Hatam Sofer confirmed the ruling permitting the sale of salt by the same procedure that was recommended for the sellers of liquor, adding: "But in other shops where the problem is merely one of preventing the making of a profit, I certainly do not permit it. Anyone acting contrary to this will not benefit from his deceit. And just as a person who observes the Sabbath with delight will enjoy bounty without end, so the opposite applies to anyone not observing the Sabbath as he should, ignoring the proscriptions of the sages."[45] The assumption that desisting from selling in other shops is always a matter of merely preventing the making of a profit is, of course, arbitrary. The pathos accompanying this ruling clearly demonstrates that the ban is not formally derived from the distinctions between the sale of salt and the opening of shops. Economic activity according to franchises granted by the large landowners and secular authorities was entrenched in the traditional Jewish milieu, and ways to rule permissively with certain restrictions were developed there. The shops opening onto urban markets and streets as a result of the semicitizenship awarded the Jews constituted a phenomenon that threatened the status of tradition in Jewish society. This was interpreted as severing the yoke of halakhah or an evasion of its binding authority. It gave rise to protest by those considered responsible for the guarding and fostering of halakhic tradition.

At the same time as he replied to questioners from the distant community of Wardein, the Hatam Sofer delivered a sermon before his own congregation on the subject of Sabbath observance.[46] In this sermon he defined any business transaction on the Sabbath, even though carried out by circumventing halakhic work prohibitions, as outright Sabbath desecration. He spoke of "the teachings of those who reject the rulings of the sages," according to which people learn to treat lightly the prohibition on engaging in business.[47] It seems he attributed the violations of tradition at Wardein to the influence of those Maskilim who tended

---

45. Note 14.
46. Hatam Sofer, *Sermons*, ed. Naphtali Stern (Cluz, 1929), 88a. The editor commented on the link between this sermon and the responsum to Wardein.
47. Ibid.

toward Reform; his struggle against these, headed by his opponent, R. Aaron Chorin, persisted for a long time.[48] Maskilim of this ilk were liable to grant halakhic sanction to the widening of permissive conduct, something that the conservatives considered violations of sanctified tradition.[49]

We seem to have encountered the beginning of a paradox. Those tending to [reform] adhere to the formal rules of halakhah, whereas Orthodox halakhic authorities subordinate those rules to their overall religious policy. They rule strictly or leniently not according to the original rules but rather according to their estimation of the contribution their rulings would make to the preservation of tradition or to the likelihood of their being used to undermine it.

The Hatam Sofer's method of study and style of leadership are known to have served as an example for the communities of Hungary, in which his disciples and their own disciples functioned as rabbinic leaders. Their influence was especially strong in Hungary's western provinces, except for the northeastern part of the land bordering on Galicia, whence came a stream of migrants and, together with it, the influence of several factions of the hasidic movement.[50] Neither the pious according to the school of the Hatam Sofer nor the adherents of the hasidic way of life, however, had unlimited sway over their provinces. Alongside these groups there sprang up sizable groups of would-be reformers, some of whom had abandoned halakhic jurisdiction altogether, while others planned to adapt the tradition to the changing circumstances.[51] These groups formed the kernels of the communities eventually to be organized as the Neologist movement, in the wake of their clash with the pietists at the Budapest Jewish Congress of 1868.[52]

If during the lifetime of the Hatam Sofer deviations from the traditional mode of life were still a marginal phenomenon, they became

48. See *Hatam Sofer*, pt. 6, 85.

49. That this was the system used by the first reformers, and especially that of Aaron Chorin, is emphasized by Leopold Loew, "Die Reform des rabbinischen Ritus auf rabbinischem Standpunkte," in *Gesammelte Schriften* (Szegedin, 1889), 1:15–25.

50. For the history of Hungarian Jewry at this stage, see Nathanel Katzburg, "The History of Hungarian Jewry" (in Hebrew), in the introduction to the *Pinkas ha-Kehilot: Hungary* (Jerusalem, 1976), 19–36.

51. Katzburg, "Hungarian Jewry," 32–33.

52. Concerning the congress, see ibid., 52–61.

extremely common during the next generation. The change is clearly and unambiguously reflected in the reactions of his son, who replaced him as chief halakhic authority of Pressburg, to the problems of Sabbath observance in the field of our study. R. Abraham Samuel Benjamin, the Ketav Sofer, analyzes the concepts of fear of misinterpretation and desecration of the name of God in connection with Sabbath desecration, which, as we have already noted, Maimonides interpreted as meaning the conception gained by Gentiles from the behavior of Jews, namely, that Jews do not observe the requirements of their own religion. The Ketav Sofer writes: "There is certainly no desecration of the name of God when a Gentile sees a Jew desecrate his Sabbath or festival privately, for there are many Jews, as there are Gentiles, who do not observe their religion and who desecrate their festivals." This means that the deviation of an individual from tradition is not confounding, for it is an everyday affair. What then constitutes a desecration of the name of God? When such a deed is done "openly . . . with no one protesting; when all the people, including their leaders and rabbis, see this yet refrain from protesting; or when one does not listen to the voice of his teachers—this is a great desecration of the name of God."[53] The traditional view was, of course, that even a slight deviation from the rules of Sabbath observance, such as employing Gentiles in ways other than those permitted, would cause astonishment and harm the reputation of the Jew. But according to the Ketav Sofer it is only indifference to Sabbath desecration on the part of community leaders or their inability to prevent it that would attract attention. Now, if by this interpretation the Ketav Sofer is inadvertently imposing the experience of his generation on concepts conceived of in the past, in other places he writes of the change for the worse that took place in his day, not only with respect to antiquity, but even since the days of his father, the Hatam Sofer.

In a responsum given to a rabbi who wanted to base a ruling upon the Hatam Sofer's reasoning adduced above, that in a place where Jews dwell no one would suspect a Jew of employing Gentiles on the Sabbath but that one would assume rather that he was doing so "according to a halakhic permit,"[54] the Ketav Sofer points out that times had changed:

53. Abraham Samuel Benjamin Sofer, *Ketav Sofer Responsa on Orah Hayyim* (Pressburg, 1873), 41 (39b).
54. N. 20 above.

It seems to me that when my late father wrote that responsum, the people were not so exposed to public Sabbath desecration. But nowadays, Jews desecrating the Sabbath publicly are, unfortunately, more common, violating Torah prohibitions with the shops being kept open, and in some communities they are not ashamed to do so. Neither do they obey parents, teachers, or others who protest.[55]

Statements made in 1809 were no longer valid in 1866. The fifty-odd years that had passed mark a fundamental upheaval in the history of European Jewry in general and in the life of Hungarian Jewry in particular. It is thus no wonder that, even as an auxiliary concept in making practical halakhic decisions, the term "unruly generation" came to occupy a more weighty position in the writings of the son, the Ketav Sofer, than it had in those of his father, the Hatam Sofer.

In three cases in which his tendency might have been to rule permissively by virtue of the relevant details, the Ketav Sofer actually refrained from doing so because of the "unruly generation." One of these cases resembled one in which the Hatam Sofer had ruled permissively—to hand over a block of apartments to a workman under a contractual arrangement in an emergency.[56] The case considered by the Ketav Sofer was far more favorable, for the landlord had stipulated that the workman not build on the Sabbath, but the latter did not fulfill the condition. The question was whether the Jew was obliged to go to court to try to compel him to do so.[57] The Ketav Sofer concludes his responsum as follows:

Actually . . . I am not worried by the permissive ruling, for it is not my innovation at all but is obvious from rulings of the great recent authorities. . . . Nevertheless, insofar as, unfortunately, the generation is exposed . . . to the desecration of Sabbaths and festivals, a phenomenon found in almost every place Jews live . . . therefore do I recoil from permitting this thing.[58]

Typical in a number of ways is the position taken by the Ketav Sofer regarding a question put by a talmudic scholar whom he calls "one of the [stalwarts] . . . of the community."[59] This scholar had "leased fields

55. Sofer, Ketav Sofer 43.
56. Nn. 18–20 above.
57. Sofer, Ketav Sofer 41.
58. Ibid., 42b.
59. Ibid., 43.

and vineyards from a certain nobleman for many years and had also rented from him those villagers who were obliged to work for him . . . for fifty days in the year, during the appropriate agricultural periods."[60] These are the same conditions as the ones we found prevalent in seventeenth-century Poland;[61] they had not yet disappeared in the provinces of the Austro-Hungarian Empire in the middle of the nineteenth century. As we surely recall, permission had at times been given for the employment of these vassals on the Sabbath under such conditions, the explanation being that the villagers chose their days of labor according to their own considerations, in which case they should be considered as if working under contract, for the Jew had no hand in determining that they work on the Sabbath. R. Meshullam Phoebus, the halakhic authority of Cracow, who was familiar with the conditions under which the vassals did their work, rejected this claim, knowing that in fact the villagers did "whatever the landowners told them at the time."[62] So it was regarded by two important rabbis, contemporaries of the Ketav Sofer, R. Moses Teitelbaum[63] and R. Ezekiel Paneth, who were asked about similar cases. The latter replied explicitly as follows:

> True . . . if the Gentiles could choose to work on whatever days they desired, and they chose of their own free will to work on the Sabbath, there would be room to rule permissively. . . . But in fact I am aware of accepted custom whereby the Jew with the lease has . . . a foreman . . . whose job it is to urge the Gentiles he is in charge of, and he commands them and orders them to do their work day after day. . . . And the Jew with the lease is aware of all this, as well.[64]

This description was written by a person known for his habit of traveling through the provinces of Transylvania to instruct the inhabitants of the villages and towns and warn them, *inter alia*, to observe the Sabbath

---

60. Ibid.
61. See chap. 6, nn. 60ff.
62. See chap. 6, nn. 61–63.
63. Moses Teitelbaum. *Heshiv Mosheh* (Lvov, 1866), 9. Rabbi Teitelbaum, a contemporary of the Hatam Sofer, died in 1841.
64. Ezekiel Paneth, *Mareh Yehezkel* (Sighet, 1875), 4; similar is the opinion of R. Teitelbaum, *Heshiv Mosheh*.

and festivals.[65] By contrast, the rabbi of Pressburg, the Ketav Sofer, never mentioned the work conditions of the villagers—indeed it is doubtful if he was aware of them. And so he relied upon the formal definition as it was brought before him by the questioner: "that these laborers have to work fifty days a year, there being no one to tell them to do so on one day or another, the matter depending upon the choice of the workers. Thus this is a real case of contracting as mentioned in the Talmud and halakhic literature, and it is therefore basically permitted."[66]

There was, however, another consideration that outweighed the permissive one and led to the rejection of the request. Moreover, the Ketav Sofer actually reproved the questioner and his brother, "a righteous and learned man," who was a partner to the leasing,[67] in a manner similar to the way R. Solomon Kluger reproved R. Israel of Ruzhyn.[68] The brothers, who were known as scholars and pious men, would set themselves up "as targets at which arrows . . . would be shot . . . by people who disparage the righteous," for the claim would be made that their desire for money motivated their request for permissive rulings. If they acted "upon the instructions of the halakhic authorities," their deeds would serve as "a justification [for others] to desecrate the Sabbath and festivals, saying that the righteous allowed themselves to do so because it is difficult for them to resist the temptation of money."[69] The rabbi thus advised the brothers-lessors to forgo the work of the villagers on the Sabbath,[70] advice that only a person detached from economic reality, especially in agriculture, could believe practical.

The reluctance to rule permissively for fear of the spreading violations of religious law, noticeable ever since the days of the Hatam Sofer, now becomes a permanent feature of the decisions handed down by his colleagues, disciples, and their disciples, though not to an equal

65. R. Ezekiel Paneth was the rabbi of Transylvanis. His biography is given in considerable detail in the introduction to the book of his son, Hayyim Bezalel Paneth, *Derekh Yivhar* (Munkács, 1893). See Joseph Cohen, R. Ezekiel Paneth's "Responsa Mareh Yehezkel," *ha-Mayan*, vol. 4 (Jerusalem, 1964), pp. 34–45.
66. *Ketav Sofer* 42 (41b).
67. Ibid., at the end of the responsum.
68. See chap. 10, nn. 31ff.
69. N. 67 above.
70. Ibid.

degree in the rulings of each. R. Judah Aszod was not a disciple of the Hatam Sofer but followed his lead in dealing with questions of contemporary significance; he went even further than the Hatam Sofer in subordinating his rulings to a policy of strictness for fear of encouraging religious violations, as may be seen from his discussion of the subject of our own study. The question was sent to him in Szerdahei, near Pressburg, from Pápa, a large community in western Hungary that had developed under the auspices of Prince Eszterhazy.[71] The case concerned "a Jewish baker who rented from the duke . . . exclusive rights to supply all his lessees with bread."[72] The franchise, of course, required the Jew to supply the bread every day of the week, including the Sabbath. The baker tried to solve the problem by means of an agreement with a Gentile baker, by which the latter would supply the bread on the Sabbath instead of the Jew. When he did not succeed, he requested permission to hand the baking of the bread in his own bakery over to a Gentile "in such a way as to let the Gentile enjoy all the profits of the Sabbath . . . he not wanting any of the proceeds of the Sabbath labors."[73] The baker claimed that his livelihood depended on such an arrangement, but the local rabbinic court[74] was afraid to allow it; Rabbi Aszod agreed with the court and confirmed its opinion.

There is no reason to wonder at the prohibition, for the work would necessarily have been performed in the home of the Jew, and such arrangements had won very limited support among halakhic authorities, as we have seen.[75] The interesting aspect of this case is not the ruling itself but the reasoning behind it. The case arose between the years 1837 and 1841, years when the community of Pápa had no rabbi,[76] so the matter came before the three *dayyanim* (religious judges) of the town. Both the judges and R. Judah Aszod, who wrote the responsum, based their decisions upon the claim of an "unruly generation,"[77] a concept

71. For this community, see *Pinkas ha-Kehilot: Hungary*, 428–430.
72. Judah Aszod, Responsa, *Yehudah Yaaleh* (Lemberg, 1873), 62.
73. Ibid.
74. The responsum is addressed to the members of the rabbinic court; mentioned by name are Israel Epstein, Menahem Mendel Rapaport, Moses Mordecai, "my longtime disciple."
75. See chaps. 7, 8, 9.
76. See n. 71 above.
77. "And especially in an unruly generation like today's, as Their Excellencies also noted," (Aszod, *Yehudah Yaaleh* 62).

already well known. Rabbi Aszod, however, with whose detailed reasoning we are familiar, did not make this ideological ground the actual basis for his decision. He invoked halakhic grounds, which demonstrates his desire to block any attempt to tip the scale in favor of a permissive decision. The fact that the baker wanted to forfeit any income accruing from the labors of the Gentile on the Sabbath did not exclude him, in his opinion, from the category of those benefiting from Sabbath work. Why so? Because the Gentile baker, while not sharing with him the proceeds of his work on the Sabbath, "would certainly be indebted to him . . . at least minimally (shaveh perutah), which is sufficient to be forbidden as Sabbath profit, as we find in the book Tosefet Shabbat, section 306."[78] If other authorities, as we have seen, used their imagination to find a loophole in the prohibitions in order to be able to rule permissively, in this case imagination was used to bolster the prohibition.

Rabbi Aszod made yet another fundamental decision in his pursuit of a prohibitive ruling. The baker claimed that if he were unable to serve his customers on the Sabbath he might lose the franchise for the entire week. To this the rabbi replied that "even if you say you will lose the franchise, this is no loss of yours, but rather merely the preventing of profit."[79] He thus employed the formal distinction between a loss—of something one already owns—and profit, the coming into possession of something as yet not belonging to him. Other scholars noted the necessary limits of such a distinction, ruling that if preventing the making of a profit on the Sabbath causes the man to lose his livelihood on weekdays as well, there can be no greater loss than that.[80] It is true that in the actual case before him the rabbi felt that the baker's not serving his customers on the Sabbath would not necessarily lead to the loss of his livelihood. He advised him to "speak with the duke" and explain his difficulties "as a Sabbath-observant Jew according to the holy Torah. . . . He will undoubtedly understand; the baker should keep in mind the verse, 'He who observes the commandments will come to no evil.'"[81]

78. Ibid., section beginning "here."
79. Ibid.
80. See chap. 9, nn. 25, 58.
81. Yehudah Yaaleh 62.

This optimistic prognostication is merely the rabbi's wishful thinking, which could perhaps soothe his conscience should the baker's livelihood be lost as a result of his ruling. At any rate, the rabbi was basically ready to adhere to his ruling although he was certainly aware of the baker's loss of livelihood. At the end of his responsum he discussed the degree of loss a Jew had to be ready to suffer in order to preserve the Sabbath according to halakhah, concluding that he "is obliged to sacrifice all his capital" rather than violate even a rabbinic ban.[82]

R. Judah Aszod's position seems similar to that of the rabbi of Würzburg and a number of his colleagues in Germany.[83] In Hungary, too, there were those who supported this approach, but this was not the dominant viewpoint. We have already encountered Maharam Schick, disciple of the Hatam Sofer, expressing his opinion in *Shomer Zion ha-Neeman* in connection with the craftsman who wanted to employ his workers in his own home. This was a problem similar to that of the baker of Pápa; that is, because of the threat to the man's livelihood, the matter was one of great loss for him in which case "there is no need to take into consideration the question of misinterpretation"[84]—this in direct opposition to the opinion of R. Judah Aszod.

At the time of the discussion in the pages of *Shomer Tsiyyon ha-Neeman*, Schick was about forty years old and still resided in the small town of Vergin, near Pressburg. His authority gradually increased, especially after he began to serve as rabbi of the town of Huszt, in the northeast part of the country, heading an academy at which hundreds studied. At the time of the split in Hungarian Jewry he was the leader of the Orthodox camp.[85] Nevertheless, he dissociated himself from the zealotry displayed by many contemporary rabbis, especially in the area of Huszt. In their opinion, every Jew faithful to Judaism was obliged to stay as far away as possible from all contact with modern life, even going

82. Ibid, the closing passage.
83. See chap. 9.
84. See n. 80 above.
85. For R. Moses Schick, see Yekutiel Grunwald, *On the Religious Reformation in Germany and Hungary: R. Moses Schick and His Day* (Hebrew) (Columbus, Ohio, 1948). For the split in the days of the Jewish Congress, see Nathanel Katzburg, "The Jewish Congress in Hungary in 1869," in *Records of the World Congress for Jewish Studies* (Jerusalem, 1969), 2:173–175.

so far as to sacrifice sources of income stemming from changing circumstances.[86]

Rabbi Schick's moderate stand is reflected in the way he treats requests for permission to cooperate economically with Gentiles. His position resembles that of his own teacher, the Hatam Sofer. Similarly, he examines questions brought before him on their merits. Thus he does not strive to invent new ways to rule permissively, as do the halakhic authorities of Poland; but wherever he finds a basis for a permissive ruling according to the accepted halakhic tradition, he makes use of it and relies on it. He is, of course, sensitive to the threat of widespread violation of traditional rules of conduct, and he untiringly reminds his questioners that consideration of the case is conducted in an age of an "unruly generation." At any rate, he carefully refrains from imparting any weight to this fact in his halakhic investigation, unlike R. Judah Aszod and a number of contemporary authorities in Germany. He merely tosses in this consideration when rendering his final decision to prohibit or permit something and generally leaves the decision to the halakhic authority who placed the question before him.

We shall exemplify Rabbi Schick's system by looking at his responsa concerning a new source of livelihood—the acquisition of a new harvesting machine rented out to farmers during the fall and utilized by many of the small capitalists even among Orthodox Jewry. The machine was operated by "a Gentile foreman and workers under contract," and it obviously could not be idle two days a week. Rabbi Schick was asked about it twice, once by his friend, R. Zechariah Shapira, rabbi of the community of Darag,[87] and once by his disciple, Rabbi Zussman Sofer,[88] rabbi of Halas. Schick found ways to rule permissively, on condition that the work of the craftsman be carried out under contract or "that the Gentile have a partnership in the machine";[89] he was thus willing to settle for a simple, formal partnership. But he left it to his questioners, who were versed in their local conditions, to decide whether it would be right to rely on this ruling or whether it was nec-

---

86. Nathanel Katzburg, "A Rabbinical Court Ruling in Michaelowitz, 1896," in *Chapters in the History of Jewish Society Presented to Professor Jacob Katz*, ed. I. Etkes and Y. Salmon) (Jerusalem, 1980), 273–286.

87. Moses Schick, *Responsa* (Munkács, 1880), 96.

88. Ibid., 97.

89. Ibid.

essary to rule strictly in light of the status of Judaism at the time. For his own part, he states:

I stay away from such rulings, especially in this unruly generation, when one should be as strict as possible (and according to Hosea 14:10), "the righteous shall walk in them, the wicked shall stumble," the former will stay away from things that are forbidden and rely on God. Permissive rulings are of no help to the light-headed, for, relying on them, they permit themselves even more, saying that the pious permit it.[90]

The "light-headed" he talks about are not deliberate violators of Jewish law but rather observers of tradition whose devotion is insufficient to keep them away from opportunities to earn income that bring with them a danger of formal Sabbath desecration. The dilemma facing the halakhic authority was whether to meet these "light-headed" Jews halfway, so as to attract them and reinforce them, or to let them go their own way and to concentrate on building the community of the future on the basis of the minority ready for any sacrifice in order to meet halakhic requirements uncompromisingly. At this point the zealots and the moderates among the leaders of the new Orthodox community parted ways. Rabbi Schick presented the dilemma to his questioners with sufficient clarity but refrained from accepting responsibility in their stead, and we may doubt if he ever resolved this dilemma even for himself.

Only once did Rabbi Schick express an unambiguous opinion in favor of prohibiting something because of the widespread violation of traditional law. This was in reply to a question put to him by R. Jekuthiel Judah Teitelbaum of Sighet in 1873. The question concerned the carriage used to transport passengers from the railway station into town. The owner of the carriage wanted to operate it on the Sabbath "by selling his horses and all necessary equipment to a Gentile."[91] In this case, the excuse of "an unruly generation" would have sufficed, according to Rabbi Schick, in agreement with his questioner, to prohibit the arrangement,[92] even if there were a well-grounded permissive ruling that was in fact missing here, for the case related to a "well-known occupation

90. Ibid., end of responsum.
91. Ibid., 104.
92. Ibid.

carried out in a well-known place." In this instance even contracting does not suffice. The owner of the carriage, however, did not base his request for a permissive ruling on contracting but rather on the sale of his property, as was customary in neighboring Galicia.[93] It may be assumed that in Sighet there were those who were ready to support such a permissive ruling, for otherwise why would Rabbi Teitelbaum, the leading halakhic authority of the town and a famed hasidic rabbi in his own right, have to request the assistance of an outside authority?

This seems to have been a factor in the struggle over the use of the bill of sale that raged in Hungary ever since it became known that R. Hayyim of Zanz approved of it. It will be recalled that R. Hayyim wrote to one of his questioners that if the leading Hungarian halakhic authorities "intended to adopt a strict line," that is, to forbid the use of such a document in the area under their jurisdiction, "they deserve all the blessing for it."[94] In fact nothing seems to have been done collectively in this matter, but doubtless it was discussed among themselves by various rabbinic authorities. Whereas some found it necessary to make use of this convenient implement and relied upon R. Hayyim's extraordinary authority to justify it, the majority of contemporary Hungarian scholars maintained their disapproval (though out of the respect they felt for its inventor they refrained from disputing the subject with him). R. Jekuthiel Judah, who was related by marriage to R. Hayyim of Zanz,[95] found an opportunity to express his vehement opposition to the use of the bill of sale ("It should never be introduced into this country to rule permissively"),[96] and his appeal to Rabbi Schick in the matter of the carriage was merely another expression of this viewpoint. He received the assistance he sought from his colleague, Rabbi Schick, who testified that he "had never permitted anything by means of a bill of sale"[97]—a clear indication that the question of ruling permissively by means of the bill of sale had come before him previously.

R. Hayyim of Zanz's ruling was undoubtedly known in Sighet and in Huszt prior to the publication of his book in 1875. It is equally clear

93. Ibid.
94. See chap. 10, n. 68.
95. The son of R. Hayyim Baruch of Gorlice married the daughter of the rabbi of Sighet. See Isaac Alfasi, *Sefer ha-Admorim* (Tel Aviv, 1961), 89.
96. Jekuthiel Yehudah Teitelbaum, *Avnei Tsedek* (Lvov, 1885–1886), 26.
97. R. Moses Schick, *Responsa* 96.

that halakhic authorities had discussed this innovation among themselves. As mentioned above, a faint echo of this device had reached Hungary during the lifetime of the Hatam Sofer.[98] But prior to the 1860s there is no sign of widespread attention being paid to it, even though the problem of leasing that it was designed to solve was already causing difficulty for the Jews, especially in the communities of Transylvania, the source of the eventual reaction to R. Hayyim's ruling. It seems that the lessors of Transylvania had been accustomed to act permissively from a very early time. The leasing of fields and their cultivation by means of vassals was a common source of livelihood.[99] Indeed, there was no careful rabbinic supervision there; and the appointment of R. Ezekiel Paneth to the post of rabbi of the province in 1823 is considered the beginning of a process that would establish the Jews of Transylvania at a level of religious observance equal to that of the other provinces of the country.[100] This does not mean, however, that he was capable of enforcing his interpretation of halakhic requirements upon the community he led, and we find him and his sons—two of whom followed in his footsteps as the rabbis of the towns of Tasnad and Dés—grappling with the problems entailed in this situation and hesitating over their solution. R. Ezekiel's responsum dealing with the work of the villagers on an estate leased to a Jew was sent to his third son, who was not a rabbi.[101] The subject under discussion was not some particular case. The son was interested in knowing whether justification for the common permissive custom could be found.[102] It is possible that he wanted to engage in leasing, so that his question might not have been strictly theoretical. As we recall, his father replied negatively but gave advice as to how the problem could be solved practically: "The Jew should arrange an exchange with a Gentile with a lease of his own . . . the Jew lending him his Gentile vassals to work on the Sabbath,"[103] advice that may not actually have been practical at all.

Once again leasing was brought before R. Ezekiel, this time in con-

---

98. See chap. 10, n. 24.
99. Bela Vágo, *An Introduction to Pinkas ha-Kehilot: Rumania* 2:3–7.
100. See Joseph Cohen, n. 65 above.
101. See n. 64 above.
102. That the question is worded in the plural proves this is so. "Being asked about the leasing of estates . . . you tried to give a basis for permissive ruling," ibid.
103. Ibid.

nection with a concrete incident. The intermediary was his young son, Menahem Mendel, a recognized halakhic authority, later to be rabbi of Dés and the author of the books *Shaarei Tsedek, Mishpat Tsedek*, and others.[104] The question was asked by his in-law, "the illustrious R. Leib of Paza."[105] The ruling handed down was permissive. The rabbi applied the rule of contracting to the work quota of the farmers, and he proposed other reasons for leniency as well but based his conclusion on his father's opinion, which—as we have seen—seems to contradict the ruling of the son. This last question is dated 1843, while R. Ezekiel's reply to his other son is undated. It is at any rate certain that Menahem Mendel was not aware of his father's reply on the subject, and we have no knowledge as to whether he received his father's approval or not.

It appears that those raising questions about leasing came from scholarly circles, which were expanding at this time in the provincial communities. They were familiar with the halakhic problems involved, whereas the majority of the lessors relied upon their ancestral customs, which considered leasing according to accepted conditions permissible. We may conclude that such was the case from a question that arose when conditions changed, after the revolution of 1848. These matters are described by R. Ezekiel's oldest son, Hayyim Bezalel, rabbi of Tasnád and writer of a book of responsa, *Derekh Yivhar*.[106] This description is very interesting from a number of points of view.

> Recently the farmers, workers of the land, became free of their lords and no longer have to work for them; thus those Jews possessing villages, fields, and many servants have had to buy oxen and hire servants to cultivate the land they rent from the landlords. Some of these lessors have asked what to do on the Sabbath, for if the servants and oxen rest on the Sabbath and then again on the following Sunday they will suffer a great loss, especially since the work to be done is considerable. . . . And if it rains during the week and they refrain from working on a clear day, the loss will be great and may even be irreparable. For this reason these Jews have come with their question: Perhaps it is possible to find a way to allow them to work without violating the prohibition of Sabbath desecration,

104. See Joseph Cohen, "The Responsa of the Rabbis of Transylvania in the Nineteenth Century" (in Hebrew), *Areshet* 5 (1972):288–297.
105. Menahem Mendel Paneth, *Responsa Shaarei Tsedek* (Munkács, 1884), 35.
106. See in this connection Joseph Cohen, "Rabbis of Transylvania," 277–278.

for it is absolutely impossible for them to accept an obligation to have them rest.[107]

On the surface it appears that the fact that from now on the Jewish landowners would have to purchase the animals and hire the servants themselves is what caused them to come with their questions, whereas as long as the owner of the estate provided them with all necessary aids, including the workers who were his vassals, operating the estate was considered permissible without a doubt. It is, of course, possible that in connection with the original conditions some may have defined the work as being done under contract, and the rabbi then ruled permissively about it. He, then, must have pointed out to them that the new conditions invalidated this ruling—although the source before us contains no indication that this indeed was the case. At any rate, the lessors insisted that a ruling permitting work to be done on the Sabbath was a condition for the economic viability of the farm. The rabbi heard a similar claim from Jews engaged in the manufacture of potash. If they had to pay "the workman for the time he was idle, they would incur a great loss. Also, the potash is sometimes exposed to the elements and if it rains, the material is spoiled, and so the rate of work may have to be hastened."[108] A complete cessation of labor on the Sabbath was impossible for two reasons: technical and economic. Furthermore, "they said they have an old permissive ruling and will not accept a prohibition."[109] It is thus clear that the Jewish landlords rely on their traditional permit without inquiring into its nature or origin. This apparently describes the situation concerning the leasing of estates as well, the lessors' request of the rabbi presuming that despite the change in circumstances, the permissive ruling remains valid. This was the rabbi's response: "If they are honest when saying that afterward they will not desecrate the Sabbath, we should really renew the permissive ruling so as to save them from violating a biblical prohibition."[110] Regarding the

107. Hayyim Bezalel Paneth, *Responsa Derekh Yivhar* (Munkács, 1893), 3.

108. Ibid., 4, at the end of the responsum. Here the question is not addressed to the rabbi; rather it sets out to deal with the question of renting out, as it were, theoretically, discovering in the end that according to the conclusion there is some justification for the deeds of the landlords.

109. Ibid.

110. Hayyim Bezalel Paneth, *Derekh Yivhar* 3.

animals, he recommends selling them "to an employee of theirs, the money to be payed being considered a loan for a fixed period of time," a circumvention of the prohibition that is rooted in halakhic tradition, as will surely be recalled.[111] Concerning the fields, he advises "to stipulate with the Gentile that he [the lessor] gives him some of what grows, even if just a little," that is, a fictitious, tenantlike arrangement since the tenant does his work according to his own decision.[112]

The interesting aspect of the discussions of the three Paneth scholars, which were held before 1848, is that no mention is made of the bill of sale, which might have been of assistance in solving their problems. In 1867, R. Abraham Grünbaum, rabbi of Hasasa, turned to R. Menahem Mendel for advice regarding what to do about "people who will not rest even on the Sabbath in respect of having a fire lit for the distilling of brandy"; he proposes "to lighten their punishment somewhat by means of a fictitious bill of sale."[113] The rabbi addressed replied: "I do not know how a bill of sale can help save them, even slightly, from the violation of a prohibition."[114] It is unclear whether he really did not know or whether perhaps he did not want to make use of the proposed device. The very same year R. Joshua Aaron Zevi Weinberger, rabbi of Marghita,[115] replied to another scholar, who also sought a way to permit the use of a fire in the preparation of brandy, as follows: "I, too, have heard for a few years now of the permissive ruling handed down by the holy rabbi of Zanz, but I have not seen it yet."[116] These were the years of the correspondence between R. Hayyim and the two rabbis of Transylvania, mentioned in the previous chapter.[117] The case of the bill of sale was thus well known over ten years before it was published in R. Hayyim's book, Divrei Hayyim, but the halakhic authorities of Hungary were still reticent about it even after its publication. The reaction of R. Amram Blum—the author of the book of responsa Beit Shearim, who took over in Huszt for Rabbi Schick for a few years—is typical. One of his disciples informs him that two landowners with fields asked him

111. Ibid. See chap. 5, nn. 8–9.
112. Ibid.
113. Shaarei Tsedek 32.
114. Ibid.
115. In this connection, Joseph Cohen, "Rabbis of Transylvania," 297–304.
116. Joshua Aaron Zevi, Responsa of R. J. A. Z. Schossburg 23.
117. See chap. 10, nn. 66–71.

to write them a bill of sale so as to permit them to be cultivated on the Sabbath. The disciple refused but reports that another rabbi (rendered anonymous by the editor of the book) agreed to do so; the disciple doubts the validity of the document.[118] R. Amram Blum praises the step taken by his disciple, adding that he had always stayed away from similar things and, at any rate, anyone wishing to rely upon the fiction of *Divrei Hayyim* should use the bill of sale, "though I have not seen it."[119] When it got around that "there was some kind of permissive ruling using a bill of sale for working on the Sabbath,"[120] those interested begged their halakhic authorities to provide them with this convenient document. With the broadening of civil rights in the 1840s, and especially since the emancipation in 1867, the Jewish buyers or lessors of estates became plentiful,[121] including observant Jews who were apt to be relieved from their predicament by the bill of sale. The story of R. Moses Grünwald, the writer of *Arugat ha-Bosem*, who in his old age was appointed rabbi of Huszt, is typical.

> I know that a few years ago when R. Mordecai Matalon was in our community of Ratsfert . . . he stayed with a landlord who had an estate. The landlord asked him for a permissive ruling by means of a bill of sale to let him work his lands on the Sabbath, and the rabbi promised him to do so. When I stayed with him, he consulted me in this matter, about which I argued with him . . . and he agreed with me and went back on his promises.[122]

If that landlord needed a permissive ruling from a visitor from afar, the halakhic authorities in his immediate vicinity must have refused to give him one. But turning to the guest might bear fruit, for he was

---

118. Amram Blum, *Responsa Beit Shearim* 89 (Munkács, 1909).

119. Ibid. From another responsum (89) it is clear that R. Amram felt that frequent use of the services of a Gentile would uproot the concept of Sabbath: "And so I say, telling a Gentile incidentally on a Sabbath or festival to do some labor is a rabbinic ban, but if every Jew on every Sabbath and festival regularly does all his work by means of a Gentile . . . this is a violation of the Torah prohibition, "No work shall be done on them" . . . as the interpretation of the Mekhilta."

120. R. Moses Grünwald (*Arugat ha-Bosem* [Sualiue, 1912], 51), when describing how the lessor of the estate came to request a permissive ruling. For the case itself, see below.

121. Katzburg, "Hungarian Jewry," p. 38.

122. Grünwald, *Arugat ha-Bosem* 51, at the end of the responsum.

none other than the son-in-law of R. Hayyim of Zanz, R. Mordecai Dov of Hornistopol, who, like his father-in-law, was both a hasidic rebbe and the writer of halakhic works that conferred on him some degree of halakhic authority.[123] We can learn of the arguments used by R. Moses Grünwald to combat the use of the permissive ruling of R. Hayyim of Zanz from the way he tells the story of that landlord. He was asked by R. Joseph Elimelech ha-Kohen, the rabbi of the community of Zsadány, what to do in the case of a newly observant Jew who has given up his profession as a lawyer "and conducts himself properly as a Jew, which is amazing for he was not raised in this manner in his parents' home."[124] This penitent Jew was now making his living as a renter of an estate, but he does not rest the household on the Sabbath, "for he has a great deal of work and cannot possibly rest; neither do his workers want to." When this newly observant Jew heard that "there was a permissive ruling involving a bill of sale," he asked Rabbi Kohen to provide him with such a document. The rabbi admits that "he had always refrained from giving that kind of a permissive ruling." But now he was in a dilemma from which he did not know how to escape: "It is clear that if he gives him such a bill of sale, then the few renters of estates who hitherto used to rest on the Sabbath will now request the bill of sale, as well," whereas if he did not give it, "he was afraid of sinning in that he may prevent the penitent Jew from conducting himself correctly." It seems, however, that this dilemma existed apart from the special case of a newly observant Jew, "for unfortunately the few who rest on the Sabbath conduct themselves leniently in a number of things, whereas the vast majority work on the Sabbath."[125] The situation reflected in this description is that most of the lessors of estates had no hesitation about operating their estates, and the minority who rest them do not refrain from doing things that are defined as Sabbath desecration by the halakhah. It was almost impossible to refrain completely from doing certain things on an agricultural estate, and the awareness of this fact is what led R. Hayyim of Zanz to confirm the permissive ruling of the bill of sale. This problem had bothered the rabbi of Zsadány ever since, and the case of the newly observant Jew merely underlined the confusion he tried to dissipate with the advice of R. Moses Grünwald.

123. See Alfasi, *Sefer ha-Admorim* 30.
124. *Arugat ha-Bosem* 51.
125. All this—ibid.

R. Moses Grünwald ruled unambiguously to prohibit such a step. He said: "Concerning the very fact of permitting the lessors of estates to cultivate their fields and vineyards by a fictitious sale—halakhic authorities have already spoken out strongly against it."[126] The subject had obviously occasioned strong protest on the part of its opponents; R. Moses joined their numbers emphatically. The fictitious character of the sale is clear here to all: "It is known that one does not usually sell a business upon which one's livelihood depends."[127] The difficulty encountered in disqualifying the bill of sale absolutely stemmed from the explicit permissive ruling of R. Hayyim of Zanz. R. Moses Grünwald thus set out to neutralize this authority with the help of three retorts presented in logical order. "The author of *Divrei Hayyim* was not in favor of ruling permissively; he did so merely because he felt it better to violate a lesser prohibition than a greater one, and there is much to be said for that."[128] The author of *Arugat ha-Bosem*, accustomed as he was to inquire into the roots of every regulation in depth,[129] was ambivalent toward R. Hayyim's halakhic reasoning but maintained silence about his objection. He was, of course, right in saying that "anyone studying his words in all his responsa concerning this will be clearly aware how difficult it was for him to bring himself to rule permissively."[130] Nevertheless, the fact was that in the end R. Hayyim permitted it. R. Moses now resorts to one of R. Hayyim's responsa to a questioner from Hungary, in which he apparently informs him that he has retracted,[131] although this retraction meant only that he was sorry he had sent the bill of sale for the residents of Hungary. Second, R. Moses claims that the permissive ruling was originally intended only for those lessors of estates who shut down their estates on the Sabbath but who were concerned that on account of "the complicated affairs of the estate with their many servants and because of the labors of some animal or the like it might be impossible for them to assure that the Sabbath was

126. Ibid.
127. Ibid.
128. Ibid.
129. His book, *Arugat ha-Bosem*, is written as a consecutive discussion of matters pertaining to *Shulhan Arukh, Orah Hayyim*, and the responsa are integrated into the discussion.
130. Ibid.
131. He meant *Divrei Hayyim* 2:30.

not desecrated;[132] this interpretation clearly contradicts the straight-forward meaning of R. Hayyim's ruling. According to the interpretation of R. Grünwald, at any rate, as handed down to the newly observant Jew and others who until now had operated their businesses on the Sabbath and have need of the bill of sale merely to ease their consciences, "it never occurred to anyone to rule permissively by means of a bill of sale."[133]

The debate concerning the bill of sale in Hungary focused on the leasing of lands, concerning which Sabbath observance was extremely problematic. However, halakhic authorities one generation after the emancipation were asked to consider many other questions of this sort. The writer of Arugat ha-Bosem was asked, besides the matter of leasing, about a barrel factory, a shoe workshop, steam-operated millstones, a machine for the manufacture of butter, and another machine for the sawing of wood.[134] His contemporary, R. Shraga Zvi Tennenbaum, the author of Neta Sorek, studied the problems of "a business of millstones for the grinding of flour and the preparation of oils,"[135] millstones driven by steam and by water, a mechanical plow, and a factory for sawing wood.[136] Similar problems are dealt with by the writers of responsa, whose large number is significant especially when seen in contrast to the number of such authors in the countries of eastern Europe, where the Jewish population was still largely functioning in a traditional at-mosphere.[137] Here, as early as the time of the community schism, only half the Jewish population belonged to Orthodox communities, and over the years that group became a minority.[138] The phenomenon testifies, first of all, to the deep involvement of the Jews in the general economic life of Hungary, including Orthodox Jewry. Second, this is a sign of the awareness of the need for halakhic discipline that developed as a result of the struggle of Hungarian Orthodoxy against the Neologist reformers

132. Arugat ha-Bosem 51.
133. Ibid.
134. Ibid., 47–53.
135. Shraga Zvi Tennenbaum, Neta Sorek (Munkács, 1898–1899), 1:12.
136. Ibid., 1:13–20.
137. It is easy to see this according to the Otsar ha-Sheelot u-Teshuvot, ed. Menahem Nahum Kahana-Shapira (Jerusalem, 1981), to Shulhan Arukh 243–247.
138. See Nathanel Katzburg, "The Jewish Congress of Hungary 1868–1869," in Hungarian Jewish Studies, ed. Randolph L. Braham (New York, 1969), 2:20–21.

and other Jews breaking their ties with tradition. The status of the rabbis as counselors for the individual in his religious behavior was greatly strengthened, as demonstrated by the multitude of questions on the topic under discussion.

It is difficult to find basic innovations in the solution of problems addressed by the Hungarian halakhic authorities. With varying individual degrees of independence, erudition, and fear of making a decision, they repeat the lines adopted by their great forerunners, the Hatam Sofer and Maharam Schick. The motif of "an unruly generation" plays a leading role in their deliberations, sometimes almost preventing serious consideration of the halakhic merits of the case. Someone who is called "an outstandingly learned young rabbi" by the author of *Neta Sorek* puts to the rabbi a question concerning a master carpenter who wanted to entrust his workers with the preparation of windows and doors.[139] Since the work is to be performed under a contractual arrangement and in the home of the Gentile, the questioner has no doubts about it being permissible: "He was merely afraid that this might be the beginning of a permissive trend that could have disastrous consequences, with people engaging in Sabbath labors against halakhah."[140] The rabbi's reply acknowledged that "in an unruly generation . . . there is room for worry. Nevertheless, we are not authorized to prohibit something clearly allowed and to invent unprecedented decrees that our sages did not think of, a step that is clearly sinful."[141]

The permissive rulings, when handed down, were based mainly on two principles: the employment of the Gentiles on a contractual basis, more or less taking into consideration the question of loss, and the partnership—real or formal—with the Gentile in the business.

However, after all is said and done, the bill of sale as a means of ruling permissively did not disappear from the scene. The authority of

139. *Neta Sorek* 1:17.
140. Ibid.
141. Ibid. The Orthodox rabbis of Hungary, too, were not always able to enforce halakhic detail. R. Abraham Shag (*Ohel Avraham* [Jerusalem, 1880], 4) replies to a questioner from the community of Mattersdorf where the bakers were accustomed to allow their Gentile workers to begin to knead the dough on the Sabbath before nightfall, claiming that if they want to bake on Sunday such a step is necessary. The rabbi replies that he ignores this matter, "thus maintaining the rabbinic rule: 'Just as it is obligatory to say something that will be listened to, etc.'" See too R. Jacob Tennenbaum, *Naharei Afarsemon* (Paks, 1898), *Orah Hayyim* 10.

its writer, R. Hayyim of Zanz, sufficed to ensure that anyone choosing to rely on it could not be prevented from doing so. We can conclude from the strong protest lodged by the writer of *Arugat ha-Bosem* concerning the land leasing that others did rely on it, and no collective ban was in force. He considered it in connection with the industrial plants mentioned above;[142] and although his conclusion was negative, his rejection of it was not as emphatic as was his ruling in connection with the estate. He was, of course, one who tended to rule strictly or, rather, one of the school that tended to make a permissive ruling dependent upon the ability of the halakhic authority to satisfy all the different halakhic points of view, almost ignoring the consequences of his ruling for the questioner. His system is reminiscent of the approach of the pious rabbis of Germany and of R. Judah Aszod in his country, the difference being that he surpasses them in his matched mastery of halakhic tradition,[143] a mastery exploited not to uncover new ways to rule permissively but rather to bolster prohibitions.

A single example of Rabbi Grünwald's approach will suffice. In the matter of the barrel factory brought before him by his younger brother, Eliezer David, who was also his disciple, he examines the possibility of the workmen performing their work under a contractual arrangement.[144] In that event the only outstanding problem would be that of fear of misinterpretation, a problem ignored by halakhic authorities when considerable loss was involved. Unlike R. Judah Aszod[145] and other authorities, the author of *Arugat ha-Bosem* concedes that the fear of losing one's livelihood turns the prevention of making a profit into a matter of loss. Nevertheless, as long as the labor of the workmen has to be done in the home of the Jew, he refuses to rely on the permissive ruling that was so readily available. Selling the workshop to the workman does not help either, for this is merely a fictitious sale. The only possibility is for the workmen to rent themselves a separate workshop in which they would be permitted to engage in their labors under con-

142. N. 134.
143. The writer of *Arugat ha-Bosem* clarifies the halakhic topics and rulings relevant to his responsa, which deal with questions of "telling a Gentile" before he begins to reply; his responsa are thus exemplary for precise and thorough analysis. See *Arugat ha-Bosem*, secs. 41–46.
144. Ibid., 47.
145. See n. 78.

tract. He relates that "something of this sort came before me here in our town and I permitted it in this fashion, but not in the workshop of the Jew where they work throughout the week. And even though it may be difficult for the questioner to meet such an expense, do not worry about it, 'for one who incurs extra expense for the Sabbath, the Sabbath will repay it for him' [Shabbat 119a], and a person observing the Sabbath properly is granted all his wishes."[146] Rabbi Grünwald clearly envisioned the observant Jews of his generation as a minority willing to make far-reaching sacrifices without compromise.

Strangely enough, despite everything, we find him using the bill of sale in the case of a question brought before him by his son, the rabbi of Mako, concerning steam-powered millstones.[147] After excluding alternative approaches, he says, "The only way to rule permissively is on the basis of renting or selling to a Gentile,"[148] and then supplies the proper wording for the bill of sale. This wording is none other than that of the bill of sale of R. Hayyim of Zanz[149] with alterations appropriate to the details of the case. This does not mean that Rabbi Grünwald changed his mind concerning the doubtful status of this ruling: "At any rate, a pious Jew will take care and not rely on rulings based on fictitious sales." But he does say "that a bill-of-sale ruling has already been accepted by a number of millers,"[150] and he does not want to clash with the accepted custom. It seems that his reservations concerning the bill of sale were actually limited to the leasing of estates, with their variegated types of work and the almost unavoidable involvement of the Jew himself. In businesses like milling, by contrast, the owners could be away from the premises and leave the work in the hands of the Gentile craftsman. Although from a halakhic point of view, this distinction carried no weight, as regards the feelings of the Sabbath observer affected by these problems, this was not so. These feelings eventually became decisive with the simple folk, and we perceive here that even the most meticulous halakhic authorities sometimes went along with these feelings—which is the central thesis of this study.

146. See *Arugat ha-Bosem* 47, end of the responsum.
147. Ibid., 50.
148. Ibid.
149. See chap. 10, n. 52.
150. *Arugat ha-Bosem* 50.

12

Appendix: "If a Person Dies on the First Day of a Festival, the Body Must Be Cared for by Gentiles"

An offshoot of the discussion of the Sabbath Gentile concerns the burial of a person who dies on a festival day—an instructive example of the overriding of regulations that are explicit in talmudic tradition but that conflict with one's emotional state or one's adherence to patterns of ritual behavior. "One who dies on the first day of a festival must be cared for by Gentiles; on the second day, by Jews." This statement by Rava (*Betsah* 6a) is unopposed. The disagreement between Mar Zutra and Rav Ashi merely concerns the question of whether this permissive ruling covers every corpse or only such whose burial has been or is about to be delayed. It is unclear if it refers to both rulings concerning the treatment by Gentiles or only the one concerning the treatment by Jews on the second day of the festival.[1] Mar Zutra supports the second opinion; Rav Ashi, the first. According to Rav Ashi there are no restrictions on the permissive ruling for the second day: "Although it was not delayed . . . what is the point of the second day for the dead, for the sages have equated it with regular weekdays" (ibid.). Thus it is permitted to

---

1. This doubt was raised by the *rishonim* adduced below, but it does not touch on the problem at hand.

engage in all the labors needed for the burial, such as cutting cloth for the corpse or picking myrtle boughs to put on the coffin. To complete the picture, we must adduce two instances in which amoraim refrained from making use of this ruling. Concerning Levi we read that he was asked by people of Bashkar: "What rules apply to a person who dies on a festival day?" The reply was: "Neither Jews nor Gentiles must take care of him, neither on the first day of the festivity nor on the second" (*Shabbat* 139a). The Talmud did not consider this opinion to be a contradiction of Rava's permissive ruling. This teaching was explained as depending upon the religious status of the questioners, "as the people of Bashkar are not Torah scholars" (ibid., 139b). At the end of the amoraic period, Ravina is quoted as saying that "now that there is compulsory service this must be considered" (*Betsah* 6a): The new Persians forced "the Jews to do their work. But on festival days the Jews would be excused by telling them that it is a festival day, and if they see them burying their dead they will force them to work" (Rashi, ibid.).

According to the accepted rules of halakhic decision making, the binding conclusion is based on Rava's unopposed statement, as defined by Rav Ashi, who takes precedence over Mar Zutra. This, indeed, is what was accepted by Nahmanides: "The geonim write that it makes no difference if the festival comes right before the Sabbath or if it falls on any other weekday (that is, whether it [burial] was delayed or not). If he dies on the first day of festival, he must be cared for by Gentiles; on the second day, by Jews."[2] Nevertheless, Nahmanides knew that this ruling was not universally accepted. The part permitting Jews to engage in the burial of the dead on the second day had been limited by the *Sheiltot* to cases where no Gentile was available, "but if there are Gentiles, then the Gentiles should care for him."[3] With reference to the ruling that Gentiles should care for the dead on the first day of the

2. Nahmanides, *Torat ha-Adam*, in *The Writings of Rabbenu Moses ben Nahman*, ed. Hayyim Dov Chavel (Jerusalem, 1964), pt. 2, 111; see *Otsar ha-Geonim*, *Betsah* 7a. The writings of R. Isaac Ibn Ghayyat, *Shaarei Simhah Hilkhot Evel* (Füerth, 1862), 2:56, testify to the antiquity of the practice in Spain.

3. *Hiddushei ha-Ramban, Shabbat* 139a. The section from the *Sheiltot* adduced above in the text is from the *Aharei Mot*. The printed version before us does not include this restriction in the *Sheiltot*, but all the *rishonim* refer to Nahmanides' version. See Aptowitzer's note to R. Eliezer ben Joel ha-Levi (Ravia, 1958), 421 n. 5); and see Naphtali Zevi Judah Berlin, *Haamek Shealah* on the *Sheiltot* (Vilna, 1861) 2:158b–159a.

festival, he was, however, aware that "some say that the Gentiles are needed only for the actual burial and sewing of garments or for similar principal forms of labor. But as for carrying the body and taking it out on a bier to the cemetery, Jews are permitted to do these things."[4] Concerning the custom common on the second day of the festival, Nahmanides writes: "And it is now the custom for Jews to care for the dead, including digging his grave, even though Gentiles are available."[5] Just as the ruling permitting Jews to care for the dead on the second day of the festival is unlimited, so the obligation to have non-Jews do everything for the dead on the first day is absolute.[6] This ruling was supported by the greatest halakhic authorities of Spain: R. Solomon ben Abraham Adret,[7] R. Nissim ben Reuben Gerondi,[8] and R. Isaac ben Sheshet Perfet.[9]

Outside of Spain—in Provence, in the north of France, and in Germany—this unambiguous ruling did not prevail. In Provence the accepted custom followed the alternative opinion of "some say" (above), which was rejected by Nahmanides.[10] And a similar custom was accepted by R. Eliezer ben Nathan of Ashkenaz: "On the first day of the festival Gentiles do it all, with Jews taking the body out, carrying it to the graveside, and putting it in the grave and then Gentiles covering it up."[11] Rabbenu Tam expressed reservations concerning the ruling permitting one to act on the second day of the festival as if it were a regular weekday in connection with the care for the dead: "In the days of Rabbenu Tam there was a case where they led the body beyond Sabbath

4. Nahmanides, *Torat ha-Adam* 2:11 and *Hiddushei ha-Ramban, Shabbat* 139a.

5. *Hiddushei ha-Ramban* 139a.

6. In both sources mentioned in n. 4 above. See n. 37 below.

7. *Hiddushei ha-Rashba, Shabbat* 139b: "This was the custom everywhere, for Gentiles to deal with the dead on the first day, and on the second, Jews, even though burial was not delayed and even in respect of digging a grave for him."

8. Rabbenu Nissim on R. Isaac Alfasi, *Shabbat* 139a (Vilna, 1881) 57a.

9. R. Isaac ben Sheshet Perfet, *Responsa* 487.

10. See n. 34 below, the Meiri. Similarly in Rabbenu Meir ben Simeon ha-Meili of Narbonne, *Sefer ha-Meorot* (New York, 1967), *Betsah* 6a: "If one dies on the first day of a festival, non-Jews care for him . . . taking the body out on the first day may be done even by a Jew . . . as we find in the *hashlamah* to chapter *Tolin* (twentieth chapter of *Shabbat*). . . . This is the custom in Narbonne, and washing the body is also performed by Jews." See *Temim Deim* 120b.

11. R. Eliezer ben Nathan of Mainz, *Mashkin* 3b. The wording in the text is that cited in R. Eliezer ben Joel ha-Levi 718, (Ravyah, Berlin 1913), 423.

THE "SHABBES GOY" 220

limits on a festival day, and the people of Melun rode after them to care for the dead, and Rabbenu Tam was displeased—even with those who had gone on foot, not on horseback."[12] Rabbenu Tam was more extreme than any of his colleagues. He wanted his contemporaries to be considered the equals of the people of Bashkar[13] and therefore sought to prohibit Jews from caring for the dead at all on the second day of a festival. He found support for his view in the words of Ravina, saying that in his day, too, he feared that Jews burying their dead during a festival would encourage the authorities to compel Jews working in the service of the kings or princes to work on such days.[14] The sons of Melun, however,

12. *Mordekhai, Shabbat* 426. Similarly, Tosafot *Betsah* 6a, beginning with the words "and now." According to a different tradition, the case was "in Melun, before R. Meshullam in the days of Rabbenu Tam," Tosafot, *Shittah Mekubbtset*, at the end of the book by R. Joshua Zomrin, *Nahalah li-Yehoshua* (Constantinople, 1731), adduced by Ephraim E. Urbach, *Baalei ha-Tosafot* (Jerusalem, 1980), 613 n. 70. This was the custom, too, of the writer of *Orhot Hayyim, Hilkhot Yom Tov* 25: "Some of the French halakhic authorities permit the accompanying of the dead beyond Sabbath limits even on horseback on the second day of a festival. . . . Many testify that this was done in the days of R. Meshullam." It thus seems that there is here another dispute between Rabbenu Meshullam and Rabbenu Tam, in addition to those listed in their biographies (see Urbach, pp. 71–83). This would explain the strong language used by Rabbenu Tam.

13. It would seem that Rabbenu Tam merely compared the inhabitants of Melun with those of Bashkar in that they were not Torah scholars, which is what Urbach understood (*Baalei ha-Tosafot*, 70). However, insofar as he ascribed halakhic significance to this comparison, he undoubtedly applied it indiscriminately to all those of later times. Those disputing this view, such as R. Isaac (see n. 17 below), found it necessary to come to the defense of the later generations so that they not be viewed as devoid of Torah scholarship.

14. See sources adduced in n. 12 above. It seems that from a halakhic standpoint Rabbenu Tam's proof rests on Ravina's statement, with the comparison with the inhabitants of Bashkar being used only to give additional weight. If this were the major proof, burial by means of a Gentile should have been prohibited as well, a ruling the community could not have abided. All those who adduce Rabbenu Tam's thesis assume, therefore, that he did not think of forbidding burial by means of a Gentile. See R. Meir of Rothenburg, n. 21 below. The writer of *Orhot Hayyim* (see n. 12 above) adduced the opinion of "R. Isaac Corbeil, that if a person dies on the second day of the festival Jews should not care for him, as Rabbenu Tam rules." This means that Gentiles must care for the dead. The same source adds that "Rabbenu Tam would only allow one or two to accompany the dead modestly, on foot," i.e., Jews to accompany the Gentile gravedigger. According to *Haggahot Maimoniyot* (*Hilkhot Yom Tov* 1, 70), "wherever there are Gentiles, Rabbenu Tam ruled that a Jew may not bury the dead even on the second day of a festival, because we are not Torah scholars, as Levi sent to the inhabitants of Bashkar." In his opinion, Levi did not intend to

were not the only ones who disagreed with him, even among his con-temporaries.[15] A story is told of the brothers R. Judah and R. Joseph, sons of R. Yom Tov, who ruled contrary to R. Tam, "and Rabbenu Tam wondered how they could permit it."[16] His disciple, R. Isaac ben Samuel of Dampierre, rejected his dependence upon the example of the people of Bashkar and the fears of Ravina,[17] and during the next generation few supported his ruling.[18]

Nevertheless, in Germany the difference in practice between the two festival days was steadily reduced. R. Eliezer ben Joel ha-Levi of Bonn rejected the ruling of Sheiltot forbidding Jews to bury their dead on the second day as long as this could be done by Gentiles; but he accepted the opinion of his grandfather, R. Eliezer ben Nathan, that Jews should lead the body to the grave even on the first day.[19] In contrast, the Or Zarua favored the ruling of the Sheiltot.[20] R. Meir of Rothenburg tried to combine the two rulings,[21] and his disciple, Rabbenu Asher,

---

prohibit burial by a Gentile either, and if he did, it was an exception to the rule, "He found a valley where they scoffed very much at a prohibition, so he fenced it off." According to Rabbenu Tam, as well, it should not be used as a precedent. In our Tosafot (n. 12 above), it seems that Rabbenu Tam's turning to the inhabitants of Melun was based on their being compared with those of Bashkar, whereas the ref-erence to Ravina comes as a kind of an afterthought. This may be precisely what took place. However, in the Tosafot of Rabbenu Asher, Shabbat 139b (Jerusalem, 1978), the reference to Ravina is adduced as if it were the main thing. In addition, it says there: "Rabbenu Tam also sent them word [that] the inhabitants of Bashkar are not Torah scholars," and this order reflects the intended halakhic reasoning.

15. To the opinion of R. Isaac of Corbeil (n. 14 above), who was of the same opinion as Rabbenu Tam, the writer of Orhot Hayyim adds: "But in many places the custom follows that of Rabbenu Joseph Bekhor Shor, who rules permissively." Rab-benu Tam's opinion thus contrasts with the accepted ruling in previous generations. It seems that Rashi too ruled permissively, at least when the funeral was delayed. The ruling ascribed to him by the rishonim, according to which the digging of a grave was forbidden, even on the second day of a festival, is not to be found in the wording of Rashi before us. See Aptowitzer, R. Eliezer ben Joel ha-Levi, Rawyah (1958), 422 n. 7.

16. Adduced in Sefer Mitsvot Gadol, Hilkhot Yom Tov, negative injunctions 72 (Venice, 1547), 25c; Haggahot Maimoniyot, Hilkhot Yom Tov 1, ayin.

17. Sefer Mitsvot Gadol, Hilkhot Yom Tov, negative injunctions 72; Tosafot Betsah 6a.

18. Rabbenu Jehiel seems to support his ruling; see Tosafot Betsah 6a.

19. R. Eliezer ben Joel ha-Levi, Rabiah 718.

20. Or Zarua 2:331.

21. Hilkhot Semahot ha-Shalem (Jerusalem, 1976), par. c (pp. 13–15).

tells in his own writings of the practice in Germany concerning the second day of a festival: "A Gentile digs the grave and prepares the coffin and shroud and does whatever is biblically forbidden, but Jews bring out the body and carry it."[22] But in a responsum he says that "a Jew prepares a shroud on the second day if the non-Jew does not know how to do so."[23] The *Mordekhai*, however, obliges the Gentile to prepare the shroud, even on the second day,[24] which eventually became the accepted custom, as noted by the author of *Terumat ha-Deshen*.[25] Other preparations were made by Jews, even on the first day, as Rabbenu Asher confirms in his responsum: "Even on the first day, Jews lift the body on their shoulders and carry it to the grave and bury it."[26] The author of *Terumat ha-Deshen* gives advice regarding the procedure for cleansing the body without wringing out cloths, an action prohibited biblically, this in order not to leave the cleansing process to "completely unclean Gentiles."[27] In practice, then, the difference in custom between the two days vanished, except for the theoretical situation in which no Gentile were available to perform the burial itself, in which case a Jew would be permitted to do this on the second day but not on the first.

The difference between the customs of Spain, on the one hand, and of Provence, France, and Germany,[28] on the other, is certainly not to be explained on the basis of an assumption of two different traditions, which is the usual schematic way to explain such differences in scholarly research. The deviation from the straightforward talmudic tradition is not uniform in the three countries mentioned. Neither is it peculiar to them, for it starts with the ruling of the *Sheiltot* requiring, if possible, the use of a Gentile on the second day of a festival, contrary to the sense of the original talmudic statement. The reason for the deviation must be sought in the problematic nature of both halves of the talmudic ruling: They are unusual, they do not jibe with the general atmosphere of

22. Rabbenu Asher, *Betsah* 1:5.
23. Rabbenu Asher, *Responsa* 23:2.
24. *Mordekhai, Shabbat* 426.
25. *Terumat ha-Deshen* 82.
26. Rabbenu Asher, *Responsa* 23:2.
27. *Terumat ha-Deshen* 82.
28. H. J. Zimmels, *Ashkenazim and Sepharadim* (London, 1958), 184, comments on the differences in custom between Ashkenaz and Sepharad without discussing the reasons.

the ritual, and they come up against psychological obstacles in their implementation.

The ruling permitting work in connection with burial on the second day of a festival is based formally on the prohibition itself in that the status of the day is rabbinic. However, so permissive a conclusion is unparalleled. The regulations concerning a second day of a festival are in every detail the same as those governing the first day.[29] This is not only a formality but is rooted in the collective consciousness of the community. Those celebrating the festival did not regard the sanctity of the second day as being any less than that of the first, for the feeling of sanctity was not rooted in the halakhic definition of the formal status of the festival but rather in the restrictions and symbols, in the work prohibitions and religious rituals that set the day apart from other days of the year. In these respects, there was no difference between the two days.[30] Accordingly, performing labor for the dead on the second day was deemed to be a desecration of its sanctity, and the formal permission granted by halakhic tradition did not easily overcome the reluctance to accept it. It is obvious that this reticence was more powerful with the simple people who adhere to accepted customs than with talmudic scholars who follow the abstract thought of halakhah. This situation is reflected in a story related by R. Isaac Or Zarua: "I heard that R. Isaac ben R. Asher allowed his disciples even to dig [a grave]. He went with them to the cemetery and he began to dig, then he left, and his disciples finished digging the grave."[31] R. Isaac, like many other halakhic authorities, accepted the straightforward Talmudic ruling, according to which all labor for the dead is permitted on the second day of the festival. But it was only his personal example of digging that could overcome the reticence of the many who viewed the performance of labor as a desecration of the holy day.

The other portion of the halakhic tradition, "If he dies on the first

29. *Orhot Hayyim, Hilkhot Yom Tov* 25, adduces the opinion that garments of the mourners are torn on the second day of a festival, but this is rejected by Maimonides, *Hilkhot Yom Tov* 6:23. This, too, is the opinion of Nahmanides; see *Maggid Mishneh*, loc. cit. This, too, is the ruling of *Shulhan Arukh, Orah Hayyim* 526:11. See Hatam Sofer, *Responsa, Orah Hayyim* 145.

30. See Jacob Katz, "Decisions in the Zohar Concerning Halakhah" (in Hebrew), *Halakhah and Kabbalah*, 48.

31. *Or Zarua* 2:331.

day of the festival, Gentiles are to care for him," encountered an obstacle of a different kind. The use of the services of a Gentile was solely instrumental and excluded all matters of ritual. Ritual slaughter of animals for food, writing a Torah scroll, phylacteries, mezuzot, and the like are acceptable only when performed by Jews, or "partners to the covenant," as they are called—a concept that indicates the sociological nature of this limitation, which flows from the exclusivity of the religious group in its unifying ritual and ceremonial activity. Now, burying the dead and especially washing the body and attiring it—"purification," as it came to be known[32]—were rituals, and handing over these operations to Gentiles seemed disrespectful. This feeling is certainly what led R. Eliezer ben Nathan and others who ruled similarly, especially the halakhic authorities of Provence, to restrict the Gentile's care of the dead even on the first day of a festival to the burial itself. Moreover, the "purification" of the body and the carrying of it to the graveyard, which they defined as a kind of "requirement of the *mitsvah*" ("which may be a requirement of the *mitsvah* even though it is not the *mitsvah* itself"),[33] they took away from the Gentile and returned to Jewish hands. This feeling is made explicit by R. Menahem ha-Meiri in his defense of the custom of the sages of Provence as opposed to that of the disciples of Nahmanides, who tried to impose their teacher's ruling, which, as we have seen, made no such distinctions.[34] We shall consider his reasoning shortly. We learn of the extent of this reluctance to make use of the services of a Gentile in caring for the dead from a story told about R. Abraham ben David, "who delayed the burial of a scholar out of respect for him until the second day of the festival, so that Jews would care for him."[35] This contradicted the halakhah. The Meiri explains this as a sort of emergency ruling, "for the deceased was a great talmudic scholar, and he did not want Gentiles to care for his

---

32. The *rishonim* mention the washing of the dead, dressing him, but in *Terumat ha-Deshen* 82, there is mention of *tohorah*, "purification"; Ben-Yehuda's dictionary does not list this connotation.

33. R. Menahem ha-Meiri, *Magen Avot*, ed. Isaac ha-Levi Last (London, 1906), 34. In *Sefer ha-Meorot* (n. 10 above), it says "for it is required as a *mitsvah*." The concept of *kevod ha-beriot*, "human dignity," is also found in ha-Meiri; see *Beit ha-Behirah, Betsah*, ed. Lange-Schlesinger (Jerusalem, 1956), 35–41.

34. Ibid., pp. 32–38.

35. Ibid., p. 35. The case is also mentioned in *Orhot Hayyim, Hilkhot Yom Tov* 27.

needs, even digging his grave, for it is considered disrespectful to the dead in those regions."[36]

Internal religious pressures thus brought about changes in these two halakhic points, but not all halakhic authorities gave in to this pressure. As we have seen, Nahmanides and later Spanish scholars supported the original halakhic instructions. And, as we have already noted, there were also some scholars of Ashkenaz who interpreted the regulations precisely. These represent a school of thought that we may call halakhic-dogmatic. They reasoned that the existence of an explicit talmudic ruling meant that such a halakhah possessed authority like that of a divine decree and defined the boundaries of appropriate and fitting behavior. Nahmanides refers to those who claimed that a Gentile caring for the needs of the dead was disrespectful. He says that once it has been decreed by heaven that a person is to be buried on the first day of a festival, so that the burial must be carried out by a Gentile, there is no further reason to make a distinction between caring for the body and burying it, "for as long as the final stage of the burial is to be done by Gentiles, it is not respectful for a Jew to carry out the body and for a Gentile to bury it."[37] In Spain this dogmatic approach was maintained, whereas in Ashkenaz it was the compromising approach that won out: Burial by Jews was banned on the second day of a festival as well, whereas in the preparations for the funeral Jews were allowed to engage even on the first day.

36. Ibid.
37. *Hiddushei ha-Ramban, Shabbat* 139a. The permissive ruling is formally based on the principle of *mi-tokh*, "since," *Betsah* 12a. However, this principle is applicable only if it is required by the day or by a *mitsvah*, this being the crux of the dispute.

13

Summary: The Limits of Halakhic Flexibility

After this review of the emergence of problems connected with the phenomenon of the Sabbath Gentile throughout the ages, it would be proper to return and redefine these problems with clarity and precision in order to determine what can be learned from them.

The root of the Sabbath Gentile phenomenon is to be found in the nature of the Sabbath as a uniquely Jewish religious precept. The Jew himself as well as his male and female servants and his beasts of burden are forbidden to labor on the Sabbath; this does not apply to other people, who have neither accepted Judaism nor fallen under Jewish jurisdiction, such as slaves or servants. We do not know whether in biblical or early Second Temple days a Gentile happening to be in a Jewish settlement was prevented from violating the Sabbath atmosphere by laboring in public. In tannaitic literature—the Mishnah, the Tosefta, and halakhic midrashim—that reflects the reality of Jews and Gentiles coexisting as an everyday affair, there is no sign of such a trend. The Jewish religion was not perceived to be a form of ritual or a set of customs obligating the inhabitants of a particular region. Rather it was perceived as an obligation of the Jewish nation stemming from the acceptance of the Torah at Mount Sinai, and Sabbath observance was a part of this unique obligation. Gentiles were thus undoubtedly allowed to engage in their occupations. The question of whether Jews were permitted to employ Gentiles in their own labors was bound to arise and demand a practical answer. It is possible and perhaps probable that during the initial stages of shaping the nature of the Sabbath during the Second Temple period, during the formative stage of "normative Judaism," an unambiguous, negative answer to this question was handed down. Nevertheless, from the tannaim, whose teaching determined the nature of the Sabbath for the future, we discern a differential-casuistic answer. Prohibition and permission were determined in each individual case, and it is not possible to determine with complete certainty just what it was that led to a positive or negative answer. Consequently, the amoraim were themselves uncertain in their determination of the boundaries between prohibition and permission, even differing in their interpretation of the statements of their predecessors that served as the basis for their discussions. It is thus unnecessary to note that their exegesis—occasionally itself in need of explanation and interpretation—did not resolve all the doubts and did not result in the formation of a clear conceptual picture that would have served as a convenient and secure basis for ruling in every future case resulting from changes in the conditions under which the Jewish people were to live.

At any rate, one principle did crystallize during the amoraic period: that the prohibition on employing Gentiles is not included in the Sabbath observance as laid down in the Torah. The rule, "telling a Gentile [is forbidden as] shevut," was not intended to determine the prohibition itself, but rather its degree [of strictness]. In other words: A prohibition is in force, but it is not included in those defined as biblically prohibited. It is merely a rabbinic prohibition. This distinction between the two kinds of prohibition is central, of course, in the talmudic codification of halakhah, but researchers are probably right (even though, surprisingly, research on the subject is as yet not sufficiently clear or detailed) in concluding that it is the result of the later development. During the initial stages of the development of normative Judaism, all the restrictions accepted as obligatory in order to guarantee Sabbath rest (and similarly to guarantee the other explicit Torah precepts) are considered part of the Torah precept itself.[1]

---

1. See chap. 1, nn. 5ff. I adduced an example of a late differentiation between a biblical prohibition concerning the taking of interest and a rabbinic one in my lecture before the Third World Congress of Judaic Studies, Abstracts of the Lectures in the Field of Jewish History (Jerusalem, 1961), VI–VI3.

SUMMARY 229

Nevertheless, this early stage in the development subsided as time passed. The midrash attributing the prohibition of employing a Gentile on the Sabbath to the verse making Sabbath observance obligatory (Exodus 12:16: "No work at all shall be done on them") disappeared and was forgotten. Once rediscovered, it was interpreted contrary to its simple meaning and redefined as a mere scriptural support.[2] Only rarely was it suggested that some of the labors performed by the Gentile in the service of the Jew might be considered Sabbath desecration according to the original intent of the Torah. The assumption that the entire prohibition was rabbinic in origin was the basis as early as the talmudic period for the reasoning behind certain permissive rulings. This assumption established the halakhic basis for the relative flexibility seen in the discussions by halakhic authorities of problems with no precise precedents in talmudic tradition.

The source of problems of this nature was, as we have already noted, changes in the conditions under which people lived—migration, on the one hand, and the availability of new sources of livelihood, on the other. The talmudic precedent that involved the use of a boat belonging to a Gentile seaman discusses setting sail by sea, which reflects the needs of the inhabitants of Palestine. By contrast, the Jews of other lands—Babylonia, Egypt, Spain, France, or Germany—had a greater need of sailing down rivers. The crucial question was whether the rules affecting sailing at sea could be applied to means of transport by river. The Jews who had remained in Mediterranean countries were living in climatic conditions similar to those of Palestine. They were able to live with the ban on the use of fire for cooking and heating and no more thought of permitting the making of a fire by means of a Gentile than of performing any other labor. In northern lands—France, Germany, or England—this was more difficult. Yet just here, the household of Jews of the upper stratum was dependent upon the services of "man- and maidservants" throughout the week. They were permitted to kindle a fire for their own needs. Were their masters permitted to warm themselves at their fires? Talmudic tradition contained no direct precedent to resolve doubts; yet the problem had to be solved. Most of the problems arose, of course, as a result of having recourse to new sources of livelihood unimagined by previous generations. Some of the questions resulted from technical innovations, such as the manufacture of glass or silk, where work has to

2. See chap. 1, n. 11.

proceed uninterrupted. The economic value of most of these manufacturing plants, and more so of agricultural farms, was dependent upon the plant not being idle two days a week, on Sunday, the day of rest of the craftsmen and laborers, and on the Sabbath, the sanctified day of the Jewish owner.

If no precedents that applied to the new conditions could be found, how was it decided if they were permitted or forbidden? Before dealing with this question, we must clarify the ways in which the tradition was conveyed from one generation to the next, not necessarily in connection with the matter under discussion here.

We review the process of the transfer of tradition by studying the various branches of halakhic literature. This leads one to believe that this literature—or, more precisely, the writers of this literature, the halakhic authorities—were the conveyors of tradition. The fact is, these writers transmitted the knowledge of halakhic give-and-take and its conclusions, conveying it from one generation to the next. However, the give-and-take of halakhic discussion is not the same thing as its practical existence, and the bearers of its actual existence were not only the halakhic authorities. The halakhic authorities were the sole and unique transmitters of tradition only in those areas that, by their very nature, were restricted to experts, such as the writing of a Torah scroll, phylacteries, and mezuzot, in which experts depend entirely on scribes and scrolls. By contrast, the observance of Sabbaths and festivals is an example of ritual and precept transferred from one generation to the next, from one place to another, even from one exile to another by virtue of its being deeply rooted in the lives of the individual and community. A Jew trained to observe the Sabbath from childhood, and even more so, an entire Jewish community remaining faithful to Judaism, will continue observing the Sabbath even if conditions have been altered because of a change of residence or any other reason, although there will be some adaptation to the new conditions.

At first glance, both individual and community living under the new conditions would be obliged to ask the opinion of a recognized halakhic authority in order to know if the adjustments in practice meet the requirements of halakhah. Indeed, there were cases where such questions were brought before the authorities initially, that is, before the adaptive process generated generally accepted behavioral patterns. In such cases, the behavioral patterns may be said to have been shaped by formal halakhic principle. It is, however, certain that things did not develop this way all the time. Some behavioral patterns seem to have developed incidentally, whereas others may have come about on the advice of learned people who were, however, unversed in the control of halakhic ruling as practiced by authorized halakhic experts. The role played by such dilettantes, who, in the absence of recognized halakhic authorities, became the crutch of the community in its religious conduct, was greater than we usually imagine. The numerous cases encountered in our study of the community relying on anonymous rulings illustrate this point amply.[3]

Nevertheless, guidance provided by such laymen or even behavioral patterns that were shaped incidentally are not really products of chance. Nor are they a simple result of compromises imposed by existential pressures, for even without the supervision of recognized halakhic authorities the trend of the pious never abandoned their striving to ensure the survival of tradition, even though it adapted itself to the changed conditions. Nonetheless, we still ask: If it was not halakhic rules that guided the adapters and their advisers, who or what directed them in determining the limits of adaptability? Our reply is that there was at work here what may be called a ritual instinct, to be illustrated by the topic under consideration. This ritual instinct deters a Sabbath-observant Jew from doing something that has the appearance of work. He will not milk his cows or light his oven, and he will refrain from settling with his debtor who has come to pay his debt and collect his collateral, and so on. However, this selfsame instinct did not rebel against having these jobs done by a Gentile, especially when the Jew did not need to instruct him on the Sabbath about what to do, the Gentile being sufficiently trained to act on his own initiative.

This ritual instinct, acting innocently, was able to establish a custom prevalent in the community but could not give it formal halakhic sanction. This could come only from recognized halakhic authorities, whose task it was to examine the custom in the light of written halakhic tradition. The fact that a custom had already become prevalent in the community had a certain degree of importance according to halakhic rules but was certainly not decisive. If the custom was found to contradict halakhic tradition explicitly, it was uprooted—unless a reason

---

3. For an example from the geonic period, see chap. 2, n. 53; from later periods, see chap. 6, nn. 6–7, 61–62; chap. 7, nn. 43–44; chap. 11, n. 37.

could be found to justify it in retrospect or to accept it on the basis of the rule, "It is better for them to act erroneously than to sin deliberately." Retroactive approval of a custom depended upon the mastery and independence of the halakhic authority in his field, while application of the rule that "it is better to act erroneously" was dependent upon the severity of the contradiction between established custom and halakhic requirements—and no less upon the halakhic authority's evaluation of his ability to override the established custom. At any rate, the determination of the severity of the prohibition according to the accepted halakhic criteria, the most basic being the difference between a biblical prohibition and a rabbinic one, was of no small significance in deciding whether or not there was justification for sanctioning a permissive custom generated by ritual instinct.

Restricting the definition of a prohibition was, however, insufficient to determine its details. In the Talmud itself, the rule of "telling a Gentile—*shevut*" does not appear as a basic principle from which various halakhic rules are derived. The halakhic rules were worded casuistically, as were all the rules of the Mishnah and the *baraitot*, that is, each individual case and its relevant ruling were given, the reason for the particular prohibition or permission being only rarely indicated. The rule of "telling a Gentile—*shevut*" is enunciated almost by chance, in the midst of halakhic give-and-take, to explain an apparently strange ruling permitting the purchase of land in Eretz Israel on the Sabbath (*Gittin* 8b) and the carrying—or heating—of water to facilitate a circumcision (*Eruvin* 67b); that is, instructing the Gentile to do these things is merely a rabbinic prohibition, and the rabbis did not make such decrees where the performance of biblical precepts was involved. This rule was not able to serve even post-talmudic halakhic authorities as a basis for their decisions. At best, they could rely on it in cases of doubt: In such a case, had the prohibition been biblical, one would have been obligated to rule strictly, but had it been rabbinic, one could rule leniently.

However, most of these questions did not involve doubts where the halakhic authority had to decide if the rule inclined permissively or prohibitively. The questions concerned unprecedented cases, and the halakhic authority had to draw analogies from cases considered in the Talmud. With regard to renting, the Talmud mentions a field in a permissive context and a bathhouse prohibitively (*Avodah Zarah* 21b). In later periods, however, we encounter projects of other kinds: millstones,

SUMMARY 233

olive presses, shops, and factories. The prohibition against telling a Gentile was not applicable in situations involving biblical precepts. The precepts mentioned are circumcision and purchasing land in Eretz Israel, and the question arose as to whether analogies could be drawn from these to any action included in the concept of religious precept: bringing an *etrog* from outside Sabbath limits, lighting a candle, or bringing a book for purposes of study. Whether or not the cases under consideration were found to parallel ones mentioned in the Talmud was a matter of interpretation, of defining the basis for the permissive or prohibitive ruling handed down explicitly in the Talmud. Some viewed the bathhouse as being banned because it was a permanent location and known by the Jew's name. Accordingly, any enterprise of a similar kind would be prohibited as well. Another authority might attribute unique characteristics to a bathhouse, in which case the ban on the former would not apply to the latter.[4] The application of the permissive ruling given in the Talmud in connection with those two specific precepts to the other precepts depended, in turn, upon the question of whether the permissive ruling was considered conditional upon the unique characteristics of those two precepts—circumcision and purchasing land in Eretz Israel being considered so important that they overrode Sabbath restrictions—or whether it stemmed from their very nature as precepts, in which case analogies may be drawn to any other precept as well.[5]

Not all the cases serving as bases for analogy were taken from talmudic literature. Rulings handed down by early halakhic authorities played the same role relative to their successors. When R. Meir of Rothenburg sanctioned the custom of allowing the lessors of tax-collecting rights to substitute a Gentile on the Sabbath, on condition that the Gentile collector receive a certain percentage of the sum he collected, he made it possible to draw analogies from this case to similar ones. However, the resemblance of this case to the others depended upon the explanation of the basis of R. Meir's permissive ruling. Did he rule permissively because had he done otherwise the tax collector would himself have collected the taxes, thus violating a rabbinic ban, or did he rule permissively merely because he feared the tax collector would have need to write something down, a biblical prohibition? Another reason for the

4. Chap. 2, nn. 35–39; chap. 5, nn. 39–41.
5. Chap. 4, nn. 76–82; chap. 7, nn. 3–7.

permissive ruling was R. Meir's evaluation of the loss the tax collector might incur. But was this only because the man had already invested money, in which case he would lose that which had previously been his, or was the danger to his future income sufficient?[6]

As our study shows, R. Meir of Rothenburg's ruling served as a point of departure for the consideration of requests for permissive rulings no less than did the examples adduced in the Talmud. The denominator common to all discussions of this type was that the analogy with the concrete example and the reliance on the principle underlying it are intertwined. If instead of ruling in the case of the tax collector, R. Meir of Rothenburg had ruled that any prevention of future profit—or, on the contrary, only a loss of capital—would justify overriding the ban on "telling a Gentile," he would have done away with the doubts surrounding the meaning of his decision. In so doing, however, he would have deviated from the talmudic casuistic method and impeded the way to future development of halakhic decisions, for the relative flexibility of halakhah derived from its lack of systematization. Students of halakhah interested merely in the theoretical aspect encounter a lack of consistency of every kind among its rules. The subject we are considering here is very rich in contradictions that commentators have tried at length to resolve, but without success.[7] One prominent example of this will suffice. It was ruled as a matter of principle that a Jew was forbidden to benefit from wages earned on the Sabbath, that is, any income accruing from an activity itself permitted on the Sabbath. Accordingly, all the permissive rulings adduced to enable a Gentile to work in a plant owned by a Jew were useless, for the income from such activity should have been banned. Since talmudic sources contain cases of permissive rulings, such as renting one's field to a Gentile, the commentators concluded that there were exceptions to the ban on Sabbath in-

---

6. Chap. 5, nn. 77ff. The *Magen Avraham* 244:17 provides an explanation for R. Meir's permissive ruling (not indicated in his own words), according to which handing over the collection of taxes to a Gentile on the Sabbath is no more than the sale of the rights the Jew had previously bought from the ruler. According to him, this precedent is limited to cases of this kind.

7. The perplexities are reflected in the works of commentators on the *Shulhan Arukh* and their successors who do not refer to concrete questions, but rather compare paragraphs of the accepted regulations. See R. Raphael Meislisch, *Tosefet Shabbat* (Frankfurt am Oder, 1797), and from more recent times, R. Jacob Shalom Sofer, *Torat Hayyim* on *Hilkhot Shabbat* 242–265 (Paks, 1911).

come. Indeed, in the Talmud itself we find that such income was permitted if it was all-inclusive, that is, that the wages for a Sabbath work was "swallowed up" in the income of a week or month. The commentators added other qualifications derived from casuistic rulings of the talmudic and post-talmudic halakhic literature. Rabbenu Nissim ruled, according to the example of the renting out of a field, that if the Gentile labors for his own benefit, the profit of the Jew accruing, as it were, incidentally, the ban on Sabbath income is not valid.[8] Nevertheless, despite such fine and meticulous distinctions, the writings of later commentators reveal more than a little confusion when they attempt to interpret every case where earlier halakhic authorities had allowed or forbidden Sabbath-day income in ways that make them appear to be derived purely logically. Yet the question of Sabbath-day income was merely one of many such questions that proves that the abstract rules applying, at first glance, to the matter of a Sabbath Gentile are incapable of explaining the details of the relevant halakhic rulings.

Pure logic is certainly far from being the only guide to the rulings of the halakhic authorities in deciding permissively or prohibitively. While analogies drawn from the early sources are always involved in the making of halakhic decisions, they do not exhaust the process. Motifs other than logical reasoning have their effect as well. The incentives for breaching the defined prohibition or for limiting the extent of the permissive ruling in public life are intermingled with the argumentation of the halakhic authorities among themselves or in negotiations with others. Methods of making a living, personal convenience, taking into account relationships with non-Jewish neighbors, and so on, on the one hand, and recoiling from personal participation in the labor, on the other hand, guide the community in its search for a way to satisfy both sides of the dilemma. The selfsame factors confront the halakhic authority in his attempt to guide the community in the said dilemma. But in his search for a solution he must grapple as well with the abstract halakhic tradition, in addition to the factors relevant to the community. Wherever this tradition includes rulings concerning the permissive and pro-

---

8. Rabbenu Nissim on R. Isaac Alfasi, *Avodah Zarah* 21b, beginning with the words "and that which we have heard"; and see *Migdal Oz* to Maimonides, *Hilkhot Shabbat* 6:12. Here it seems that in the case under consideration R. Abraham ben David, unlike Maimonides, worries about Sabbath income.

hibitive aspects of employing a Gentile on the Sabbath, the ruling handed down by the halakhic authority had to be based on them. The aforementioned existential pressures might prompt him to make a more serious intellectual effort to bridge the gap between them and the desired permissive ruling. But he could not ignore them, and the ability to arrive at compromise solutions is not unlimited. Sometimes the written halakhic guidelines forced the halakhic authority to rule negatively even though he desired to rule positively in cases of already entrenched permissive customs and conduct. "Ritual instinct" and halakhic interpretation are not always compatible, although the conflict between them does not always adopt the same pattern. It even happened, as we have seen, that the incompatibility of forces acting in the two planes yielded an opposite result. The halakhic authority, by virtue of his study of the sources, came up with a permissive solution, whereas the community, acting according to its ritual instinct, rejected it—as in the case of joining a caravan that leaves three days before the Sabbath[9] or by warming a room by directly instructing a Gentile to do so.[10]

At any rate, the development of halakhah in both planes, the custom prevalent in the community and the handing down of decisions based on theoretical give-and-take, both advanced and hindered one another. The dynamic nature of this development, that is, the need to examine new situations and to arrive in each case at a binding conclusion, was dependent upon the historical circumstances. The restriction of Jewish economic activity, such as the limitation of Jewish employment in medieval Germany to commerce and loans, minimized the problems that had to be dealt with, whereas broadening Jewish economic involvement, as occurred in Poland following Jewish entry into leasing deals, made them more common.

However, intellectual productivity, which left clear traces in halakhic literature down through the ages, was itself dependent upon the degree of supervision the halakhic authorities enjoyed over community proceedings and the community's need for scholarly guidance in everyday activity. The numerically few questions that were posed in the Middle Ages in France and Germany enriched halakhic literature with more innovative laws and legal reasoning than did the many problems that

9. Chap. 3, nn. 67ff.
10. Chap. 4, nn. 46–48.

plagued the Jews of seventeenth- and eighteenth-century Poland. The Ashkenazic Middle Ages were characterized by strict and spontaneous subordination of the community at large to the bearers of halakhic authority. The situation in Poland of the sixteenth through eighteenth centuries was different. Instead of the small, isolated communities of the Middle Ages, here we have large communities surrounded by settlements, many of which were scattered among the villages and estates belonging to aristocrats and landlords. The supervision of individual activities was in the hands of community organizations and national committees, with the halakhic authorities acting as mere advisers, counselors, and admonishers. The leaders had at their disposal means of enforcement no less severe than the ones used in the Middle Ages, but the religious and moral authority backing up law enforcement could not be compared with that which existed when the bearers of halakhic and administrative authority were one and the same. At any rate, it is certain that the gap between halakhic requirements, as laid down in halakhic codices, and their application in the community at large was greater here than it was in the Middle Ages. The community could very well settle for maintaining those limitations it adhered to by virtue of its "ritual instinct," whereas it tended to disregard the minutiae of the rulings, which the halakhic mind produced according to some system. This is very clear in the subject under discussion in this study. The community's use of the Sabbath Gentile, which from a halakhic standpoint was a violation of restrictions, reached unprecedented dimensions and set an example for the future, as we learned from contemporary documentation and from a review of developments in later generations.

It is true, of course, that the evolution of new kinds of employment throughout the sixteenth to eighteenth centuries, as contrasted with the situation in the Middle Ages, fueled the drive for permissive rulings unheard of in earlier times. However, what characterizes this period is not the large number of such rulings but rather their popular nature, for many of them did not result from the consideration of halakhic authorities of questions put to them by the relevant parties; they were instead enacted by the interested parties themselves, incidentally, as it were. The halakhic authorities were aware of what was going on, and some of them tried to correct this trend by determining the boundaries between what they considered permissible according to halakhic tradition and what they considered forbidden or between what they felt could be approved of retroactively and what had to be rooted out under any and all conditions. However, as far as the implementation of their halakhic rulings was concerned, they had to rely either on the powers of enforcement enjoyed by the lay leadership or on the persuasive effort of their own reproofs. These two methods of persuasion, even when acting in consort, were not sufficient to restore religious observance to the level desired by the halakhic authorities.

The sixteenth to eighteenth centuries are generally considered the final stages in the era in which tradition dominated Jewish society in an absolute sense. In the second half of the eighteenth century the first cracks in the wall of tradition become apparent, and from then on there was a widening of the areas in which individuals and groups could express their Jewish identity by means of Jewish symbols of their own choice or even abandon all conscious signs of their Judaism. As to the commonly held concept of tradition being identical with the rule of halakhah, one gains the impression that the outstanding feature of the modern period is a curtailment of the power of halakhah and with it a corresponding decline in the influence wielded by its interpreters, the halakhic authorities.

This impression, however, only partially fits the facts. It is true that ever since man's relationship to religion became a matter of his own free will, which is one of the most outstanding features of modern society, the number of Jews living according to the rulings of halakhic authorities has diminished. However, the number of people obeying halakhic rulings determines only the extent of its dominion. The profundity of its influence is conditional upon the degree of its adherents' dedication to it. This dimension, instead of diminishing, has become greater and deeper ever since those faithful to halakhah have begun to view themselves as a community struggling to maintain the original Jewish tradition, in the face of its abandonment by those who reject it. This situation remained valid both at the time the rejectionists were a mere minority whose influence the majority strove to nullify, as in the days of the early Maskilim, and also when the observers of halakhic tradition had become an Orthodox minority entrenched in its separate institutions and developing its own unique way of life. Under such conditions the halakhic authority came to play a central role in the consolidation of his community, with the criterion for consolidation being one's personal loyalty to the most precise halakhic rulings.

The weakening of the restrictive framework of traditional society, which made it possible for others to cast off the halakhic yoke, motivated the Orthodox to harness themselves to it all the more tightly. Precisely because from this time on a compelling social pattern no longer existed, accepted community practice and written halakhic rules, together with the halakhic authorities who expounded them, assumed a unique status, almost unprecedented in previous generations. An observant Jew, unqualified to find his way through the complexities of halakhic literature—those making such an effort were always a minority, and even they refused to rely on their own opinions where questions requiring searching study were involved—had no choice but to turn to recognized halakhic authorities, his local rabbi or a renowned halakhic expert, who were willing to give a ruling in every case of uncertainty.

This state of affairs led to an apparently surprising development: Responsa literature, instead of diminishing as ever larger segments of the community rejected halakhic domination, actually underwent tremendous expansion. This is to be explained by the fact that those remaining under the jurisdiction of halakhah accepted its yoke in shaping their lives to a greater extent than in earlier generations.

This development is further apparent in the shift in topics considered in these responsa. Until modern times the legal rules of the third part of the *Shulhan Arukh, Hoshen Mishpat,* played a central role in responsa collections, with most of the actual replies dealing basically with civil law. In recent generations, most of the scholarly responsa fall under the headings of *Orah Hayyim* and *Yoreh Deah,* that is, they relate to the observant Jew's personal conduct and his religious ritual.

The topic we are discussing here demonstrates this phenomenon clearly. The responsa literature compiled by recent authorities is full of responsa aimed at solving problems of employing Gentiles in the service of Jews or in partnership with them. These problems arose, of course, as a result of Jews having entered new economic areas and having recourse to newly invented technical instrumentalities. These novel activities provided other sections of Jewish society with an excuse to cut their ties with halakhah, for the latter made economic life more difficult and limited the exploitation of opportunities that opened up before the generation of the emancipation. However, the observers of halakhic tradition desired to conduct themselves in accordance with the counsel of their halakhic authorities: "Engage in the one without abandoning the other." They wanted to benefit from the new means of earning a livelihood to whatever extent halakhic restrictions made it possible, even if this meant pushing back the boundaries of these restrictions to the very utmost.

However, the determination of these limits did not lie within the power of authority of those directly involved. If they desired to be considered members of the Orthodox community, they had no choice but to have resort to the opinions of those halakhic authorities recognized by the community. The dependence of a modern Orthodox Jew upon his religious mentor, his halakhic authority, is thus greater than was that of his forefathers, the ghetto dwellers, upon the halakhic authorities of their time. Furthermore, this situation has imposed upon the halakhic authority far greater responsibility in deciding between permission and prohibition. In addition to the usual considerations deriving from the details of the particular case in light of halakhic tradition, there is also the additional dilemma posed by the possibility that a restrictive ruling might lead to the exclusion of the questioner from the Orthodox community, whereas a permissive one might be interpreted as acquiescence in the breach of the wall of religion, a fear that has plagued the adherents of the old-style form of Judaism ever since they realized that the power of their words was insufficient to put an end to the disruption of a unifying traditional framework. Thus we find in modern times that those who deal with questions of permitting work on the Sabbath done by Gentiles face this dilemma: Some are influenced in their final decision by the first part of the dilemma, but the majority are influenced by the second.

The problem of employing a Gentile in the service of a Jew on the Sabbath has been, ever since, the fulcrum for forces pulling in two directions. The need to alleviate the consquences of the cessation of work from both a personal and an economic point of view always carried weight. But at the same time, the fear of misinterpretation, circumvention of the law, and deceiving both man and God alike pulled strongly in the opposite direction. The halakhic authorities thus had to integrate into their decision-making process the evaluation of economic, social, and moral data to a greater extent than in most other topics requiring halakhic decisions. At the same time, they attempted to disguise the relationship of their rulings to contemporary contingencies and to present them as the application of principles firmly planted in sanctified halakhic tradition. Otherwise, their rulings would have lost their authority in the eyes of the community that was required to comply with them and was willing to do so.

It is clear that the methods adopted by halakhic authorities do not obligate the historian. If, because of his tendencies and purposes, the halakhic authority had to emphasize the relationship of his rulings to the sources and to minimize their dependence upon exigencies of the times, the historian is expected to present and evaluate unbiasedly the roles played by both factors. The development in most halakhic areas proceeds practically independently of external factors, leaving the historian but little to describe. The matter of the Sabbath Gentile is extraordinary in that its development was involved in changes and shifts that took place at various levels of existence. This seems to be the reason why the study of the history of this topic—to the surprise of the researcher himself—has proved to be extremely fertile and fruitful.

Index